The Civil Rights of Teachers

"Critical Issues in Education"
Under the Advisory Editorship of Louis Fischer

The Civil Rights of Teachers

Louis Fischer, LL.B., Ph.D.
David Schimmel, J.D.

University of Massachusetts, Amherst

Harper & Row, Publishers
New York, Evanston, San Francisco, London

To our Barbaras

THE CIVIL RIGHTS OF TEACHERS

For information address Harper & Row, Publishers, Inc., 10 East 53rd Street, New York, N.Y. 10022.

Standard Book Number: 06-042072-3

Library of Congress Catalog Card Number: 72-11495

Contents

Editor's introduction

In a diverse, pluralistic culture the institutions, policies, and practices of education will be influenced by the major disagreements of the times. Education in America, a diverse nation searching to define its brand of pluralism, most certainly reflects the major conflicts of the culture.

The dominant tradition of our past attempted to keep the public schools above or away from the controversies of the times and attempted to transmit a common core of learnings. Those tranquil days are gone, perhaps forever. Today, consistent with John Gardner's phrase that "education is the servant of all our purposes," various interest groups attempt to influence and even control public education. Such groups represent political and economic diversities; racial, ethnic, and religious preferences; business interests, conservationists, internationalists, isolationists; proponents of women's liberation, sex education, and sensitivity training, to name but the best-known voices. In addition to these influences from the culture at large, developments more indigenous to schooling must also be considered. Among these are the various forces urging innovation, accountability, professionalism for teachers, and community control. They are also concerned with combating institutional racism and sexism, violence in the schools, and the civil rights of teachers and students.

Teachers must become informed about these issues and conflicts if they are to function as professionals. Toward this end, a beginning must be made in teacher education programs and continued into a teacher's maturing years. The titles in this series were conceived with such a goal in mind. Each volume can stand on its own, yet the several volumes are easily relatable. This arrangement maximizes flexibility for professors who may select one or more volumes, while the student's budget is also respected.

The authors were selected on the basis of their competence as well as their ability to write for an audience of nonspecialists, be they teachers, prospective teachers, or others interested in the dominant issues in our culture that influence the schools.

Louis Fischer
Amherst, Massachusetts

Preface

Several years ago, when the California Board of Education established a committee on teaching about the Bill of Rights and directed the creation of a curriculum guide on that subject, the California Teachers Association publicized the project as "Education for Freedom." It was clear then, and it is clear now, that an important key to student understanding and acceptance of civil rights is the teacher who has freedom to act in accordance with his values as a professional and as a person.

Because teachers are so close to children and in so decisive a role as their mentors, they hold a special position of trust and responsibility. What they say and what they do, not only in the classroom but often elsewhere, can unlock the best or the worst in young people. We hope they will always function as examples of the way in which individuals in a democracy ought to behave.

In this complex society, however, it is not easy to determine what is the right thing to say or do in every circumstance. The teacher's right of academic freedom must be balanced against the need to maintain reasonable school discipline. His or her right to personal privacy must be balanced against the consequences of public behavior that are considered unacceptable.

A teacher must exercise his own judgment in finding such

a balance, and those who supervise his performance must also exercise judgment. Sometimes they go too far, and sometimes teachers are intimidated. Fear to discuss new ideas may be as unhealthy for education as extreme statements or extreme behavior.

Those of us who have had a part in events of the past two decades will read this thoughtful book by Louis Fischer and David Schimmel with particular interest. The authors have explored the various issues the courts have faced in connection with teachers' rights under the First and Fourteenth Amendments. Through insightful selection of recent decisions as well as landmark cases they have arrived at conclusions about the state of the law that will be highly useful to teachers, administrators, and trustees who confront similar questions.

Equally valuable are the authors' insights regarding the constant development of new attitudes as society shifts toward acceptance of new behaviors. Teachers today, they observe, are better educated, more organized, and more willing to claim the rights accorded their fellow citizens. Yet clashes of interests arise, and we ignore traditional restrictions at our peril.

Racial discrimination is a major area of violation of due process, even today, when so much has been accomplished to validate the right of a minority-group educator to equal opportunity for any teaching or administrative position. While the courts have been firm on this principle, say the authors, schools and communities have found many ways to frustrate the spirit of the law. This and other areas of conflict that the book explores make it clear that the struggle for civil rights is an unending one.

While cases are cited from many states, I am gratified that several important questions arose in the school systems of California and that the answers, as interpreted by the authors, indicate a trend toward increased recognition of teachers' rights.

As never before, schools need teachers who have a sense of their own dignity and worth, who recognize the value for themselves and their students of a faithful observance of the democratic process, and who behave in such a way that their own civil rights and those of every other person are protected. Such educators will derive substantial benefit from this book.

Wilson Riles
Superintendent of Public Instruction
State of California

Introduction

The civil rights of teachers are often ignored and sometimes openly violated in the schools and communities of our nation. It is paradoxical that in the schools, which have as one of their major purposes "the preparation of citizens for effective participation in a democracy," civil rights have never been consistently applied.

One reason for this inconsistency is that teachers are generally unaware of their rights. A recent survey in Massachusetts, for example, indicated that the law gives teachers a much wider range of freedom of speech and action than most teachers realize. Some even believe that they voluntarily give up many of their rights when they sign their teaching contracts.

These factors tend to reinforce and perpetuate one another. If teachers are unaware of their rights or believe they have given them up, they will fail to assert these rights when they are ignored. By not challenging or even questioning those who violate their rights, teachers help make such violations more likely and more frequent.

Since many teachers see themselves as having few rights, they are often unsympathetic to demands that students' rights be respected. "After all," comments one, "I don't see why my students should have any more rights than I do."

As a result of these attitudes, schools often teach a lack of concern for civil rights. This, of course, is not part of the curriculum. But institutions, like parents, teach more by what they do than by what they say. Thus, despite the schools' formal commitment to teach the Bill of Rights, they do the reverse when administrators don't uphold the rights of teachers and when teachers don't respect the rights of students. As several studies have shown, students, teachers, and the public know many facts about our Constitution but are all too willing to curtail the rights of those with whom they disagree.[1]

If teachers were more conscious of their civil rights, they could more effectively assert and protect them. And by legally asserting them they would teach students how these historic rights can be protected today.

In addition, a study of civil rights cases can help teachers develop a better understanding of how our educational, political, and legal systems work. First, some teachers who realize that their rights are being abridged feel unable to do anything about it. They think they must choose between resigning or conforming. This book suggests other alternatives.

Second, parties to a conflict frequently identify their own interests with the Bill of Rights. It is then easy to use the rhetoric of constitutional rights as a cover for asserting personal interests or as an excuse for simplistic thinking. A study of civil rights cases forces the reader to go beyond this easy rhetoric and to realize that the conflict is rarely that of right against wrong but usually involves a tough choice between conflicting values.

Although this book is aimed primarily toward teachers and prospective teachers, it is also intended for others interested in the subject. It can be used for several purposes.

1. *To learn the law.* Chapters can be read selectively to learn what courts have said about specific issues such as freedom of speech, personal appearance, political and union activities, loyalty oaths, and due process. For this purpose each chapter is self-contained. Although the chapters move progressively from the relatively simple issue of freedom of speech to the more complex question of due process, they are not interdependent.

[1]For a brief but disturbing account of the schools' ineffectiveness in teaching the Bill of Rights, see H. H. Remmers and R. D. Franklin, "Sweet Land of Liberty," *Phi Delta Kappan*, October 1962; for more thorough documentation, see H. H. Remmers and D. H. Radler, *The American Teenager*, New York, Bobbs-Merrill, 1957.

2. *To learn about current controversies.* Through the use of court cases, the book examines a wide range of recent constitutional conflicts between teachers and educational administrators or school boards. The cases illustrate such controversial teacher behavior as homosexuality, drug use, excessive drinking, membership in subversive organizations, refusal to sign loyalty oaths, use of obscenity in class, refusal to conform to school rules concerning dress and personal appearance, and discrimination on the basis of race or sex.
3. *To learn the reasons courts give for their decisions.* By presenting more than the facts and the legal rulings, the book attempts to illustrate the ways judges reason. And by borrowing generously from court opinions, we have attempted to show how judges "think through" a case from the conflicts presented to the conclusions reached.

This book is intended to communicate with laymen about the law. But lawyers, like teachers and other professionals, often use a technical vocabulary of their own. This jargon, or "legalese," serves as a shorthand to facilitate communication among lawyers but becomes a barrier to communication between lawyers and laymen. We have tried to minimize this problem by translating legalese into English wherever possible.

The Case Approach. Typically the law is explained to educators and laymen by means of a "text" approach. A text usually starts by stating the statutory or case law on a subject and then giving a few examples of how it applies and any exceptions that might exist. This method has the advantages of brevity and simplicity; it states the conclusions of the courts and provides answers to legal questions. The problem with this method is that it seems abstract, "legalistic," and somewhat divorced from human controversy.

Instead, we generally use the "case" method. Rather than starting with the legal answers, this approach begins by presenting an educational and legal controversy. Most of the cases are recent. All describe real and complex situations that teachers and school systems have been unable to resolve. After outlining the facts of the case, we pose several questions to be considered in order to understand the implications of resolving the case for or against the teacher. Then we summarize the opinion of the court, which includes the reasoning that led the judges to their decision. By accompanying the judges on their journey from statement of facts to legal conclusions, the reader should be better able to understand the philosophy behind the law.

Generally we have not chosen easy cases with obvious answers. Most of the cases do not present clear examples of right against wrong; rather, they illustrate rights in conflict. Many are on the cutting edge of the law, in areas where it is changing. They raise questions about which reasonable educators and judges differ, and the answers are neither simple nor precise.

Because this book focuses on areas of conflict and change, a reader might conclude that most of the law is controversial and confusing. In fact, however, the reverse is true. In over 95 percent of the cases that arise, almost all lawyers and judges agree on the law to be applied. The facts are often in dispute, but usually the law has been established through prior decisions of the legislature or the courts. However, since this book focuses on areas of change and controversy, the cases we present are not typical.

A case approach to a legal question takes more time than a text approach, which can neatly lay out the law. But because the world of educational conflict is not a neat one, court cases provide the reader with situations he can recognize and perhaps identify with. We believe the problems this approach might pose for someone unfamiliar with it are more than offset by the lively realism it provides.

By the time this book is published, some of its conclusions may be outdated by more recent cases.[2] Therefore, it is important to note that our purpose is not to present all the current law dealing with the civil rights of teachers. Rather, our aims are: (1) to help teachers understand the legal issues in a civil rights controversy—to ask the right question, not to teach the final answer; (2) to indicate the trend of judicial decision, not the latest case on each issue; (3) to present representative cases in the field, not a comprehensive statement of the law; and (4) to focus on the legal aspects of cases rather than on their educational, economic, political, or sociological aspects.

The civil rights revolution, which dominated America during the 1960s, had a variety of manifestations. Analysts have explored its consequences for our nation's minorities and its youth, for the women of America and of the world, for the inmates of our prisons

[2]The legal decisions in this book reflect most of the major cases on the subject as of July, 1972.

and even for members of the armed forces. But it is almost impossible to find a book that systematically explores the impact of the civil rights revolution on teachers. This volume is intended to help fill that gap.[3]

We wish to acknowledge and thank those who helped us in this effort: Pat Burke, Pamela Centauro, Nancy Frazier, Steve Guild, Bruce Hood, Elliott Lichtman, David Matz, Daniel Pollitt, Gordon Schimmel, and George Urch, who criticized the manuscript; the members of the State of California Professional Standards Commission for the years 1967–1969 and Vivian Monroe of the Constitutional Rights Foundation of Los Angeles, for focusing our concern on this topic; Ellis Horvitz, who brought interesting cases to our attention; and Pat Gordon, Sue Winkler, Nancy Burnett, and other helpful members of the Center for Secretarial Services at the University of Massachusetts School of Education, for their expert typing. And to our wives, Barbara Bree Fischer and Barbara Barlin Schimmel, who supported us in this effort, we dedicate this book.

Louis Fischer
David Schimmel

[3]A pamphlet entitled *Protecting Teacher Rights* is a good introduction to the topic. It was published in 1970 by the National Education Association, Washington, D.C.

The Constitution guarantees freedom of thought and expression to everyone in our society. All are entitled to it; and none needs it more than the teacher.

—*Mr. Justice William O. Douglas*
in *Adler* v. *Board of Education*

Teachers of the public schools being the important element of our population that they are, the sooner and more completely they are advised of their rights or lack of them, the better.

—*The Supreme Court of Texas*
in *Woods* v. *Reilly*

The Civil Rights of Teachers

1

Are teachers second-class citizens?

A BRIEF PERSPECTIVE

Pedagogue was the Greek word for a kind of slave, but to us it means *teacher*. Although no rational person contends that the conditions of teachers in the United States of America today are like those of slaves, until very recently teachers were certainly second-class citizens. The following excerpts from a teacher's contract illustrate conditions that were not uncommon in the 1920s.

I promise to take a vital interest in all phases of Sunday-school work, donating of my time, service, and money without stint for the uplift and benefit of the community.

I promise to abstain from all dancing, immodest dressing, and any other conduct unbecoming a teacher and a lady.

I promise not to go out with any young men except in so far as it may be necessary to stimulate Sunday-school work.

I promise not to fall in love, to become engaged or secretly married.

I promise not to encourage or tolerate the least familiarity on the part of any of my boy pupils.

I promise to sleep at least eight hours a night, to eat carefully, and to take every precaution to keep in the best of health and spirits, in order that I may be better able to render efficient service to my pupils.

I promise to remember that I owe a duty to the townspeople who are paying me my wages, that I owe respect to the school board and the superintendent that hired me, and that I shall consider myself at all times the willing servant of the school board and the townspeople.[1]

In many localities teachers are still second-class citizens. Let us look briefly at some historical antecedents of these social and legal deprivations, keeping in mind that the values of a culture change slowly—certainly much more slowly than its material and technological aspects. Many of the values, beliefs, and attitudes of a hundred years ago are still with us, though we've replaced stagecoaches with jets, frontier lawmen with a computer-assisted FBI, and lap-held slates with overhead projectors, videotapes, and "talking typewriters."

For our purposes a brief and general glance into history will suffice. For more detailed study we highly recommend Howard K. Beale's *Are American Teachers Free?*[2] and Willard S. Elsbree's *The American Teacher*[3] as two interesting and thorough works on this subject.

THE BURDENS OF THE PAST CENTURY

Teaching as an occupation is struggling to shake off a burdensome legacy of nineteenth-century restrictions. In frontier America, as well as in rural towns and villages across the nation, a powerful tradition developed that prevented separation of a teacher's private life from his occupational life. This tradition remains strong in rural America and influences the urban scene as well. Significant changes have occurred and continue to occur; however, many of our leaders grew up in rural settings and accepted the dominant values of their childhood environment. In fact, millions of people who today live in urban centers spent their formative years on farms or in small towns. Consequently, though the majority of our population currently resides in metropolitan areas, values and attitudes formed in rural agricultural settings still influence the behavior of urban and suburban dwellers.

"Boarding 'round"

In the middle of the nineteenth century, it was common practice for teachers to live with the families of children who attended their schools. They would spend about a week at a time in the home of each family in lieu of higher cash wages. "The extent of boarding around was large. In 1862 the number of teachers in Vermont who were subjected to this mode of life was 3354, or 68 percent of all those employed. Connecticut reported a similar situation earlier. The proportion of winter teachers boarding in 1846 constituting 84 percent of those reporting . . . reliable statistics are not available for other states, but the policy appears to have been a common one before the Civil War."[4] Although many claims have been made for the benefits as well as the shortcomings of "boarding 'round," the arrangement undoubtedly encouraged the general attitude that teachers have no private lives at all.

With or without boarding around, a teacher's life has always been similar to that of a goldfish in a bowl. Like ministers—but unlike lawyers, physicians, businessmen, or plumbers—teachers were closely regulated by public rules and expectations.

"The explanation for this lies in the nature of the business in which they are engaged. Entrusted with the responsibility of instructing the young, they stand *in loco parentis* before the law and the public and are expected to keep themselves above reproach and to be subservient to the wishes of the most pious patrons in the community."[5] Thus, the teacher was seen as an adult model, a role he is expected to fulfill to some extent even today. Another reason for regulating the lives of teachers has to do with the constant face-to-face relationships that were integral to the folk culture of rural America. Urban centers provide anonymity, which tends to separate one's work from his home and make it more possible for a teacher to conduct his private life according to the dictates of his conscience.

Specific areas of restriction

Since the Civil War period a wide variety of restrictions have surrounded the lives of teachers. These restrictions often paralleled the folkways and mores of the times but were more strictly applied to teachers. In fact, teachers risked dismissal for engaging in some activities (even away from school) that were perfectly acceptable for others. A brief catalog of common restrictions follows.

Drinking. Although in colonial times teachers drank alcoholic beverages quite openly, the later temperance movement brought severe and lasting restrictions. Drunkenness almost certainly cost a teacher his* job, and applicants for positions usually faced the questions, "Do you drink?" and "Do you smoke?" Contracts forbade drinking and smoking, and even an occasional drink in a private home could lead to chastisement or dismissal. As in most other restrictions small towns were more severe than cities, and the Northeast was less restrictive than other parts of the country.

Smoking. The use of tobacco, particularly by women, was frowned upon. In many places this was a specifically forbidden practice whose violation led to dismissal. There are schools today that will not hire women who smoke, and many states still require teachers to teach the "evil effects of smoking and alcohol."

Theater. It comes as a surprise to many that theater attendance was a forbidden form of amusement in many communities. In fact, such restrictions lasted until about 1920.

Dancing. Dancing and card playing were frowned upon even more than attending the theater. In connection with any socially marginal or questionable behavior, a much higher degree of abstinence was required of teachers than of their pupils' parents.

Divorce. Divorce would generally lead to dismissal and a change of profession. "After all, divorce is immoral, and you don't want an immoral teacher influencing your children." Gambling and swearing were similarly treated.

Marriage. Oddly enough, marriage could also lead to dismissal, particularly in the case of women teachers. Until the 1920s and 1930s, contracts tended to prohibit marriage, but later these were eliminated as unreasonable and against public policy.

Sexual immorality. Sexual immorality was almost always disastrous. Whether it consisted of adultery or fornication, or even rumors of such conduct, dismissal would follow.

Late hours. Going out on school night or staying out until late at night was forbidden. In fact, "keeping company" was against the rules in many communities, while others specified in their contracts

*In our culture it is conventional to use the pronoun *he* to refer to the third person singular. Yet in teaching, an occupation with large numbers of both women and men, the historical feminine stereotype often leads writers to refer to the teacher as "she." We purposely alternate *she* and *he* throughout the book, except when teachers are specifically identified. The reader might pursue this and related matters in a companion volume in this series, Nancy Frazier and Myra Sadker, *Sexism in School and Society*, New York, Harper & Row, 1973.

that a woman teacher might "keep company" with only one man and that he might not be another teacher.

Gossip. Rumor or gossip, however unfounded, tended to be sufficient for dismissal, particularly if it were related to sexual immorality. Since a teacher was expected to be a model adult, she could be dismissed if her *reputation* for good character were tainted.

Publicity. If the behavior of a teacher brought any unfavorable publicity to the school, his career was in jeopardy. Any unconventional behavior or nonconformity was treated as sufficient evidence of immaturity, inability, or immorality.

Grooming. The personal appearance of teachers was closely controlled. Cosmetics, gay colors, bobbed hair, sheer stockings, short skirts, low-cut dresses, and the like, were forbidden.

Racism. White teachers, particularly in small communities, were dismissed if they were seen in public with blacks or visited their homes. In the South white school boards would ignore sexual behavior on the part of black teachers that would lead to the dismissal of white teachers.

Organizations. Membership in organizations was a very sensitive matter with many local variations. For example, in some communities a teacher had to join the Ku Klux Klan to keep his job. In others, membership in the KKK led to immediate dismissal. There were many controversial and therefore "unsafe" organizations, including the American Civil Liberties Union. Teachers were not to take part in open, public criticism of issues, leaders, or organizations. The widely accepted exercise of free speech, press, or assembly were denied them. Any type of activity related to labor organizations was discouraged, and membership in teachers' unions would typically lead to dismissal.

Duties. At the same time, a variety of formal and informal obligations were imposed on a teacher's private life. For example, if he was invited to a social function he could not decline. His contract often obligated him to Sunday School teaching, Scout work, or 4-H club leadership. Amazingly enough, teachers tended to submit to these restrictions, meekly accepting them and helping to enforce them against their fellow teachers.

TOWARD GREATER FREEDOM

Without a doubt giant strides have been made away from these restrictive practices. The reasons for increased freedom in the lives of teachers and in the occupation of teaching are many, and they are inseparable from general cultural developments in the United States. The major factors in this development are the demographic shift to urban centers, the development of teacher organizations, the influence of the mass media, and the increased militancy of teachers in pursuit of their constitutional rights.

To illustrate the dramatic shift in cultural attitudes and the increased public willingness to separate teachers' private lives from their occupational role, here is an example from a recent public meeting of the school board in a tiny community in rural New England.

In this small community of about 400 inhabitants, a controversy arose regarding the teaching of Mr. B, a vigorous young man just two years out of an excellent Ivy League university. Objections arose to his eagerness to teach some ideas and concepts in the general area of "sex education" to his fourth graders. During the meetings that were called, of both formal and *ad hoc* parent groups, a very conservative faction crystallized with Mr. M as the spokesman. In his presentation to the school board, Mr. M made it quite clear that the objections were only to Mr. B's behavior in the school. Then he proceeded to say, "We don't care if he goes skinny-dipping on his own time. That's his own life."

As we shall see, not all communities are willing to make this clear a separation, even today, between a teacher's occupational role and his private life.

Today's teachers, employed mostly in urban and suburban centers, tend to be fairly well protected by their organizations as well as by the anonymity of mass living. They find ludicrous the conditions of employment readily accepted by their forefathers two generations ago. However, the preceding material must not be dismissed as being merely historical information. History is not just "one damn fact after another." We are still influenced by earlier cultural patterns, and in many informal ways we are controlled by their consequences. One of the authors, for example, had the following conversation with the associate superintendent of public instruction for the state of California in 1969:

Superintendent: Teaching is a privilege, not a right. If one wants this privilege, he has to give up some of his rights.

Author: Just what constitutional right does one have to give up in order to enter teaching?

Superintendent: Any right his community wants him to give up.

In other words, this educational leader (though no longer an associate superintendent) believes the civil rights provisions of the Constitution do not apply to teachers the way they do to businessmen, physicians, lawyers, taxi drivers, or plumbers. Is he correct in his beliefs? Do others share his convictions? What civil rights must one surrender in order to teach children and youth?

CURRENT PRACTICES

The educational leader just mentioned is not alone in his conviction that local communities can and should control the behavior of teachers. These controls, though well meant, often lead to at least partial revocation of the Bill of Rights for teachers. Specific cases and controversies are described in later chapters, while some rather widespread practices are noted here. These practices are particularly invidious when they are applied in a covert, unstated, and even dishonest fashion.

Extreme examples of control over teachers' private lives are found in many small communities where one religion is dominant and the selection of teachers and particularly administrators is systematically influenced by religious affiliation. Practices that occur at the point of *selection* are peculiarly difficult to eliminate or even attack, since selection committees are necessarily called upon to exercise discretion and make qualitative judgments when hiring people. For example, in a recent interview for an elementary school teaching position in the state of North Carolina, a well-qualified graduate of an excellent school was asked whether or not she smoked. This turned out to be the most dangerous question in the interview. The wisdom of smoking aside, no school board in the country would propose to dismiss a teacher who smoked outside the classroom or away from school. Yet despite the common acknowledgment of the right to smoke, the overall qualitative judgment at the initial screening or selection stage often obscures violation of this right.

A more common example is the current concern about beards, mustaches, and long hair. Although the courts tend to protect a teacher's right to wear a beard, candidates for teaching positions are often passed over because of this factor. Many a young candidate faces a serious personal conflict when his friends or advisors tell him, "Shave your face and you'll get the job. Once the principal and the community come to appreciate your talents, you can grow your beard again."

Membership in certain organizations or political parties has similar consequences. While we generally proclaim freedom of conscience and political commitment, open membership in the Socialist Party or the John Birch Society is an insurmountable barier to initial employment in thousands of school districts throughout our "free" country. Moreover, many nontenured teachers are dismissed for membership in such organizations, though the stated reason for nonrenewal of a contract may be insufficient knowledge of the "new math" or the "new English," or some other apparently legitimate ground.

A known history of social dissent, though peaceful and lawful, is also commonly viewed with suspicion by hiring authorities. Screening committees and administrators are concerned with the efficient functioning of their schools. They tend to view social activists as potential troublemakers who will interfere with the smooth running of a "tight ship." Viewed with suspicion is a history of activism in "peace movements," "Black Power," "Women's Liberation," "World Federalism," and perhaps most suspect of all, "Gay Liberation."

Open support of similar causes by teachers often leads to harrassment, disciplinary actions, and at times, dismissal. Most teachers do not fight unwarranted disciplinary action, choosing rather to negotiate a quiet resignation with a positive letter of recommendation that makes possible a new job and, therefore, economic survival in some other community. Most administrators would rather "settle" the matter in the same way in order to avoid public controversy, which might endanger the next bond issue. Thus, in a way both teachers and administrators contribute to the erosion of civil rights.

Vigorous participation in controversial political elections and local community issues, and outspoken criticism of school policies and practices are other legally protected activities that in practice are often abridged. The extent of such curtailment is not known. Inferences can be drawn from the cases that reach the courts, from the many incidents reported by the press, and from the files of the two major educational organizations, the National Education Association (NEA) and the American Federation of Teachers (AFT). Both the NEA and AFT are seriously concerned with the practices mentioned in the preceding paragraphs. The NEA, for example, has created the Dushane Fund to focus on the variety of problems and issues dealing with the rights of teachers. The concerns of the NEA and the AFT are broader than those of this volume, however, since we confine ourselves to the civil rights of teachers while these organizations are also concerned with a variety of contractual rights, welfare issues, and other professional matters.

SOME CONTROVERSIAL CASES

The following well-publicized cases should illustrate the stridency of civil rights controversies related to education. They are presented for three reasons: (1) They illustrate the range of issues that will be examined in the following chapters; (2) they sensitize the reader to current controversies in this area; (3) they illustrate rights in conflict —that is, the ways in which the interests of a community may clash with those of teachers.

Controversy 1. A high school teacher in a city with a population of over a quarter million wrote a play. She wrote it on her own time, away from school, to be performed by a nonprofessional group in the city completely independent of the schools. The play turned out to be a controversial one and was considered by some people to be offensive in its references and implications concerning sex, religion, and interracial relationships. Other groups in the community considered the play to be completely acceptable and inoffensive in light of contemporary public morality. The state superintendent of public instruction entered the controversy to investigate whether or not the teacher's certificate should be revoked or suspended, or she should be disciplined in some other way.

It is clear that a lawyer, a physician, a plumber, or a business executive has a well-protected right to write such a play. Its performance, though controversial, would not jeopardize their jobs or state licenses. However, a teacher is regarded as a model who stands in a special relationship of example and trust to the children and the community. In her special position, is it not proper that higher standards of conduct be expected of her?

Controversy 2. A high school teacher in a town of thirty thousand had a letter to the editor published in the local paper. In it he made a series of powerful statements criticizing the superintendent and the school board. His letter claimed that the superintendent "crammed POP (Performance Objective Program) down the teachers' throats"; that the school board foolishly spent public money on useless but expensive "pseudo-educational gadgets"; and that disproportionate portions of the budget went for showy but useless innovations. Since the letter contained both negative personal opinions and mistaken facts, the school administration proposed that he be dismissed for "unprofessional conduct."

The teacher involved in this controversy claimed that as a private citizen he had the right to speak and write his opinions like anyone else. The superintendent and the school board, on the other hand, contended that such a letter, "outside the chain of command," damages the schools, creates a negative public image, interferes with efficient administration, and therefore hurts the schools and the community.

Controversy 3. A high school social studies teacher wanted to explain and develop the concept of taboo with his class. As one of several examples he wrote the word *fuck* on the board, eliciting from the class its socially acceptable equivalent, *sexual intercourse.* Some parents objected to his selection of instructional ideas and methods, and insisted on his dismissal. The school administrators agreed with the parents. The teacher claimed the right to choose his own teaching methods as part of his academic freedom, an application of the free-speech guarantee of the First Amendment. Does the First Amendment of the Constitution apply to the classroom? Should it so apply? Chapters 2 and 3 examine cases and legal principles related to the three controversies just described.

Controversy 4. Two middle-aged male teachers shared a house and taught in the junior high schools of a large city for over ten years. Both were tenured and known to be competent teachers and willing workers. On the basis of secret surveillance, the local police accused them of homosexuality. In a closed hearing in the superintendent's office, the teachers admitted to being homosexuals but stated that their private lives had no connection to their teaching and thus were irrelevant to the superintendent. The superintendent wanted to dismiss them "in order to protect the moral development of the students and to protect the schools from an angered and outraged community." Are teachers protected in their private sexual lives? Are there overriding public interests to be protected that outweigh whatever private rights exist in the situation?

Controversy 5. A black high school teacher grew a beard, which he refused to remove despite repeated requests and orders from his principal. The principal, on behalf of the community, claimed that the teacher was an improper model for students and that his having a beard made it difficult to enforce the "no beard" policy for students. The school board wanted to fire the teacher for "insubordination." Should he submit his personal appearance to the control of the principal? Is his beard "symbolic speech" and thus protected under freedom of speech? Do the same principles apply to teachers of any race, or do cultural and racial characteristics influence one's civil rights?

Controversy 6. In a junior high school in a midwestern community, the principal notified two of the teachers that their attire tended to be too colorful, flamboyant, and "in general not a proper professional way of dressing." Mr. A, liked to wear bell-bottom pants, colorful shirts and jackets, and loud neckties or none at all. Miss W frequently wore miniskirts or pantsuits. The principal informed them in a friendly manner that if they wanted to be rehired for the next year they must dress in a manner "consistent with other teachers in the school, like members of the business community."

Should the teachers accept conservative community standards of attire? Is there a right to dress to suit one's own taste? Or does the community have the right to specify the adult models it employs in its schools? Chapters 4 and 5 examine cases and legal principles related to the private lives of teachers and their personal appearance and attire.

Controversy 7. Mr. B, an elementary school teacher, became an active member of the Black Panthers. His activities, though well known throughout the community, took place on his own time and away from school. His school is racially integrated, but his chapter of the Black Panthers advocates racial separation. The principal, also black, requested Mr. B to leave the organization or resign from his teaching position.

Should Mr. B have to choose between a teaching career and membership in the Black Panther Party? Does he have a right to do both? Can a community require that its teachers not join controversial organizations?

Would it make any difference if Mr. B were a member of the KKK? of the American Communist Party? of the American Fascist Party? of the American Civil Liberties Union?

Controversy 8. In a hotly contested school board election, Mr. M, a high school teacher, worked very hard in behalf of the losing candidates. After the election he received notice of termination of employment. He was told that he should not have taken a partisan stand in a controversial school board election because he thereby "undermined his effectiveness as a teacher," and that he would "no longer be able to work effectively with either the Board or those parents who were on the other side in the election."

Should a teacher's political behavior be so circumscribed? Must he remain politically silent or only stay out of school-related elections?

Controversy 9. Mr. Smith was a probationary teacher at Hillview Elementary School. During his first two years of teaching, his supervisor and principal recommended that he take part in a variety of in-service education programs to strengthen his techniques of teaching and classroom management. Smith followed these suggestions and tried to improve the quality of his work. He also became a very active member of a coalition of teachers combining local affiliates of the NEA and the AFT. Together these groups were demanding that the school board negotiate a contract with them on behalf of all the teachers in the school system. During his third year at Hillview, Smith received written notice that his contract would not be renewed and that it would be in his own best interest to look for a position in another school district.

Smith claimed that the nonrenewal of his contract was in retaliation for his organizational activities, while the school board asserted that it was due to the unsatisfactory quality of his work. What are the competing rights in the situation and your reactions to them? Chapters 6, 7, 8, and 9 examine cases and legal principles related to controversies 7, 8, and 9, as well as conflicts about loyalty oaths for teachers.

Controversy 10. Mrs. M was in her second year of teaching in the elementary schools of Middletown. Early in the spring she received notice from her principal informing her that her contract would not be renewed for the following year. When she asked the reasons for her dismissal, she was told that as a probationary teacher she did not have to be given any.

Mrs. M was dissatisfied with this nonexplanation. She wondered whether she could be dismissed without any notice of her deficiencies and perhaps a hearing to present her side of the matter. Does a probationary teacher have a right to "due process" before being dismissed? Should she have such a right? Would it be too inefficient and costly for a school system to provide reasons and a hearing before probationary teachers could be dismissed?

Controversy 11. Mrs. C was a married high school teacher in her seventh year of competent service. When she became pregnant she received notice from the school administration that she must take a maternity leave at the end of her fourth month of pregnancy. Mrs. C and her physician claimed that she was quite healthy and vigorous, and that on medical advice she could finish teaching the entire school year, since she would be in her seventh month of pregnancy when the summer vacation began. The school board insisted on adherence to the policy in order to maintain discipline, to avoid a variety of complications related to teaching by pregnant women, and to continue effective operation of the school. Mrs. C claimed that the policy was unfair and violated the equal protection clause of the Constitution.

Controversy 12. School District Delta desegregated its schools and combined the racially separate schools into a single system. During this process it became clear that there were too many teachers for the unitary system, and the school board proceeded to dismiss some of them. Among them was Mr. Smith, a black teacher. Smith claimed that since the school board used no objective standards to determine competence, his dismissal represented racial discrimination and violated his civil rights. The board claimed that since there were no objective standards by which to judge teaching competence the school administration must decide according to its best judgment. The board claimed that if it did not have such discretion it could not run the schools. Chapter 10 examines cases and legal principles related to controversies 10, 11, and 12.

Evidence of further controversies involving the civil rights of teachers can be found in any metropolitan newspaper. This volume cannot address all of them, but if educators come to understand the principles we analyze as well as their applications, we believe that some progress will have been made toward fuller realization of the ideals of our Constitution.

NOTES

[1]Quoted by T. Minehan, "The Teacher Goes Job-Hunting," *The Nation, 124,* 1927, p. 606.

[2]Howard K. Beale, *Are American Teachers Free?* New York, Charles Scribner's Sons, 1936.

[3]Willard S. Elsbree, *The American Teacher*, New York, American Book Co., 1939.

[4]*Ibid.*, p. 288.

[5]*Ibid.*, p. 296.

2

Freedom of speech outside the classroom

Congress shall make no law . . . abridging the freedom of speech or of press, or the right of the people peaceably to assemble and petition the Government for a redress of grievances.

—*The First Amendment of the Constitution*

The Fourteenth Amendment provides that "no State shall . . . deprive any person of . . . liberty . . . without due process of law." It has been held that the freedoms of speech and of the press are among the Fourteenth Amendment "liberties."[1]

—*Charles Black, Jr.*

The First Amendment was designed to protect the freedom of speech of citizens in a democratic society. It protects the freedom of an individual to speak and write critically about governmental policies and public officials. Whether the criticism is balanced or biased, careful or sloppy, constructive or destructive, it should not jeopardize a citizen's job unless he knowingly makes false accusations.

Is a teacher equally free to criticize public officials and government policy? Or does a person give up certain First

Amendment rights when he accepts employment in the public schools?

If an employee of a private business were discharged for publicly "blasting" his boss, he would have no constitutional right to re-employment. Should a public school teacher have more freedom than his counterpart in industry?

Doesn't public criticism of educational matters by a teacher carry more weight than similar statements by the average citizen? If so, does a teacher have a greater responsibility to check the accuracy of his public coments? And if he fails to exercise this responsibility, does a school board have the right to dismiss him?

These are some of the questions posed by the cases in this section. We begin by examining the landmark case of *Pickering* v. *Board of Education.* The Pickering case not only confronts a wide range of free-speech issues for teachers but also illustrates one route for legally resolving constitutional conflicts: the local court, the state appeals courts, and finally the U.S. Supreme Court.

THE PICKERING CASE: A CRITICAL LETTER TO THE EDITOR

Marvin Pickering was a high school teacher in Will County, Illinois. He was critical of the way the superintendent and the board of education had tried to raise money for new schools and of their expenditures for athletic purposes. He did not want his opinions to be restricted to the teachers' lounge, so he sent the following controversial letter to the local newspaper:

Dear Editor:

I enjoyed reading the back issues of your paper which you loaned to me. Perhaps others would enjoy reading them in order to see just how far the two new high schools have deviated from the original promises by the Board of Education. First, let me state that I am referring to the February thru November, 1961 issues of your paper, so that it can be checked.

One statement in your paper declared that swimming pools, athletic fields, and auditoriums had been left out of the program. They may have been left out but they got put back in very quickly because Lockport West has both an auditorium and athletic field. In fact, Lockport West has a better athletic field than Lockport Central. It has a track that isn't quite regulation distance even though the board spent a few thousand dollars on it. Whose fault is that? Oh, I forgot, it wasn't supposed to be there in the first place. It must have fallen out of the sky. Such responsibility has been touched on in other letters but it seems one just can't help noticing it. I am not saying the School shouldn't have these facilities, because I think they should; but promises are promises, or are they?

Since there seems to be a problem getting all the facts to the voter on the twice defeated bond issue, many letters have been written to this paper and probably more will follow, I feel I must say something about the letters and their writers. Many of these letters did not give the whole story. Letters by your Board and Administration have stated that teachers' salaries total $1,297,746 for one year. Now that must have been the total payroll, otherwise the teachers would be getting $10,000 a year. I teach at the high school and I know this just isn't the case. However, this shows their "stop at nothing" attitude. To illustrate further, do you know that the superintendent told the teachers, and I quote, "Any teacher that opposes the referendum should be prepared for the consequences." I think this gets at the reason we have problems passing bond issues. Threats take something away; these are insults to voters in a free society. We should try to sell a program on its merits, if it has any.

Remember those letters entitled "District 205 Teachers Speak," I think the voters should know that those letters have been written and agreed to by only five or six teachers, not 98% of the teachers in the high school. In fact, many teachers didn't even know who was writing them. Did you know that those letters had to have the approval of the superintendent before they could be put in the paper? That's the kind of totalitarianism teachers live in at the high school, and your children go to school in.

In last week's paper, the letter written by a few uninformed teachers threatened to close the school cafeteria and fire its personnel. This is ridiculous and insults the intelligence of the voter because properly managed school cafeterias do not cost the school district any money. If the cafeteria is losing money, then the board should not be packing free lunches for athletes on days of athletic contests. The taxpayer's child should only have to pay about 30¢ for his lunch instead of 35¢ to pay for free lunches for the athletes.

In a reply to this letter your Board of Administration will probably state that these lunches are paid for from receipts from the games. But $20,000 in receipts doesn't pay for the $200,000 a year they have been spending on varsity sports while neglecting the wants of teachers.

You see we don't need an increase in the transportation tax unless the voters want to keep paying $50,000 or more a year to transport athletes home after practice and to away games, etc. The rest of the $200,000 is made up in coaches' salaries, athletic directors' salaries, baseball pitching machines, sodded football fields, and thousands of dollars for other sports equipment.

These things are all right, provided we have enough money for them. To sod football fields on borrowed money and then not be able to pay teachers' salaries is getting the cart before the horse.

If these things aren't enough for you, look at East High. No doors on many of the classrooms, a plant room without any sunlight, no water in a first aid treatment room, are just a few of many things. The taxpayers were really taken to the cleaners. A part of the sidewalk in front of the building has already collapsed. Maybe Mr. Hess would be interested to know that we need blinds on the windows in that building also.

Once again, the board must have forgotten they were going to spend $3,200,000 on the West building and $2,300,000 on the East building.

As I see it, the bond issue is a fight between the Board of Education that is trying to push tax-supported athletics down our throats with education, and a public that has mixed emotions about both of these items because they feel they are already paying enough taxes, and simply don't know whom to trust with any more tax money.

I must sign this letter as a citizen, taxpayer and voter, not as a teacher, since that freedom has been taken from the teachers by the administration. Do you really know what goes on behind those stone walls at the high school?

Respectfully,
Marvin L. Pickering

Questions to Consider

1. Did Pickering have the right to publish letters criticizing his superintendent and school board? If so, should he have gone through channels before making his criticism public?
2. Did Pickering have a duty of loyalty to his superiors? Should he have been careful not to damage their professional reputations?
3. If Pickering's public criticism was correct, should this protect him? If some of his criticism was incorrect, does this justify the school board in dismissing him?

4. Are there sometimes reasons for limiting a teacher's right of free speech? Or should a teacher have the same rights as any other citizen?

School board action

Angered by the publication of the letter, the board of education prepared formal charges against Pickering. The charges stated that his letter to the newspapers contained

many untrue and false statements and comments which directly and by innuendo and without justification, questioned and impugned the motives, honesty, integrity, truthfulness, responsibility and competence of this Board of Education and the School Administrators of this District in carrying out their official duties . . . seriously involved and damaged the professional reputations of said Administrators and Board and are and will be highly disruptive to the discipline of the teachers and morale and harmony among teachers, administrators, Board of Education and residents of this District.[2]

After a full hearing on these charges, the board dismissed Pickering because it determined that publication of his letter was "detrimental to the efficient operation and administration of the schools of the district." But Pickering contended that the letter was protected by his constitutional right of freedom of speech, and he took his case to court.

The Illinois courts

The local court affirmed the decision of the school board. Pickering then appealed to the Illinois Supreme Court, which found that a number of the statements and charges made by Pickering in his letter were untrue and misleading. The Illinois Court also pointed out that Pickering "never made a formal or informal protest or report to any of his superiors about the subject matter of his accusations and charges."[3]

The Court acknowledged that citizens generally have the right to openly criticize public officials. Moreover, such officials can take no action against members of the public for making false statements if the critics believed their statements were true. But in this case the Court said Pickering could not be considered "a mere member of the public." On the contrary, "he holds a position as teacher and is no more entitled to harm the schools by speech than by incompetency, cruelty, negligence, immorality, or any other conduct for which there may be no legal sanction."[4]

The question, said the Court, is not whether the public has the right to criticize school officials but whether the school board must continue to employ a teacher who publishes misleading statements which might be detrimental to the schools. The Illinois Court answered this question negatively. It reasoned that Pickering's acceptance of a teaching position obliged him to refrain from making statements about the operation of the schools that he would have had the right to make had he not been a teacher.

Thus, the Illinois Court concluded that "a teacher who displays disrespect toward the Board of Education, incites misunderstanding and distrust of its policies, and makes unsupported accusations against the officials is not promoting the interests of his school . . ."[5] Since there was no indication that the board's action was capricious or arbitrary, the Court refused to set aside the school board's decision to dismiss Pickering.

The Supreme Court

Despite the ruling of the Illinois Court, Pickering still believed his letter was protected by the First Amendment. He therefore, appealed to the United States Supreme Court.

In its argument before the Supreme Court, the school board contended that a teacher, "by virtue of his public employment has a duty of loyalty to support his superiors" in attaining the goals of education, and that if he must speak out publicly he should do so accurately. Pickering, on the other hand, argued that since teachers have the same rights as other citizens, public officials should be able to take action against a teacher's false statements only if they are defamatory —i.e., if the teacher knew they were false or made them with reckless disregard for their accuracy.

In view of these conflicting claims, Justice Marshall wrote on behalf of the Court that the problem was "to arrive at a balance between the interests of the teacher, as citizen, in commenting upon matters of public concern and the interests of the State, as an employer, in promoting the efficiency of the public services it performs through its employees."[6] The Court then examined the two major questions presented by this case.

First, it considered whether Pickering could be dismissed for making critical comments in public. Can public criticism, even if it is true, disrupt discipline and loyalty, and therefore form a basis for dismissal?

The Court found that the statements in Pickering's letter consisted mainly of criticism of the school board's allocation of funds and of both the board's and the superintendent's methods of informing (or not informing) the taxpayers of the real reasons why additional funds were sought for the schools. Such statements, said the Court,

> *are in no way directed towards any person with whom appellant [Pickering] would normally be in contact in the course of his daily work as a teacher. Thus no question of maintaining either discipline by immediate superiors or harmony among coworkers is presented here. Appellant's employment relationships with the Board and, to a somewhat lesser extent, with the Superintendent are not the kind of close working relationships for which it can persuasively be claimed that personal loyalty and confidence are necessary to their proper functioning.*[7]

Thus, the Court "unequivocally" rejected the board's position that critical public comments by a teacher on matters of public concern that are substantially correct may furnish grounds for dismissal.

Second, the Court considered whether Pickering could be dismissed if the board found that some of his statements were incorrect. These centered on Pickering's exaggerated claims regarding the costs of the athletic program and the suggestion that teachers had not been paid on occasion. The only completely false statement was his claim that $50,000 a year had been spent to transport athletes; the correct figure was about $10,000. Concerning these statements the Court wrote:

> *The Board's original charges included allegations that the publication of the letter damaged the professional reputations of the Board and the superintendent and would foment controversy and conflict among the Board, teachers, administrators and the residents of the district. However no evidence to support these allegations was introduced at the hearing. So far as the record reveals, Pickering's letter was greeted by everyone but its main target, the Board, with massive apathy and total disbelief.*[8]

The board must therefore have decided that Pickering's statements were harmful to the operation of the schools by equating the board members' own interests with that of the schools. However, the accusation that administrators are spending too much money on athletes cannot be regarded as "detrimental to the district's schools." Such an accusation, wrote Justice Marshall,

> *reflects rather a difference of opinion between Pickering and the Board as to the preferable manner of operating the school system, a difference of opinion that clearly concerns an issue of general public interest. In addition, the fact that particular illustrations of the Board's claimed undesirable emphasis on athletic programs are false would not normally have any necessary impact on the operation of the schools, beyond its tendency to anger the Board.*[9]

More important, the question of whether a school system requires additional funds is a matter of legitimate public concern in which the judgment of the school administration cannot be taken as conclusive. On such a question, wrote the Court,

> *Free and open debate is vital to informed decision-making by the electorate.* Teachers are, as a class, the members of a community most likely to have informed and definite opinions as to how funds allocated to the operation of the schools should be spent. Accordingly, it is essential that they be able to speak out freely on such questions without fear or retaliatory dismissal. . . .[10]

In this case Pickering made erroneous public statements on current issues. The statements were critical of his employer but were not shown to have impeded his teaching or to have interfered with the operation of the schools. Therefore, the Court concluded,

> *In a case such as this, absent proof of false statements knowingly or recklessly made by him,* a teacher's exercise of his right to speak on issues of public importance may not furnish the basis for his dismissal from public employment.[11]

How Far Does the Pickering Case Extend? The decision by the Supreme Court not only led to Pickering's reinstatement as a teacher but also indicated how other courts might rule on related issues.

Does the Pickering case mean that a school board could never restrict a teacher's right to publicize his views? Probably not. In fact, Justice Marshall wrote,

It is possible to conceive of some positions in public employment in which the need for confidentiality is so great that even completely correct public statements might furnish a permissible ground for dismissal. Likewise, positions in public employment in which the relationship between superior and subordinate is of such a personal and intimate nature that certain forms of public criticism of the superior by the subordinate would seriously undermine the effectiveness of the working relationship between them can also be imagined.[12]

Although Justice Marshall did not indicate how the Court would rule in these situations, he did note that such cases would pose significantly different considerations than those of the Pickering case. We can thus infer that a school board might restrict a teacher's right to publicize his views if it could show compelling need for confidentiality or demonstrate that the employee's relationship with his superior is of such a personal nature that public criticism would destroy that relationship.

Would the Pickering decision protect teachers against being dismissed for unintentionally erroneous public criticism? Generally, but not always. Suppose a teacher carelessly made false statements about the operation of the schools that had a harmful impact and would be difficult to counter because of the teacher's presumed access to the facts. A high school teacher, for example, might carelessly charge that guidance counselors were using obsolete and descredited tests as a central part of the college advising program. In such a case the school board might require that the teacher make substantial efforts to verify the accuracy of his statements before publishing them. If a teacher failed to make such efforts, he might be dismissed. This would be quite different from the case of Pickering, who reported erroneously on athletic expenditures that were a matter of public record. Pickering's position as a teacher gave him no greater authority than any other taxpayer, and the school board could easily have refuted his erroneous statements by publishing the accurate facts.

What if a teacher published a letter that had no factual basis? In such a case questions might be raised about his fitness to teach, and the letter could be used as evidence of the teacher's general incompetence. But he could not be dismissed simply for writing the letter. Other evidence of incompetence would have to be examined.

Would the First Amendment protect a teacher who published statements that he knew were false about an issue of public importance? Probably not. As Justice White pointed out in a separate opinion on the Pickering case, "Deliberate or reckless falsehoods serve no First Amendment ends and deserve no protection under that Amendment."[13] And as the Supreme Court stated in a previous case, "The knowingly false statement and the false statement made with reckless disregard of the truth, do not enjoy constitutional protection."[14]

THE SEWARD CASE: A LETTER THAT UPSET THE COMMUNITY

In 1969 two Alaska teachers published a controversial "open letter" to the Seward School Board. The letter, which led to their dismissal, raised First Amendment issues similar to those considered in the Pickering case. But different facts led the Alaska Supreme Court to a different ruling.

The letter made allegations about ten incidents concerning the superintendent that the writers charged were "definitely detrimental to the morale of our teaching staff and the effectiveness of the local educational system."[15] Several of the allegations were false; these included the charge that the superintendent ordered a custodian to do electrical work "beyond his skill in a dangerous building" and threatened "to get one-third of the faculty this year and half of the remainder the next year." The open letter also charged that the superintendent was "upsetting the school system" and "bringing teachers and others into public disgrace and disrespect."

Although this case appeared to be similar to *Pickering,* the Court pointed out that it differed in several important ways. First, these teachers' statements *did* concern their immediate superior. This is because the superintendent in Seward's small two-school system had a close working relationship with teachers and students, with whom he dealt frequently and directly. Second, the false statements in the open letter were *not* about matters of public record that could easily be corrected by the school board. Instead, the harmful impact of the false charges and allegations proved very difficult to counter. Third, unlike the Pickering letter, which was greeted with "massive apathy," this letter led to intense public controversy involving teachers, the school board, and the public—controversy that lasted more than a year. Fourth, the false accusations in the open letter "were not consistent with good faith and were made in reckless disregard of the truth." For these reasons, the Court upheld the dismissal of the Alaska teachers.

RELATED ISSUES AND CASES

Must a teacher's public criticism of his school system be couched in moderate terms to be entitled to constitutional protection? Not according to the Court of Appeals of New York. In a case decided in 1969, the Court held that "indiscreet bombast in an argumentative letter," without damage to the operation of the school system and without proof of reckless or intentional error, was not sufficient to sanction disciplinary action.[16] "Otherwise," the Court wrote, "those who criticize in an area where criticism is permissible would either be discouraged from exercising their right or would be required to do so on such innocuous terms as would make the criticism seem ineffective or obsequious."[17]

Does the First Amendment protect a teacher's right to circulate controversial petitions on school premises? Generally, it does. Beginning in January 1967 the Los Angeles Teacher's Union circulated the following "Petition for Better California Education":

> *To: Governor Ronald Reagan; Max Rafferty, State Superintendent of Public Education; and the Los Angeles City Board of Education: We, the undersigned certificated employees of the Los Angeles City School District, do hereby protest the threatened cutback in funds for higher education and imposition of tuition at college and university campuses. We further petition you to increase, not cut, the revenues for public education at all levels to meet our soaring enrollments and big city problems—by overhauling our tax structure now, not by violating California's proud claim to free public education for all.*[18]

The school board prohibited the circulation of the petition because the subject was controversial, would "cause teachers to take and defend opposing political positions, thereby creating discord and lack of harmony," and would disturb and distract teachers doing lesson planning, since "discussions between petition circulators and off-duty teachers will inevitably involve some disagreements and resultant debates."

The union asked the court to prohibit the board of education from interfering with teachers' First Amendment rights. In June 1969 the Supreme Court of California issued an opinion that strongly defended the right of teachers to petition for redress of grievances. Such a petition, wrote Justice Peters on behalf of the California Court, "epitomizes the use of freedom of expression to keep elected officials responsive to the electorate, thereby forestalling the violence which may be practiced by desperate and disillusioned citizens. This is undoubtedly why it receives explicit First Amendment protection in addition to the protection afforded to freedom of expression generally."[19] Furthermore, Justice Peters pointed out, "tolerance of the unrest instrinsic to the expression of controversial ideas is constitutionally required even in the school." Then, paraphrasing the U.S. Supreme Court, he wrote, "In order for school officials to justify prohibition on school premises of a particular expression of opinion, they must be able to show that their action was caused by something more than mere desire to avoid the discomfort and unpleasantness that always accompany an unpopular viewpoint."[20] They must show that the danger justifying restriction rises "far above public inconvenience, annoyance or unrest." Moreover,

It cannot seriously be argued that school officials may demand a teaching faculty composed either [of] unthinking 'yes men' who will uniformly adhere to a designated side of any controversial issue or of thinking individuals sworn never to share their ideas with one another for fear they may disagree and, like children, extend their disagreement to the level of general hostility and uncooperativeness. Yet it is precisely the inevitable disharmony resulting from the clash of opposing viewpoints that defendants [Board of Education] admittedly seek to avoid in the present case.[21]

Before issuing the Court's ruling, Justice Peters made the following timely and important observation:

The rights of students and teachers to express their views on school policies and governmental actions relating to the schools, and the powers of the school authorities to regulate political activities of students and faculty, are of peculiar concern to our state and nation today. Education is in a state of ferment, if not turmoil. When controversies arising from or contributing to this turbulence are brought before the courts, it is imperative that the courts carefully differentiate in treatment those who are violent and heedless of the rights of others as they assert their cause and those whose concerns are no less burning but who seek to express themselves through peaceful, orderly means. In order to discourage persons from engaging in the former type of activity, the courts must take pains to assure that the channels of peaceful communication remain open and that peaceful activity is fully protected.[22]

Thus, the Court concluded that the Union's petition in this case

clearly falls within the desirable category of political activity, and their past conduct clearly evidences respect for laws and willingness to challenge them in courts rather than through disruptive channels. Absent a showing of a clear and substantial threat to order and efficiency in the school, such proposed First Amendment activity should not be stifled.[23]

Although this opinion is not binding on courts outside California, it presents a strong and persuasive case for the protection of teachers' rights to petition for redress of grievances in similar situations throughout the country.

Can a teacher be dismissed for making unpopular public statements away from school on highly controversial topics such as sex education, drugs, foreign policy, or abortion? Could a school board, for example, discharge a teacher who wrote an unpopular article in a socialist magazine condemning the American economic system? Made a speech urging public support of North Vietnam? Or wrote a controversial novel condoning free love among high school students? If 51 percent of the parents were offended by a teacher's writings or speeches, would this justify dismissal? If 95 percent were offended, would the case against the teacher be stronger?

None of these incidents alone would justify firing a teacher. A teacher cannot be discharged for exercising his First Amendment rights. And it does not matter whether his writing and speech are popular or not. The fact that a majority (or even 95 percent) of the citizens or parents, pupils or administrators strongly disagree with a teacher's views does not provide ground for dismissal: Constitutional rights cannot be abridged by majority opinion.

SUMMARY AND CONCLUSIONS

The following principles emerge from recent cases concerning the rights of teachers to freedom of expression outside the classroom:

1. A teacher cannot be compelled to give up his First Amendment right to comment on matters of public interest in connection with the operation of the schools. (An exception might be made if a school board could show a compelling need for confidentiality or demonstrate that the teacher's working relationship to his superiors would be seriously impaired by public criticism.)

2. A teacher cannot be discharged for exercising his First Amendment right to speak or write outside of school on controversial issues that are not related to education.
3. Even if public criticism by a teacher is incorrect, the erroneous statements cannot form a basis for dismissal unless they were made knowingly or recklessly.
4. The First Amendment also protects a teacher's right to circulate controversial petitions on school premises during his free time unless such activity poses a serious and imminent threat to order and efficiency in the schools.

In conclusion, a teacher cannot be discharged for exercising his First Amendment right of freedom of speech, whether his views are popular or not. For the civil rights of teachers are guaranteed by the Constitution of the United States; they are not privileges granted by the citizens or administrators of each school district. Thus, a teacher cannot be fired for writing a controversial novel or play, for expressing unpopular political or economic views, or for publicly discussing unconventional ideas outside of class. The extent to which his freedom of speech can be limited in the classroom is considered in Chapter 3.

NOTES

[1]Charles Black, Jr., *Perspective in Constitutional Law*, Englewood Cliffs, N.J., Prentice-Hall, 1963, p. 85. Thus, the courts have incorporated the First Amendment protection of free speech into the Fourteenth Amendment, and they have protected citizens against abridgment of their free speech by state or federal governments.

[2]*Pickering* v. *Board of Education*, 225 N.E. 2d 1, 7 (1967).

[3]*Id.* at 6.

[4]*Ibid.*

[5]*Ibid.*

[6]*Pickering* v. *Board of Education*, 391 U.S. 563, 568 (1968).

[7]*Id. at* 569–570.

[8]*Id.* at 570.

[9]*Id.* at 571.

[10]*Id.* at 572 (emphasis added).

[11]*Id.* at 474–475 (emphasis added).

[12]*Id.* at 570.

[13]However, White's opinion suggests that to fire a teacher a school board might have to prove not only that the teacher's statements were knowingly or recklessly false but also that they had some harmful impact on the schools. *Id.* at 583–584.

[14]*Garrison* v. *Louisiana*, 379 U.S. 64, 75 (1964).

[15]*Watts* v. *Seward School Board*, 454 P.2d 732, 733 (1969).

[16]*Puentes* v. *Board of Education of Bethpage*, 250 N.E. 2d 232, 233 (1969).

[17]*Ibid.*

[18]*Los Angeles Teachers Union* v. *Los Angeles City Board of Education*, 455 P. 2d 827, 828 (1969).

[19]*Id.* at 832.

[20]*Ibid.*

[21]*Id.* at 833.

[22]*Id.* at 836 (emphasis added).

[23]*Ibid.*

3 Freedom of speech in the classroom

Teachers and students must always remain free to inquire, to study, and to evaluate to gain new maturity and understanding; otherwise our civilization will stagnate and die.

—*Chief Justice Earl Warren*
in Sweezy *v.* New Hampshire

A reluctance on the part of the teacher to investigate and experiment with new and different ideas is anathema to the entire concept of academic freedom.

—Parducci *v.* Rutland

To impose an intellectual straitjacket on our educational leaders, wrote Chief Justice Warren, "Would be to imperil the future of our nation." Since new social, aesthetic, and scientific discoveries can always be made, it is important that teachers remain free to evaluate and criticize the values, styles, and truths of the past and the present. This is the purpose of academic freedom. It includes not only a teacher's right to speak and write freely about her subject but also the right to select appropriate teaching materials and methods.

Academic freedom is based on the First Amendment and on the

need, in a democratic society, to protect the freedom of teachers and students to challenge established concepts. It was the process of challenging established concepts that gave rise to the controversies presented in this chapter.

May teachers assign books or articles that offend parents or school authorities? May they use teaching methods that are not acceptable to the majority of citizens in their community or to members of their profession? Should they be permitted to express controversial personal views to students in the classroom? These are the major issues confronted by the following cases.

THE KEEFE CASE: OFFENSIVE LANGUAGE AND ACADEMIC FREEDOM

Robert Keefe taught high school English in Ipswich, Massachusetts. He was a creative teacher who wanted to do more than the curriculum required. He sought to expose his students to relevant and provocative contemporary writing. Therefore, on the first day of school in September 1969 he gave each member of his class a recent issue of *The Atlantic*. He assigned the lead article, entitled "The Young and the Old," which discussed dissent, protest radicalism, and revolt.[1] The article contained the term *motherfucker* which was repeated a number of times. Keefe explained the origin and context of the term and told the class that any student who considered the assignment distasteful could have an alternative one.

The following excerpt from the controversial article illustrates its language, style, and tone.

Of enormous importance for these rebellions is another basic component of the protean style, the spirit of mockery. . . .

The mockery can be gentle and even loving, or it can be bitter and provocative in the extreme. Here the Columbia rebellion is illuminating. What it lacked in graffiti it more than made up for in its already classic slogan, "Up against the wall, motherfucker!" I make no claim to full understanding of the complete psychological and cultural journay this phrase had undergone. But let me at least sketch in a few steps along the way:

1. The emergence of the word "motherfucker" to designate a form of extreme transgression. The word might well have originated with the black American subculture, and certainly has been given fullest expression there and used with great nuance to express not only con-

tempt but also awe or even admiration (though an equivalent can probably be found in virtually every culture).

2. The use of the word in contemptuous command by white policemen when ordering black (and perhaps other) suspects to take their place in the police lineup, thereby creating the full phrase, "Up against the wall, motherfucker!" The mockery here was that of dehumanization, and use of the phrase was at times accompanied by beatings and other forms of humiliation. . . .

Finally, Lionel Trilling's pun, in characterizing the striking students (not without affection) as "alma-mater-fuckers," a witty example of an important principle: the mocking of mockery.

In evaluating the significance of the phrase and its vicissitudes, the classical psychoanalytic approach would, immediately and definitively, stress the Oedipus complex. After all, who but fathers are motherfuckers?

. . . But one does well to move beyond this kind of psychoanalytic explanation, to take it as at most a beginning of, rather than an end to, understanding. For if we assume that the mother in question is, so to speak, the fucker's own, we are dealing with an image of the ultimate violation of the ultimate incest taboo. Now, it has been said that this taboo is society's last inviolate principle—the only psychomoral barricade which contemporary rebels have not yet stormed. Whether or not this is true, the bandying about of the phrase "Up against the wall, motherfucker!" is a way of playing with an image of ultimate violation, and of retribution for that violation.

Questions to consider

1. If parents objected to the article and the school board asked Keefe not to use it again but he refused, would the board be justified in firing him?
2. If not, does this mean that a teacher could assign any book or article? Shouldn't school boards have some control over what publications are assigned to students? If so, how much?
3. If you were a member of the Ipswich School Board, would you vote to dismiss Keefe for assigning the article? Why or why not?

Results of the assignment

There was no evidence of negative student reaction to the article or the class discussion. However, a number of parents found the "dirty" word highly offensive and protested to the school committee. Members of the committee asked Keefe if he would agree not to use the word again in class. The teacher replied that he could not in good conscience agree. After a meeting of the school committee, Keefe was suspended and proceedings were initiated to dismiss him. Keefe, however, believed this would violate his civil rights and went to court to stop his dismissal.[2]

The case raises a number of questions regarding controversial speech in a high school classroom. This is the way one federal appeals court treated them:

Isn't an article that repeatedly uses a vulgar and highly offensive term pornographic and improper? It depends on the article. In this case the judge read the article and found it "scholarly, thoughtful, and thought-provoking." The court said it was not possible to read this particular article as "an incitement to libidinous conduct." If it raised the concept of incest, wrote the judge, "it was not to suggest it, but to condemn it," for the word was used "as a superlative of opprobrium."

Assuming that the article had merit, couldn't the teacher have discussed the article without considering the controversial word? Not in this case. The offending word was not artificially introduced but was important to the development of the thesis and conclusions of the author. Therefore, no proper study of the article could avoid considerations of the offensive word.

Can't a school committee protect students from language that the parents of some students find genuinely offensive? This would depend on the specific situation—the age of the students, the words used, and the purpose of their use. In this instance the word was used for educational purposes. Most high school seniors knew the word, and it has been used nationally by young radicals and protestors. The judge questioned whether quoting a "dirty" word in current use would be a shock too great for high school seniors to stand.

"If the answer were that the students must be protected from such exposure," wrote Judge Aldrich, "we would fear for their future." Thus, he concluded that the sensibilities of offended parents "are not the full measure of what is proper in education."

Does that mean a teacher could assign any book that is legally published? Are obscenity standards the same for students as for adults? No, the court does not go that far. The issue is one of degree. Whether the use of offensive language is proper depends on the circumstances. In fact, Judge Aldrich acknowledged that "some measure of public regulation of classroom speech is inherent in every provision of public education." But the judge concluded that the application of such a regulation in the Keefe case "demeans any proper concept of education." Thus, as the Supreme Court has pointed out, the unwarranted inhibition of the free speech of teachers not only affects the teachers who are restricted but also has an "unmistakable tendency to chill that free play of spirit which *all* teachers ought especially to cultivate and practice."[3]

The concern for the protection of academic freedom, of course, goes beyond the selective protection of offensive language. It is based on a historic commitment to free speech, on the importance of academic inquiry to social progress, and on the need of both teachers and students to operate in an atmosphere that allows free challenge of established concepts.

THE LINDROS CASE: A CONSERVATIVE INTERPRETATION OF ACADEMIC FREEDOM

A tenth-grade English teacher, Stanley Lindros, asked his students to write a short story based on a personal experience. In response to requests from his students to present an example of his own work, Lindros read a piece entitled "The Funeral." The story was a reflective description of the funeral of a young black friend, and contained the words "White-Mother-fuckin' Pig."

Although the story caused no disruption, the school board believed that the use of this "coarse and vulgar expression" showed extremely poor judgment. As a result, Lindros was not rehired. Lindros, however, believed the board's action was a violation of his academic freedom and took his case to court. He relied on the Keefe decision and argued that failure to rehire him for reading "The Funeral" violated the First Amendment and stifled creative teaching.

A California appeals court disagreed.[4] "Academic freedom," said the court, "does not signify the absence of all restraint." The Keefe case, wrote Judge Ford, did not intend "to give carte blanche in the name of academic freedom" to teaching that is "both offensive and unnecessary to the accomplishment of educational objectives." Thus the applicability of the concept of academic freedom must be determined in the light of the circumstances of the particular case.

The court ruled that *Keefe* was distinguishable from the Lindros case. Keefe was a tenured teacher, the article he assigned was scholarly and thoughtful, and the vulgar word was not artificially introduced but was central to the development of the thesis. Furthermore, the word was directly related to the analysis of a subject which was considered proper for students "who had reached the maturity of high school seniors."

In contrast, Lindros' students were in the tenth grade, he was a probationary teacher, his story was not scholarly, and the vulgar words were not central to the thesis. Under these circumstances, the court ruled that it was not unreasonable to conclude that "the embodiment of vulgarity in a model of a story of the genre which the teacher sought to have his students write substantially transcended any legitimate professional purpose and was without the pale of academic freedom." Thus the court concluded that there was sufficient reason to sustain the school board's decision not to rehire Lindros.

THE MAILLOUX CASE: CONTROVERSIAL TEACHING METHODS

The Keefe case indicated that a teacher cannot be fired merely for assigning an article that contains vulgar language that offends parents. Whether the language used is protected by academic freedom depends on the circumstances of the case—the relevance and quality of the article or story, the opinion of other educators in the field, the age and maturity of the students, and the effect on the class. Under the circumstances of the Keefe case the language was protected. But in the Lindros case the language was not.* The problem is, How can a teacher know before he assigns an article or uses controversial language whether he will be fired or protected? In the Mailloux case Judge Charles Wyzanski tried to answer this question.

Roger Mailloux was an eleventh-grade English teacher at a co-ed high school in Lawrence, Massachusetts. In the fall of 1970 his class was discussing a novel about a young teacher in rural Kentucky and his encounter with conservative local practices such as seating boys and girls on opposite sides of the classroom. During the discussion some students commented that the practice of seating boys and girls separately was ridiculous. Mailloux said that some current attitudes are just as ridiculous. As an example, he introduced the subject of taboo words and wrote the word *fuck* on the blackboard. He then,

> *. . . in accordance with his customary teaching method of calling for volunteers to respond to a question, asked the class in general for an explanation. After a couple of minutes, a boy volunteered the word meant "sexual intercourse." Plaintiff [Mailloux], without using the word orally, said: "We have two words, sexual intercourse, and this*

*The same type of language may be protected under some circumstances and not under others. In such cases where reasonable people may differ concerning what language is appropriate for certain students, a decisive variable may be the values and attitudes of the judge hearing the case.

word on the board; one is accepted by society, the other is not accepted. It is a taboo word." After a few minutes of discussion of other aspects of taboo, plaintiff went to other matters. At all times in the discussion, plaintiff was in good faith pursuing what he regarded as an educational goal. He was not attempting to probe the private feelings or attitudes, or experiences of his students, or to embarrass them.[5]

The next day the parent of a girl in Mailloux's class complained to the principal. After an investigation by the head of the English department and a hearing before the school committee, Mailloux was dismissed for "conduct unbecoming a teacher." He went to court to seek reinstatement on the ground that in discharging him the school committee deprived him of his rights under the First and Fourteenth Amendments.

After evidence was presented in court, Judge Wyzanski found that:

- The topic of taboo words was relevant to the teaching of eleventh-grade English.
- Use of the word *fuck* is relevant to a discussion of taboo words. "Its impact," commented Judge Wyzanski, "effectively illustrates how taboo words function."
- Boys and girls in the eleventh grade are sophisticated enough to treat the word in a serious educational manner.
- Mailloux's writing the word did not have a disturbing effect on the class.
- In the opinion of some educational experts, the way Mailloux used the word fuck was appropriate under the circumstances and served a serious educational purpose.
- In contrast, other qualified educators testified that Mailloux's use of the word was neither reasonable nor appropriate.

With these facts in mind Judge Wyzanski then discussed the prevailing law in such cases. The Keefe case, said the judge, upheld two kinds of academic freedom: the "substantive right" of a teacher to choose a teaching method that serves a "demonstrated" educational purpose and the "procedural right" of a teacher not to be discharged for the use of a teaching method that is not prohibited by clear regulation.

In this case the judge ruled that the teaching methods used by Mailloux "were obviously not 'necessary' to the proper teaching of the subject and students, in the sense that a reference to Darwinian evolution might be thought necessary to the teaching of biology."[6]

Mailloux certainly could have used other methods to explain the concept of taboo words. Thus, the case illustrates "the use of teaching methods which divide professional opinion."

Should the ruling of the Keefe case apply to Mailloux? The Keefe case, wrote Judge Wyzanski, "indicated that the use in the classroom of the word 'fuck' is not impermissible under all circumstances—as, for example, when it appears in a book properly assigned for student reading."[7] But when a secondary school teacher chooses a teaching method that is not necessary and is not generally regarded by his profession as permissible, it is undecided "whether the Constitution gives him any right to use the method or leaves the issue to the school authorities."

After acknowledging the national tradition of academic freedom, Judge Wyzanski fully explains why he believes the secondary school situation should be distinguished from higher levels of education. This explanation sets the stage for his ruling, which places limits on academic freedom in secondary schools.

> *The secondary school more clearly than the college or university acts* in loco parentis *with respect to minors. It is closely governed by a school board selected by a local community. The faculty does not have the independent traditions, the broad discretion as to teaching methods, nor usually the intellectual qualifications, of university professors. Among secondary school teachers there are often many persons with little experience. Some teachers and most students have limited intellectual and emotional maturity. Most parents, students, school boards, and members of the community usually expect the secondary school to concentrate on transmitting basic information, teaching "the best that is known and thought in the world," training by established techniques, and to some extent at least, indoctrinating in the* mores *of the surrounding society. While secondary schools are not rigid disciplinary institutions, neither are they open forums in which mature adults, already habituated to social restraints, exchange ideas on a level of parity. Moreover, it cannot be accepted as a premise that the student is voluntarily in the classroom and willing to be exposed to a teaching method which, though reasonable, is not approved by the school authorities or by the weight of professional opinion. A secondary school student, unlike most college students, is usually required to attend school classes, and may have no choice as to his teacher.*[8]

Bearing this in mind, Judge Wyzanski ruled that for a controversial teaching method to be constitutionally protected, it is not enough for a secondary school teacher to prove that it was done in good faith, is relevant to his students, and is regarded by some experts as serving a serious educational purpose. He must also show that the teaching method "has the support of the preponderant opinion of the teaching profession or of the part of it to which he belongs."

If this is not shown, "the state may suspend or discharge a teacher for using that method, but it may not resort to such drastic sanctions unless the state proves he was put on notice, either by a regulation or otherwise that he should not use that method."[9]

This procedural protection is afforded a teacher because he is engaged in the exercise of "vital First Amendment rights." In his teaching capacity he should not be required to "guess what conduct or utterance may lose him his position."

Since Mailloux did not know that his conduct was prohibited by any regulation or understanding among teachers, Judge Wyzanski ruled that it was a violation of due process for the school committee to discharge him. (The concept of due process is discussed more fully in Chapter 10.) The judgment therefore compensated Mailloux for lost salary and reinstated him. However, the judge noted that despite this ruling school authorities are free "after they have learned that the teacher is using a teaching method of which they disapprove, and which is not necessary to the proper teaching of the subject, to suspend him until he agrees to cease using this method."[10]

The Lawrence School Board appealed Judge Wyzanski's decision to the U.S. Court of Appeals. In September 1971 the Appeals Court agreed with the trial court's ruling that Mailloux had not received adequate notice informing him that the techniques he used would be considered improper. However, the Court rejected the guidelines Judge Wyzanski had devised, believing that "they will introduce more problems than they would resolve." Instead, the Court preferred the "balancing test." This test requires that the judge consider each case individually and balance all of the circumstances to determine whether a school board's interest in reasonable discipline is "demonstrably sufficient" to restrict a teacher's right to free speech.[11]

THE PARDUCCI CASE: CONTROVERSIAL STORIES AND ACADEMIC FREEDOM

In the spring of 1970 Marilyn Parducci assigned her eleventh-grade class a comic satire by Kurt Vonnegut, Jr. entitled, "Welcome to the Monkey House." The following day the principal and the associate superintendent of Montgomery, Alabama, expressed their displeasure with the story she had assigned. They described the content of the satire as "literary garbage" and construed the "philosophy" of the story as "condoning, if not encouraging 'the killing off of elderly people and free sex.' "[12] They advised Parducci not to teach the story in any of her classes.

Parducci was bewildered by their interpretation. She considered the satire a good literary work and, while not meaning to cause trouble, she felt she had a professional obligation to teach it. After a hearing before the school board, Parducci was dismissed for assigning materials that had a "disruptive" effect on the school and for refusing "the counseling and advice of the school principal." Parducci felt that her dismissal violated her First Amendment right to academic freedom and went to court to seek reinstatement.

In considering this case Judge Johnson first summarized the basic constitutional principles involved:

> *Although academic freedom is not one of the enumerated rights of the First Amendment, the Supreme Court has on numerous occasions emphasized that the right to teach, to inquire, to evaluate, and to study is fundamental to a democratic society. . . .*
>
> *The right to academic freedom, however, like all other constitutional rights, is not absolute, and must be balanced against the competing interests of society. . . . While the balancing of these interests will necessarily depend on the particular facts before the Court, certain guidelines in this area were provided by the Supreme Court . . . [which] observed that in order for the state to restrict the First Amendment right of a student, it must first demonstrate that "the forbidden conduct would* materially *and* substantially *interfere with the requirements of appropriate discipline in the operation of the school. . . ."*[13]

The first question considered by the court was whether "Welcome to the Monkey House" is appropriate reading for high school juniors. Although the story contains several vulgar terms and a reference to an involuntary act of sexual intercourse, the court, "having read the story very carefully," found "nothing that would render it obscene."

The court's finding that the story was appropriate for high school students was confirmed by the reaction of the students themselves. Rather than threatening or actually disrupting the educational process, the evidence indicated that the story "was greeted with apathy by most of the students." The court therefore found that the conduct for which Parducci was dismissed was not such that "would materially and substantially interfere with reasonable requirements of school discipline."

Since the school board "failed to show either that the assignment was inappropriate reading for high school juniors or that it created a significant disruption to the educational processes of this school," the court concluded that Parducci's dismissal "constituted an unwarranted invasion of her First Amendment right to academic freedom." The court noted,

When a teacher is forced to speculate as to what conduct is permissible and what conduct is proscribed, he is apt to be overly cautious and reserved in the classroom. Such a reluctance on the part of the teacher to investigate and experiment with new and different ideas is anathema to the entire concept of academic freedom.[14]

THE GOLDWASSER CASE: RELEVANCE AS A LIMIT ON ACADEMIC FREEDOM

David Goldwasser was a civilian instructor at the Air Force Language School in Texas. His job was to teach English to foreign military officers. The chief of the Language School regarded certain controversial statements made by Goldwasser in his classes as prejudicial to the interests of the U.S. Government.

The charge against Goldwasser was that

in the face of prior warnings that discussion of controversial subjects (i.e., religion, politics, race) during the class hours was contrary to Air Force policy, he made such forbidden statements on two separate occasions to his classes. One was to the effect that those who burn themselves to death as a protest against the Viet Nam War are the true heroes, and he wished he had the courage to do it himself. The other was that Jews are discriminated against in America, and that he felt such discrimination throughout his life, including his service at the language school.[15]

For this reason, Goldwasser was dismissed. But since he believed his dismissal was an infringement of his First Amendment right of freedom of speech, he went to court to appeal the Air Force decision.

Goldwasser argued that the view taken in the Pickering case by the Supreme Court "of the right of a teacher to speak his mind without forfeiting his job" applied to his situation. In response Judge

McGowan pointed out that in *Pickering* the Supreme Court recognized that public employment may involve some limitation on speech ("although there is certainly no easy leap from this to the proposition that a public employee necessarily assumes monastic vows of silence when he looks to the taxpayer for his salary").[16] The government's interest "as an employer" is in preventing a teacher from making statements that might impair his classroom performance.

"Conversely the free speech interest of the teacher is to have his say on any and everything about which he has feelings," provided there is no impairment of his efficiency. The question to be decided by the Court is, How are these competing interests to be weighed and balanced?

The court noted that Pickering was fired not for what he said in class but for writing a controversial letter to a newspaper. The efficiency with which he taught his students "was not affected by his extracurricular expressions."

In this case Goldwasser was supposed to be giving foreign officers quick training in English. Thus, the efficient utilization of time was "of critical importance." Moreover, since he was not teaching political science or sociology, his observations on Vietnam and anti-Semitism "would appear to have, at best, minimal relevance to the immediate classroom objectives." In addition, the court noted that a class of foreign officers ". . . presents special problems affecting the national interest in harmonious international relations," which could be jeopardized by a teacher's volunteering his views "on subjects of potential explosiveness in a multi-cultural group."

Thus, the court held that Goldwasser

> *was fired for what he said* within *the classroom to foreign officers who were supposed to be learning how to cope with an English-speaking dentist or garage repairman, not for airing his views outside the classroom to anyone who would listen. There is nothing to suggest that appellant [Goldwasser] was required to keep his opinions to himself at all times or under all circumstances, but only in the immediate context of his highly specialized teaching assignment—and we stress the uniqueness of appellant's teaching function in our disposition of this case. In view of that uniqueness, we cannot say that any of the interests underlying the First Amendment were served by appellant's insistance upon intruding his personal views into the classroom, or that his employer was disabled by those interests from imposing and enforcing the very limited restriction emerging from this record. Much greater limitations upon the civil freedoms of*

public employees generally have heretofore been sustained."[17]

With this statement the court concluded its opinion and affirmed the action of the Air Force in dismissing Goldwasser.

Comment

It would appear from the Goldwasser case that teachers have less freedom of expression in class than out of class. Yet freedom of speech in class is essential to academic freedom: the right to express controversial views to students in class. Presumably Judge McGowan would respond to this concern by pointing out that academic freedom is not the right to say *anything* in class but the freedom to say anything reasonably related to the subject matter.

While it may be clear how *Goldwasser* can be distinguished from *Pickering* on the basis of where the teacher's opinions are expressed, how can it be reconciled with the concept of academic freedom? The *Goldwasser* opinion suggests three possible situations in which the broad right of freedom of speech in class can be modified: (1) when the comments of the teacher are not related to academic objectives, (2) when those being taught are not ordinary students who have chosen that subject, and (3) when there are unique circumstances that might call for special rules.

THE PYLE CASE: ARE RISQUÉ REMARKS PROTECTED?

Six months after being hired as a band instructor at a Florida high school, Robert Pyle was suspended for incompetency and immorality. The suspension followed an investigation in response to complaints by several parents and students. These included objections to remarks he had made in a co-ed class relating to sex, virginity, and premarital sexual relations.

Pyle claimed that the suspension violated his constitutional rights and took his case to court. The court, however, said there was competent evidence to support the school board's action. Concerning Pyle's controversial statements the court commented: "There was evidence of unbecoming and unnecessary risqué remarks made by the petitioner [Pyle] in a class of mixed teenage boys and girls which we agree with the School Board were of an immoral nature."[18]

In an extraordinary concluding statement blending social commentary, judicial criticism, and legal opinion, the Florida court upheld the decision of the school board.

It may be that topless waitresses and entertainers are in vogue in certain areas of the country and our federal courts may try to enjoin our state courts from stopping the sale of lewd and obscene literature and the showing of obscene films, but we are still of the opinion that instructors in our schools should not be permitted to so risquély discuss sex problems in our teenage mixed classes as to cause embarrassment to the children or to invoke in them other feelings not incident to the courses of study being pursued."[19]

Thus, like *Goldwasser*, the Pyle case indicates that academic freedom does not protect a teacher's opinions and comments if they are not related to the subject being taught.

SUMMARY AND CONCLUSIONS

The cases described in this chapter emphasize that academic freedom —the right to teach, to inquire, and to evaluate—is fundamental to a democratic society. Judicial protection of academic freedom is based on the First Amendment, on the importance of academic inquiry to social progress, and on the belief that teachers and students should be free to question and challenge established concepts. Like other constitutional rights, however, academic freedom is not absolute; it must be balanced against the competing interests of society.

The Keefe case held that a teacher cannot be fired simply because he assigns a controversial book or article, or uses vulgar language in the classroom. Whether or not such language is protected by the First Amendment depends on the circumstances of each case. The circumstances a court would consider include the relevance of the controversial language or publication to the subject being taught, the teacher's method and purpose, the age and maturity of the students, the quality of the book or article used, and the effect on the students. While the Keefe case provided an example of protected speech, the Lindros case illustrated a situation in which controversial language was not protected by the courts.

According to the Mailloux case, if a teacher uses vulgar language (or assigns a controversial book or article) that is not necessary to the teaching of the subject and is not generally regarded as permissible by his profession, constitutional protection is uncertain. Judge Wyzanski ruled that to be protected by the First Amendment a public school teacher must prove that his use of a controversial method or material has the general support of the teaching profession or of educators in his field. If, however, there is a difference of opinion among educators, school boards have the right to prohibit controversial publications and language, and to discharge teachers who violate these prohibitions—provided that the teachers have clear notice of what is prohibited. Judge Wyzanski's rule is probably being used as a practical guideline by some school administrators, though it has not been accepted by the courts.

The Parducci case applied a different test. For a school board to restrict a teacher's First Amendment rights, it must demonstrate that the teacher's conduct would "materially and substantially interfere with reasonable requirements of school discipline."

The Goldwasser case held that under some circumstances schools can prohibit a teacher from discussing controversial topics if they are not related to the subject being taught or if there are certain unique circumstances in the educational situation.

The Pyle case indicated that the courts will not protect a teacher who is dismissed for using controversial language that is not related to the subject and is not appropriate for the students involved.

As Judge Johnson pointed out in the Parducci case, "when a teacher is forced to speculate" as to what speech is permissible and what is prohibited, he is "apt to be overly cautious" in the classroom. A fear to experiment with new and controversial ideas is contrary to the concept of academic freedom. Therefore, the courts in the Parducci and Mailloux cases provided certain tests or guidelines that could be used to determine what classroom speech is protected by the Constitution.

Judge Wyzanski's test in the Mailloux case, which allows school boards to prohibit methods or materials that are not supported by a majority of the teaching profession, has advantages and disadvantages. It has the advantage of clearly letting teachers know in advance the probable consequences of their actions, but it has the disadvantage of inhibiting innovation and narrowing the range of academic freedom for public school teachers. However, this test has not been generally accepted by the courts.

Thus, we are left with the "balancing test" that was used in the Keefe and Lindros cases and by most courts—a case-by-case inquiry that balances the teacher's right of academic freedom against the competing interests of society in maintaining reasonable school discipline. In most instances this means that a teacher's use of controversial material or language is protected by the First Amendment unless a school board can demonstrate that: (1) it is not relevant to the subject being taught, (2) it is not appropriate to the age and maturity of the students, or (3) it disrupts school discipline.

The final question is, How much disruption must be tolerated? Can any parent or student who objects to a teacher's exercise of his academic freedom cause a disruption and thereby remove the protection of the Constitution? Probably not. As the Parducci case points out: A teacher cannot be discharged for conduct protected by the First Amendment unless it "materially and substantially" disrupts the educational process.[20]

NOTES

[1]Robert J. Lifton, "The Young and the Old: Notes on a New History," Part I, *The Atlantic, 224*, no. 3 (September 1969), p. 47.

[2]*Keefe* v. *Geanakos*, 418 F. 2d 359 (1st Cir., 1969).

[3]Frankfurter, J., concurring in *Wieman* v. *Updegraff*, 344 U.S. 183, 194 (1952).

[4]*Lindros* v. *Governing Board of Torance School District*, 26 C.A. 3d 38 (1972).

[5]*Mailloux* v. *Kiley*, U.S. District Court, District of Massachusetts, 22 March 1971, p. 2.

[6]This refers to the Supreme Court's opinion in *Epperson* v. *Arkansas*, 393 U.S. 97 (1968), in which it ruled that an Arkansas "antievolution" statute was unconstitutional. That statute, which is based on the belief of certain religious groups, makes it illegal for a public school to teach that "mankind ascended or descended from a lower order of animals." It was outlawed because it conflicts with the First Amendment mandate of government neutrality toward religion. And according to Justice Stewart's concurring opinion, it is also unconstitutional because it "would clearly impinge upon the guarantees of free communication contained in the First Amendment." *Id.* at 116. (The full text of the Epperson case is reprinted in Appendix 2.)

[7]*Id.* at 7.

[8]*Id.* at 8.

[9]*Id.* at 10.

[10]*Ibid.*

[11]*Mailloux* v. *Kiley*, 448 F. 2d 1242 (1971).

[12]*Parducci* v. *Rutland*, 316 F. Supp. 352, 353–354 (1970).

[13]*Id.* at 356.

[14]*Id.* at 357.

[15]*Goldwasser* v. *Brown*, 417 F. 2d 1169, 1171 (1969).

[16]*Id.* at 1176.

[17]*Id.* at 1177.

[18]*Pyle* v. *Washington County School Board*, 238 So. 2d 121, 123 (1970).

[19]*Ibid.*

[20]Recently, the First Amendment was also used to uphold a New York teacher's right to remain silent during the Pledge of Allegiance. According to the judge, her "right to remain silent in the face of an illegitimate demand for speech is as much part of First Amendment protections as the right to speak out in the face of an illegitimate demand for silence." *The New York Times*, 19 November 1972, Section E, pg. 7.

4

The teacher's private life

There are certain professions which impose upon persons attracted to them, responsibilities and limitations on freedom of action which do not exist in regard to other callings. Public officials such as judges, policemen and school teachers fall into such a category.[1]

—Board of Trustees *v.* Stubblefield

The private conduct of a man, who is also a teacher, is a proper concern to those who employ him only to the extent it mars him as a teacher. . . . Where his professional achievement is unaffected, where the school community is placed in no jeopardy, his private acts are his own business and may not be the basis of discipline.[2]

—Jarvella *v.* Willoughby
—Eastlake City School District

"Today's morals," wrote the California Supreme Court, "may be tomorrow's ancient and absurd customs."[3] Morals certainly vary according to place and time, yet few parents would willingly have their children taught by teachers they consider immoral. And if parents expect teachers to serve as adult models for their children, shouldn't a school board have the right to dismiss a teacher who violates the community's moral standards? Moreover, if a teacher holds a special position of trust and responsibility, can't parents and administrators expect a higher standard of personal conduct from teachers than the law requires of the average citizen?

These are some of the issues raised in the cases presented in this chapter. They lie on the frontiers of public controversy, involving teachers who have violated community norms regarding sexual activity, use of marijuana, excessive consumption of alcohol, and obscene language. The conflicts arise out of a clash of rights: Teachers assert that their private lives are their own business, while school boards argue that teachers are models for their students and must meet the moral standards set by the community.

The following cases also illustrate several legal concepts. First, courts generally follow precedent. This means that if a court has ruled a certain way, the same court or a lower one feels obligated to rule the same way in a similar case. However, a court may not feel bound by precedent if it can "distinguish" the case—that is, if it can show that the case before it is significantly different from the past case, despite their apparent similarity. The Morrison and Sarac cases, discussed in this chapter, illustrate these two principles. The California State Board of Education used the "precedent" of the Sarac case in firing Marc Morrison. But the California Supreme Court rejected the board's action by distinguishing *Morrison* from *Sarac*.

These cases illustrate two other legal features. The authority of a higher court to overrule or disapprove the opinion of a lower court is exemplified by the *Morrison* opinion. And Justice Sullivan's dissent in the Morrison case illustrates how appeals courts handle disagreements among judges.

THE SARAC CASE: IS HOMOSEXUALITY IMMORAL?

In 1962 Thomas Sarac was arrested and charged with making a "homosexual advance" to L. A. Bowers at a public beach in the city of Long Beach, California.[4] Sarac was a secondary school teacher, Bowers a police officer. The arrest resulted in Sarac's conviction for disorderly conduct. Sarac was then accused of being unfit for service in the public school system because of his conduct on the beach, the criminal proceedings against him, and Bower's testimony that Sarac admited to "a homosexual problem since he was 20 years old and that the last time he had had sexual relations with a man was approximately 3 weeks earlier."

As a result, the state board of education revoked Sarac's secondary school teaching credential. Sarac went to court to compel the board to rescind its revocation. He argued that the board had acted unconstitutionally in revoking his teaching credential "because it failed to establish any rational connection between the homosexual conduct on the beach . . . and immorality and unprofessional conduct as a teacher on his part and his unfitness for service in the public schools."

The court, however, did not find Sarac's argument persuasive. Thus, Justice Cobey wrote:

Homosexual behavior has long been contrary and abhorrent to the social mores and moral standards of the people of California as it has been since antiquity to those of many other peoples. It is clearly, therefore, immoral conduct within the meaning of [the] Education Code.[5]

Furthermore, homosexual behavior constitutes "evident unfitness for service in the public school system."

In view of Sarac's duty to teach his students the principles of morality and his necessarily close association with children, the court found "a rational connection between his homosexual conduct on the beach and the consequent action of respondent [Board of Education] in revoking his secondary teaching credential on the statutory grounds of immoral and unprofessional conduct and evident unfitness for service in the public school system of this State."[6] Accordingly, the court refused to rescind the action of the board of education that revoked Sarac's right to teach.

THE MORRISON CASE: TEACHING AND HOMOSEXUALITY RECONSIDERED

Marc Morrison was another California teacher who engaged in homosexual activity that became public and resulted in the revocation of his teaching credentials. Morrison also took his case to court, but for him the results were different than for Sarac.

Morrison had been a public school teacher for a number of years before becoming friendly with Fred Schneringer, another teacher. As a result of this friendship, the two men engaged in a physical homosexual relationship during a one-week period. About 12 months later Schneringer reported the incident to Morrison's superintendent; this led Morrison to resign. More than a year later the board of education conducted a hearing concerning the possible revocation of Morrison's life diploma, which qualified him as a secondary school teacher in California. Morrison admitted that he had engaged in homosexual acts with Schneringer in his apartment. He also stated that he did not regard his conduct as immoral. He testified, however, that he had engaged in no other homosexual acts before or after this single incident. There was no evidence presented to contradict Morrison's testimony. The board concluded that the incident with Schneringer constituted immoral and unprofessional conduct that warranted revocation of Morrison's life diploma. But Morrison went to court to set aside the board's action.

Questions to Consider

1. What arguments would you use to support the board's action? To support Morrison's case for reinstatement?
2. What constitutes immoral conduct that would justify revoking a teacher's license? Any immoral conduct? Any sexual immorality? Any immoral conduct that might affect his teaching? Immoral conduct that is also unlawful?

The case against Morrison

The board used the following arguments to support its action; some were taken from the *Sarac* opinion.[7]

- A teacher stands *in loco parentis*. His students look up to him as the person taking the place of their parents during school hours and as an example of good conduct.
- State law requires all teachers "to endeavor to impress upon the minds of the pupils the principles of morality, truth, justice, [and] patriotism."[8]
- Morrison was a potential danger to his students not only because of his immoral acts, which he admitted, but also because he did not regard such acts as immoral.
- California law provides that the board of education shall revoke life diplomas and teaching credentials for immoral or unprofessional conduct.[9]
- Homosexual behavior is contrary to the moral standards of the people of California. It also constitutes unprofessional conduct, which need not be limited to classroom misconduct or misconduct with children.

The opinion of the court

Despite the arguments of the board of education, a majority of the California Supreme Court ruled in favor of Morrison for the following reasons:[10]

- It is dangerous to allow the terms *immoral* and *unprofessional* to be broadly interpreted. To many people, "immoral conduct" includes laziness, gluttony, selfishness, and cowardice. To others, "unprofessional conduct" for teachers includes signing petitions, opposing majority opinions, and drinking alcoholic beverages. Therefore, unless these terms are carefully and narrowly interpreted, they could be applied to most teachers in the state.
- The board of education should not be empowered to dismiss any teacher whose personal, private conduct incurs its disapproval. A teacher's behavior should disqualify him only when it is clearly related to his effectiveness in his job. When his job as a teacher is not affected, his private behavior is his own business and should not form a basis for discipline.

The Court therefore stated that the board cannot abstractly characterize Morrison's conduct in this case as "immoral" or "unprofessional" unless that conduct implies that he is unfit to teach. But how can a board of education determine whether a teacher's behavior indicates his fitness to teach? In making this determination the Court suggested that the board consider the circumstances surrounding the case.

In this instance there was no evidence to show that Morrison's conduct had affected his performance as a teacher. "There was not the slightest suggestion that he had ever attempted, sought or even considered any form of physical or otherwise improper relationship with any student. Furthermore, there was no evidence that Morrison failed to teach his students the principles of morality required by law or that the incident with Schneringer affected his relationship with his co-workers."

For a school board to conclude that a teacher's retention in the profession presents a danger to students or fellow teachers, its conclusion must be supported by evidence. In this case the Court ruled that the board had not presented adequate evidence to support its decision to revoke Morrison's life diploma.

The board relied heavily on the Sarac case and argued that its reasoning should apply to Morrison. But most of the justices disagreed. Thus, Justice Tobriner wrote on behalf of the majority, "The facts in *Sarac* are clearly distinguishable from the instant case; the teacher disciplined in that case had pleaded guilty to a criminal charge of disorderly conduct arising from his homosexual advances toward a police officer at a public beach; and the teacher admitted a recent history of homosexual activities."[11] This was not the case with Morrison.

The California Supreme Court recognized, however, that some of the language in the opinion of the Court of Appeals in the Sarac case seemed to indicate that any homosexual conduct on the part of a teacher could result in disciplinary action. If that were true, the *Sarac* opinion would be in conflict with the Court's decision in this case. To avoid confusion the California Supreme Court disapproved part of the *Sarac* ruling. Thus, Justice Tobriner wrote that the *Sarac* decision "includes unnecessarily broad language suggestive that all homosexual conduct, even though not shown to relate to fitness to teach, warrants disciplinary action." The proper construction of the Education Code, however, is more restricted than is indicated by the *Sarac* opinion, and *"to the extent that Sarac conflicts with this opinion it must be disapproved."*[12]

In sum, the California Supreme Court's decision does not mean that homosexuals must be permitted to teach in the public schools. It does mean that the California Board of Education can revoke a life diploma or teaching certificate only if that individual has shown himself to be unfit to teach. The Court concluded:

> *An individual can be removed from the teaching profession only upon a showing that his retention in the profession poses a significant danger of harm to either students, school employees, or others who might be affected by his actions as a teacher.*[13]

A dissenting opinion

In most cases decided by appeals courts, the judges reach unanimous agreement. Sometimes, however, this is not possible. In such cases a judge who does not agree with the majority may submit a dissenting opinion, which is published immediately after the opinion of the court. This is what happened in the Morrison case; Justice Sullivan believed that the reasoning of the Sarac case should apply to Morrison. In a strongly worded dissent Justice Sullivan wrote:

> *The majority argue that* Sarac *is distinguishable from the instant case on its facts. It is asserted that the teacher's homosexual conduct*

occurred on a public beach, whereas this petitioner's [i.e., Morrison's] conduct occurred in the privacy of his apartment. Apparently this asserted difference reflects the view that, absent a criminal offense, petitioner's private life is his own business and the state ". . . must not arbitrarily impair the right of the individual to live his private life, apart from his job, as he deems fit . . ." But the clandestine character of petitioner's acts did not render them any less homosexual acts. These still remained, to borrow the language of Sarac, *". . . contrary and abhorrent to the social mores and moral standards of the people of California . . ." It would be fatuous to assume that these acts become reprehensible only if committed in public. One would not expect petitioner and Schneringer to commit the acts here involved . . . in full view of the citizenry.*[14]

In this case, wrote Justice Sullivan, the board of education found

. . . on overwhelming evidence, indeed on the frank but unrepentent admissions of petitioner [Morrison], that he had committed homosexual acts with another teacher and concluded that these acts constituted immoral and unprofessional conduct and acts involving moral turpitude. The trial court reached the same conclusion. The majority is silent on this point.[15]

The majority does not say whether Morrison's acts were immoral or not. Unless the majority is willing to state that they were not immoral, argued the dissent, the Court could not say that there is no rational connection between Morrison's homosexual acts and his fitness to teach. Therefore, Sullivan concluded, the Court should not have upset the action of the Board in dismissing Morrison.

Comment

Despite the intensity of Justice Sullivan's dissent, the California Supreme Court reversed the action of the board of education in dismissing Morrison. It thereby took a bold and controversial step in protecting the freedom of teachers' private lives. Whether the courts in other states would rule the same way is uncertain. Many judges might find it easier to agree with the dissent of Justice Sullivan than with the majority of the California Supreme Court.

Additional Questions

1. Do you think the *Morrison* decision would have been different if Morrison's single homosexual incident had been with a consenting high school senior? Why or why not?

2. Would you feel differently about the Morrison case if Morrison had admitted *frequent* homosexual activity with consenting adults in private?
3. Should a different standard be applied to heterosexual activity? Do you think a male teacher should have his teaching credential revoked for making a sexual advance (without force) toward a young lady on a public beach?
4. Justice Sullivan seemed to feel that Morrison's "unrepentent" attitude toward his homosexual conduct made him a greater danger as a classroom teacher. Do you agree?
5. What, if any, private conduct that the majority of the community considers immoral would justify a school board in dismissing a teacher?
6. Do laws that encourage school boards to fire teachers for immoral conduct promote good education? Is it possible that "immorality laws" are unconstitutional?

Commenting on Morrison's contention that a ban on immoral conduct might conflict with a constitutionally protected right to privacy, Justice Tobriner wrote:

> *An unqualified proscription against immoral conduct would raise serious constitutional problems. Conscientious school officials concerned with enforcing such a broad provision might be inclined to probe into the private life of each and every teacher, no matter how exemplary his classroom conduct. Such prying might all too readily lead school officials to search for "telltale signs" of immorality in violation of the teacher's constitutional rights.*

Although this statement by Justice Tobriner was not essential to the decision of the Court, it may provide some hope for those who wish to eliminate "immoral conduct" as a basis for firing teachers. The following cases, however, indicate that the concept is still very much alive, despite the way it is being restricted.

THE STUBBLEFIELD CASE: SEXUAL RELATIONS WITH STUDENTS

Joseph Stubblefield was a certified teacher in a California public junior college. After teaching a class on the night of January 28, 1969, he drove a female student to a dark street near the college and parked. A little later a Los Angeles County deputy sheriff patrolling the area spotted the teacher's automobile. Because he could see no occupants, the deputy thought it was abandoned and walked over to investigate. He shined his flashlight into the car and found Stubblefield apparently involved in a sexual relationship.[16] When he recognized that the person with the flashlight was a deputy sheriff, Stubblefield shouted, "Get the hell away from me you dirty cop." He then knocked the deputy to the ground with his car door and quickly drove away. The deputy chased him at speeds of eighty to one-hundred miles per hour until Stubblefield's car finally pulled over.

Because of these events the Board of Trustees of the Compton Junior College dismissed Stubblefield on grounds of immoral conduct and unfitness to teach. Stubblefield, however, went to court to seek reinstatement. He contended that the Morrison case should prohibit his discharge because the evidence against him concerned only his conduct and did not demonstrate how that conduct made him unfit to teach.

Questions to Consider

1. Should a male teacher be dismissed because of a single, private sexual relationship with a consenting junior college student? What about a consenting high school senior?
2. Should a teacher be dismissed for such a relationship only if it affects his classroom teaching?
3. If Stubblefield had been polite to the deputy, would the case for dismissing him have been substantially weakened?
4. Does the reasoning of the Morrison case apply here? Or can this case be distinguished from Morrison?

The opinion of the court

The California Court of Appeals ruled that Stubblefield's actions constituted immoral conduct indicating unfitness to teach. The Court pointed out that in the public school system a teacher is regarded as a person whose words and actions are likely to be followed by his students. Therefore, responsible conduct by a teacher, even at the college level, should exclude "meretricious relationships with his students" and assaults on duly constituted authorities. According to the Court, a number of facts distinguish the Morrison case from this one. These include the lapse of time between the conduct and the discharge, the locations where the conduct occurred, and the status of the parties involved. In addition, the *Morrison* decision was critical of the lack of evidence to establish that Morrison was more likely than the average man to engage in improper conduct "with a student" or that publicity surrounding his conduct adversely affected his teaching.

The clear import of the *Morrison* decision, said the Court, is that a teacher may be discharged on evidence that his behavior indicates potential for misconduct with a student or has gained such notoriety that his on-campus activities would be impaired. The fact that Stubblefield and his companion were easily discovered "demonstrates the tenuous security from public attention provided by the front seat" of an automobile. Stubblefield's assault upon the officer and attempt to escape at high speeds ultimately insured further public attention. Finally, "unfitness to teach," in the sense that Stubblefield was more likely than the average man to engage in improper conduct with a student, "can be inferred from the very conduct itself." The evidence that was lacking in *Morrison* "was overtly manifested here." In conclusion the Court wrote:

The integrity of the educational system under which teachers wield considerable power in the grading of students and the granting or withholding of certificates and diplomas is clearly threatened when teachers become involved in relationships with students such as is indicated by the conduct here.[17]

THE BRENNAN CASE: TEACHERS AND MARIJUANA

Barnet Brennan was the teaching principal of a California school when one of her friends was arrested and convicted for possessing marijuana. Her friend argued that the laws making the possession and use of marijuana illegal, were unconstitutional. Brennan agreed. She therefore executed an affidavit in support of her friend that said, in part:

Marijuana is not harmful to my knowledge, because I have been using it since 1949 almost daily, with only beneficial results. . . . I have been a teacher for 30 years and at present am the teaching principal of a public school. During school hours I never feel the need of using cannabis sativa *[i.e., marijuana], however, each recess is eagerly awaited for smoking tobacco cigarettes. I do not consider marijuana a habit forming drug, but to me nicotine is . . .*[18]

Brennan urged the court "to set aside these unconstitutional laws" depicting marijuana as addictive and harmful, and "setting forth harsh and cruel penalties for its possession, sale and use." She believed she was performing a civic duty by making this statement.

Her affidavit immediately attracted publicity, and her students soon learned of its content. As a result, the board of the school district notified Brennan that she would not be reemployed. Since she believed her dismissal was unconstitutional, she petitioned the local court to compel the board to reemploy her. When the local court ruled in favor of the board, Brennan appealed on three grounds.

First, she contended that the term *immoral conduct* as applied to her was unconstitutionally vague. She relied on the Morrison case to argue that the term embraced an unlimited area. While the court acknowledged the danger of using the concept of immorality too broadly, it did not accept Brennan's argument. The court quoted with approval the statement of the *Morrison* opinion that cautioned that not every act of immorality would justify termination but only acts that "impaired the services of the teacher" in properly instructing the pupils. Thus, the court ruled that the term *immoral conduct* "is not unconstitutional in itself, and if there is evidence of unfitness to teach, it is not unconstitutional as applied to this case."

Concerning the controversial affidavit the court pointed out that Brennan's sworn statement was an admission that she had for many years used marijuana in defiance of state law. She did not merely advocate change of the law but declared her belief that violation of the law was appropriate, despite the fact that it might constitute commission of a felony. And though it was not Brennan's intention that her affidavit should receive wide publicity, it certainly was reasonable to anticipate that this would happen and that her students and their parents would learn of it.

Brennan also argued that she should not be penalized when there was no evidence that her statement had a negative effect on students. The court responded that the school board acted so promptly after learning of the affidavit that there was little time for any effect to develop. Moreover, the requirement of evidence of the deleterious effect of a teacher's conduct on the students does not mean that each student must be examined to determine the specific effect of the incident. Here, said the court, there was "competent evidence" on the "likely" effect of Brennan's conduct on the students. One witness testified, "I would be inclined to believe that the pupil would be thinking 'If my teacher can gain her ends by breaking the law, then I, too, can gain my ends by breaking the law!" Although witnesses were not unanimous, the court found there was adequate evidence to support a finding of unfitness to teach.

Brennan's third contention was that the signing of the affidavit "was constitutionally protected free speech" and therefore should not be considered against her. The court recognized that Brennan's desire to express disapproval of a state law does not render her unfit to teach. But the point in this case, said the court, is that Brennan

> *. . . has intentionally and knowingly violated the law, because she does not personally agree with that law, and then publicly declared that fact in such a way that it would reach and affect her pupils. It is not the affidavit which is the basis of this action against appellant [Brennan]. The affidavit is merely evidence of appellant's competence or lack of competence to teach.*[19]

Would the court have ruled differently if Brennan had publicly filed her affidavit opposing marijuana laws but said nothing about using marijuana? Apparently it would have. The court commented that another teacher in Brennan's school had filed an affidavit in the same criminal case and had also advocated a change in the laws regulating marijuana, which he felt were unconstitutional. The other teacher, however, "did not say he ever used marijuana." The court noted with approval that the board not only took no action against the other teacher because of his affidavit but even promoted him to replace Brennan.

Comment

Is it not inconsistent for the courts to rule differently in the Morrison and Brennan cases? Weren't both teachers punished for the same type of activity? Are courts more concerned about smoking marijuana than about homosexual behavior? Probably not. In fact, most people probably consider homosexual activity more immoral than smoking marijuana. How then can *Brennan* be distinguished from *Morrison?*

Morrison's credential was revoked for a single, private homosexual incident that occurred over two years before the board took action. There was no evidence of any relationship between the incident and Morrison's teaching effectiveness. By contrast, Brennan's dismissal was caused by her own voluntary, public admission that she frequently and regularly violated the law. This resulted in immediate and widespread publicity in which her action became known to her students, and there was competent evidence indicating the likelihood of a harmful effect on the school community. It is probable that if Morrison's controversial behavior had come to light in the same manner as Brennan's the legal results would have been the same.

THE McCONNELL CASE: PUBLIC PROCLAMATION OF HOMOSEXUALITY

In April 1970, James McConnell was asked to head the catalog division of the University of Minnesota's St. Paul campus library, with the rank of instructor. Before the offer was approved by the board of regents, McConnell told a university official that he planned to obtain a license to marry a homosexual friend, Jack Baker. The official told McConnell that his action might jeopardize the board's approval of his job offer. But McConnell, a member of FREE (Fight Repression of Erotic Expression), decided to apply for the marriage license anyway. This event was publicized on local television stations and resulted in several newspaper articles (e.g., "Prospective Newlyweds Really in a Gay Mood" and "Two Homosexuals Plan to Wed").[20] As a result, the board of regents voted not to approve McConnell's appointment on the ground that "his personal conduct as represented in the public and university news media is not consistent with the best interests of the University."

Since McConnell was well qualified for the job, he went to court to enjoin the board from refusing to employ him solely because he was homosexual. McConnell argued that the board's decision was "a clear example of the unreasoning prejudice and revulsion some people feel when confronted by a homosexual." Therefore, such action by the board, said McConnell, "subjected him to arbitrary, unreasonable and discriminatory action working a deprivation of his Fourteenth Amendment right to equal protection of the laws." The U.S. Court of Appeals did not agree.

The Court ruled that the board had ample basis on which it could reasonably conclude that the appointment was not in the best interest of the University. "This," said the Court, "is not a case involving mere homosexual propensities on the part of a prospective employee. Neither is it a case in which an applicant is excluded from employment because of a desire clandestinely to pursue homosexual conduct. It is, instead, a case in which something more than remunerative employment is sought; a case in which the applicant seeks employment on his own terms; a case in which the prospective employee demands . . . the right to pursue an activist role in *implementing* his unconventional idea concerning the societal status to be accorded homosexuals, and thereby, to foist tacit approval of this socially repugnant concept upon the employer. . . . We know of no constitutional fiat," concluded the Court, "which requires an employer to accede to such extravagant demands. We are therefore unable fairly to categorize the Board's action here as arbitrary, unreasonable or capricious."[21]

THE WATSON CASE: PUBLIC DRUNKENNESS AND TEACHER CERTIFICATION

Joseph Watson was a California teacher who had been convicted of six offenses involving the use of alcohol during the ten years preceding his application for a general secondary diploma.[22] The state board of education denied Watson's application. Since Watson believed he was a good teacher, he took his case to court. Relying on the *Morrison* ruling, Watson argued that since there was no evidence showing that his convictions affected his classroom performance the action of the board should be reversed.

The court acknowledged that the only evidence against Watson was his convictions involving consumption of alcohol. Nevertheless, it held that this amply demonstrated his unfitness to teach for the following reasons:

First, one of the main concerns of parents, administrators, and legislators is "the effect of the use and overindulgence in alcohol on their youngsters." Since the court found that Watson's use of alcohol had gotten entirely out of his control, he could not have "the proper concerned attitude necessary for successfully counseling and directing young students away from the harmful effects of alcohol."

Second, Watson's conduct was public. Being arrested as a "public drunk" or for driving under the influence of alcohol did not create in Watson "the example young people at an impressionable age need." In contrast to Morrison, whose conduct received no publicity before the board's action, Watson had persistently and publicly violated important community values and jeopardized the welfare of his students and the public.

Finally, Watson's apparent disregard for law and order was a serious concern. The court emphasized that an important part of education is the teaching "by example as well as precept of obedience to properly constituted authority." By contrast, Watson's behavior clearly indicated that he is unfit to teach and work with young people. "I don't know," said the trial judge, "what better evidence there could be of immorality than a series of criminal convictions."[23]

THE JARVELLA CASE: USE OF OBSCENE LANGUAGE

A dedicated and enthusiastic high school teacher from Ohio named Jarvella was fired for "immorality" because he wrote two private letters that became public. The teacher had an excellent rapport with his students and had received outstanding evaluations from his supervisors and fellow teachers. The letters were mailed to a former student, Ben Nicholas, who had graduated from high school the previous year.

Nicholas' mother found the letters among his personal effects. Because she was apparently shocked and angered by the language in the letters, she turned them over to the police department. Local newspapers learned of the letters and wrote several stories about them, and the prosecuting attorney was quoted as saying that he considered them hard-core obscenity and that "it seemed obvious that a person who would write letters of this kind is not fit to be a school teacher."[24] Subsequently the school board conducted a private hearing and terminated Jarvella's contract on the ground of "immorality." Jarvella went to the local court to appeal the board's decision.

After a hearing before the court, Judge Simmons ruled in Jarvella's favor. Concerning the letters the judge wrote: "They contain language which many adults would find gross, vulgar, and offensive and which some 18 year old males would find unsurprising and fairly routine."

The term *immorality,* said Judge Simmons, must refer not to "immoral conduct" in the abstract but to that which is "hostile to the welfare of the school community." The private writings of a teacher not contrary to that welfare "are absolutely immaterial" and cannot be used to justify discharging the teacher.

There was no evidence that the writing of these letters adversely affected the welfare of the schools—except after public disclosure. And this, wrote Judge Simmons, "was the result, not of any misconduct on [Jarvella's] part, but of misconduct on the part of others . . ."

The court concluded that a teacher's private conduct is a proper concern of his employer only when it affects him as a teacher; "his private acts are his own business and may not be the basis of discipline" so long as his professional achievement is not affected. The court therefore held that Jarvella should be restored to his rights under his teaching contract.

SUMMARY AND CONCLUSION

Whether a teacher can be dismissed for conduct that is generally considered immoral or illegal depends on the circumstances of the case. Circumstances that appear to be especially important are: (1) whether the conduct was personal and private, (2) whether it became public through the indiscretion of the teacher, and (3) whether it involved students.

Personal and private activity. The *Morrison* and *Jarvella* opinions held that private conduct cannot be considered immoral action sufficient to justify a teacher's dismissal simply because it is contrary to the mores of the community. Thus, evidence that a teacher has done something that many or even most people regard as immoral (e.g., homosexual activity, smoking marijuana, excessive drinking, or using obscene language) is not by itself sufficient ground for dismissal. To dismiss a teacher it must be demonstrated that his "immorality" is related to specific conduct that affects his ability to teach. As long as his competence as a teacher is not affected, his private acts are his own business and should not form a basis for disciplinary action.

Personal conduct that becomes public through the teacher's indiscretion. Courts tend to uphold the dismissal of teachers for this kind of immoral conduct. Examples we have considered include attempting to "pick up" a homosexual partner on a public beach, applying for a license to marry another homosexual, repeated arrests for drunken driving, and publicly admitting to frequent use of marijuana. Other examples might include a teacher who worked as a prostitute on weekends or a teacher found guilty of burglary.

Whether activities such as appearing in the chorus line of a burlesque theatre, working as a bartender in a controversial establishment, being a conspicuous and habitual gambler, or directing a nudist camp could result in dismissal might depend on such factors as the size and sophistication of the community, the notoriety of the activity in question, and whether the activity took place in or away from the community where the teacher is employed.

Immoral conduct with students. In such cases the courts can be expected to be quite strict. Thus, evidence of a single homosexual relationship between a teacher and a student would probably be enough to sustain a teacher's dismissal, even if the relationship had occurred years before and even if no other students, parents, or teacher knew about it. Similarly, a public school teacher who participated with his students in smoking marijuana, drinking excessively, or using obscene language would probably receive no protection from the courts.

In some situations, however, the age and maturity of the students might make a difference. Hence, the use of obscene language or perhaps even a discreet sexual relationship between a junior college teacher and a twenty-one-year-old student might be regarded far differently than such language or relationship between a junior high school teacher and his students.

Evidence to support dismissal. In the case of personal and private conduct, a teacher cannot be dismissed unless competent evidence is presented to support the charge of unfitness to teach. Where personal conduct has become public through the teacher's intention or indiscretion, evidence of the actual negative effect of his conduct on his classroom performance is not necessary; competent evidence of the "likely" harmful effect on the students is probably adequate. In cases involving immoral conduct with a student, there is no need to show that the conduct is likely to have any negative effect on classroom performance. Thus, if evidence develops concerning a single sexual relationship between a teacher and a student, the teacher could be dismissed for that conduct alone, even though he is an excellent teacher and there is no evidence that the incident has affected his teaching.

In sum, the law concerning the removal of a teacher for immoral conduct is neither neat nor precise. There are no recent opinions of the U.S. Supreme Court on this topic, and the landmark decision in the Morrison case may not be followed in all states. Nevertheless, the *Morrison* opinion probably represents the direction of the future. It recognizes that a teacher should not be penalized for his private actions unless they relate directly to his professional qualifications and have a clear impact on his effectiveness as a teacher.

NOTES

[1]94 Cal. Rptr. 318, 321 (1971).

[2]233 N.E. 2d 143, 146 (1967).

[3]*Morrison* v. *Board of Education,* 461 P. 2d 375, 385 (1969).

[4]Sarac was specifically charged with having "rubbed, touched, and fondled the private sexual parts of one L. A. Bowers, a person of the masculine sex, with the intent to arouse and excite unnatural sexual desires in said L. A. Bowers." *Sarac* v. *State Board of Education,* 57 Cal. Rptr. 69, 71 (1967).

[5]*Id.* at 72.

[6]*Id.* at 72–73.

[7]Arguments in support of the decision of the board of education are also taken from the dissenting opinion of Judge Sullivan, *Morrison* v. *State Board of Education,* 1C 3d 214, 240 (1969).

[8]Education Code, Section 13556.5. *Id.* at 247.

[9]Education Code, Section 13202, provides: "The State Board of Education shall revoke or suspend for immoral or unprofessional conduct . . . or for evident unfitness for service life diplomas, documents or credentials." *Id.* at 218.

[10]These arguments are taken from the opinion of the Court written by Judge Tobriner, *Id.* at 217–238.

[11]*Id.* at 238.

[12]*Ibid.* (Italics added).

[13]*Id.* at 235.

[14]*Id.* at 244.

[15]*Id.* at 249.

[16]In the words of the court, the deputy observed that Stubblefield's "pants were unzipped and lowered from the waist, exposing his penis. The student was nude from the waist up, and her capri pants were unzipped and open at the waist." *Board of Trustees of Compton Jr. Col. Dist.* v. *Stubblefield,* 94 Cal. Rptr. 318, 320 (1971).

[17]*Id.* at 323.

[18]*Governing Board* v. *Brennan,* 18C. A. 3d 396, 399–400 (1971).

[19]*Id.* at 402–403.

[20]*McConnell* v. *Anderson,* U.S. Court of Appeals, 8th Circuit, #20, 583, 18 October 1971, as reported in *Employment Practices Decisions,* New York, Commerce Clearing House, 1971, pp. 5174–5177.

[21]*Id.* at 5176–5177.

[22]These included four convictions for drunk driving. Watson was again arrested for drunk driving while his application was pending before the state board. *Watson* v. *State Bd. of Education,* 22 C.A. 3d 559, 561 (1971).

[23]*Id.* at 565.

[24]*Jarvella* v. *Willoughby—East Lake City School District,* 233 N.E. 2d 143, 145 (1967).

5
The teacher's personal appearance

Each teacher is expected to give proper attention to his personal appearance. A pleasing appearance in dress and manner influences the reaction of students to the teacher and to the general learning environment. . . .

—from a Louisiana School Board Regulation as reported in Blanchet *v.* Vermilion School Board *(1969)*

It seems to us that the wearing of a beard is a form of expression of an individual's personality and that such a right of expression, although probably not within the literal scope of the First Amendment itself, is . . . entitled to its peripheral protection.

—Finot *v.* Pasadena Board of Education *(1967)*

If most parents want schools to teach their children conventional standards of dress and grooming, do they have a right to make this part of the informal curriculum? If so, isn't it reasonable to ask teachers to be adult models of neatness and good taste?

A bank, a store, or a law firm can require that its employees wear business suits during working hours. Should a school board be able to make the same type of requirement for its teachers?

An increasing number of teachers argue against these requirements. They say that grooming and dress are personal matters, and that they should be allowed to dress as they like. But many school boards believe it is their responsibility to insure that a teacher's appearance is in accord with the professional standards of the community.

The cases in this chapter were brought by teachers who were dismissed for violating school policy concerning grooming or dress. They went to court to affirm what they believed were their constitutional rights.

THE LUCIA CASE: FAIR PROCEDURES FOR TEACHERS

Monson is a small town in western Massachusetts with a population of about 4,000 people. During the 1968–1969 winter vacation, a Monson teacher named David Lucia began growing a beard, which he wore to school when classes resumed in January. While the beard grew to cover Lucia's face, he kept it short, neat, and well-trimmed, and it caused no disruption in his classroom. The week after school resumed the superintendent told Lucia that there was an unwritten policy that teachers should be clean shaven on the job. The next week, following the instructions of the school committee, the superintendent informed Lucia by letter of a school policy against wearing beards and mustaches while teaching and specifically requested that Lucia shave his beard. Privately the superintendent told Lucia, "Were I you, I'd remove the beard; but the decision is up to you."[1] Next Lucia met with the school committee, each of whose members stated his reasons for feeling it was inappropriate for a teacher to wear a beard in class. After the meeting Lucia told one of the members that "Monson was 100 years behind the times."

The following week the committee met and voted to suspend Lucia "because of insubordination and improper example set by a teacher in the Monson School System." Lucia was not notified of the meeting or informed that the school committee was going to consider suspending him. Two weeks later the committee met in executive session to vote on Lucia's dismissal. Although Lucia was not notified of this meeting either, he heard about it and asked that it be postponed several days so that he could attend with legal counsel. His request was not granted, and the committee voted to dismiss him.

After his dismissal Lucia attempted unsuccessfully to secure employment as a teacher. He remained unemployed for six weeks and then worked periodically in a factory for about two-thirds of his former salary. Because of his dispute with the school committee, Lucia lost fifteen pounds, and a preexisting ulcer was aggravated. As a result of these events, Lucia went to court to reverse his "improper dismissal" and seek damages against the school committee.

The court did not decide on the question of whether or not wearing a beard was a constitutional right. Instead, it ruled that Lucia's freedom to wear a beard, especially in combination with his professional reputation as a school teacher, might not be taken from him without due process of law.

The court then noted two "substantial deficiencies" in the procedures followed in suspending and dismissing Lucia. First, he was not specifically told what the charges against him were and that refusal to remove his beard would result in his dismissal. Second, prior to Lucia's controversy with the school committee there was no written or announced policy that Monson teachers should not wear beards in the classroom. After criticizing the committee's lack of due process, the court observed:

The American public school system, which has a basic responsibility for instilling in its students an appreciation of our democratic system, is a peculiarly appropriate place for the use of fundamentally fair procedures.[2]

The lack of such fair procedures led the court to void Lucia's suspension and dismissal, order his reinstatement, compensate him for his lost salary and the costs of his court suit, and award him $1,000 of "compensatory damages" for the pain and suffering connected with the weight loss and aggravated ulcer caused by his unlawful dismissal.

From the ruling in the Lucia case, we can conclude that a teacher cannot be lawfully dismissed for wearing a beard unless: (1) there is a published school policy outlawing beards, (2) teachers are given adequate notice of the policy and the consequences of not adhering to it, and (3) a fair hearing is held to judge the specific alleged violation.

Thus, the court established certain minimum procedures of due process that would apply to a school system that wants to control whether or not teachers wear beards, mustaches, or—presumbaly—long hair. The unanswered question of whether a teacher's beard is entitled to constitutional protection is considered in the following case.

THE FINOT CASE: THE RIGHT TO WEAR A BEARD

Paul Finot taught government to high school seniors in the Pasadena, California, school system for seven years. In September 1963, when Finot arrived at school wearing a recently grown beard, the principal asked him to shave it off. Upon his refusal the board of education transferred Finot to home teaching, despite the fact that he was a challenging and effective classroom teacher. Finot branded his transfer "unconstitutional" and went to court to force the board to change its action.

The board said its action was justified on the basis of the professional judgment of the principal and superintendent, and the school's administrative policy. The policy had been in force for three years. It was based on the city's teacher handbook, which called for teachers to practice the common social amenities as evidenced by acceptable dress and grooming, and to set an example of neatness and good taste. This was related to a student handbook prohibiting beards, mustaches, and excessively long hair as "not appropriate dress for male students."[3]

The board's action was also based on the "professional judgment" of Finot's principal and superintendent. They explained that the appearance of teachers had a definite effect on student dress and that student dress had a definite correlation with student behavior—the well-dressed student generally behaved equally well. Their concern was that Finot's beard might attract undue attention, interfere with the process of education, and make the prohibition of beards for students more difficult to enforce. And they felt that wearing a beard did not meet the school's requirement of acceptable grooming or set an example of good taste.

Questions to Consider

1. Do you think the school board was justified in transferring Finot? Was it justified in expecting its teachers to provide an example of neatness and good taste? Why or why not?
2. If you were a school administrator, what, if any, rules would you issue concerning standards of grooming?
3. Should the wearing of a beard or long hair be allowed under some circumstances and prohibited under others?

4. Where in the Constitution could Finot find support for his claim that he had a right to wear a beard?

Court decisions

After hearing arguments from lawyers for the school board and Finot, the trial judge found that the board's action in changing Finot's teaching assignment was a lawful and reasonable exercise of its discretion. But Finot and the American Civil Liberties Union disagreed. Therefore they took the case to the U.S. District Court in California.

The District Court supported Finot's argument that the board's action in transferring him to home teaching was unconstitutional. The Court said that Finot's right to wear a beard was one of the liberties protected by the Fourteenth Amendment to the Constitution, which prohibits the deprivation of any person's life, *liberty*, or property without due process of law. The Court also said that "the wearing of a beard is a form of expression of an individual's personality."

Some people interpret a beard as a symbol of masculinity, authority, or wisdom. Others see it as a symbol of nonconformity or rebellion. In either case, the Court recognized that symbols, under appropriate circumstances, "merit Constitutional protection." Thus, though not within the literal scope of the First Amendment, wearing a beard is entitled to its peripheral protection as a form of symbolic speech and a "right of expression." In conclusion, the Court ruled that in the absence of evidence that a teacher's wearing a beard has an adverse effect on the educational process, beards on teachers "cannot constitutionally be banned from the classroom."

If wearing a beard is a constitutionally protected personal liberty, does this mean that a school system can set no limits upon these liberties? No. But it does mean that for a school to require a waiver of such liberties as a condition of employment it would probably have to meet three tests suggested by a California court: (1) There must be a rational relation between the restriction in question and the effectiveness of the educational system; (2) "the benefits which the public gains by the restraints must outweigh the resulting impairment of constitutional rights"; (3) "no alternatives less subversive of constitutional rights are available."[4]

In the Finot case the Court held that the school board had failed to meet the second and third tests. It ruled that the benefit in supporting school rules outlawing student beards does not outweigh Finot's right to wear a beard while teaching in a classroom. Furthermore, there are other alternatives open to the school board to deter students from wearing beards that are less subversive of Finot's rights than the administrative policy in question.

THE PEEK CASE: AN INSTANCE OF INSTITUTIONAL RACISM

Ribault Senior High School in Duval County, Florida, had one black teacher. His name was Booker C. Peek, and he wore a goatee as a matter of racial pride. As a French teacher he was considered superior.

Peek's principal repeatedly requested that he remove his goatee, and Peek repeatedly refused. Solely because of this refusal, the principal recommended nonreappointment. As a result, Peek was not reappointed to the Duval County School System for the 1969–1970 school year.

Peek believed his constitutional rights were violated by the action and went to court to seek reappointment. The school board claimed that Peek's nonreappointment was based on a reasonable exercise of the principal's discretionary power to insure appropriate dress, discipline, and deportment of students. However, no evidence was presented indicating that Peek's wearing a goatee might reasonably be expected to disrupt discipline or cause students to wear inappropriate dress.

The court ruled in Peek's favor for the following reasons:

- It referred with approval to the holding in the Finot case that the wearing of a beard by a teacher is a constitutionally protected liberty under the due-process clause of the Fourteenth Amendment. "The wearer of the goatee here," said the court, "deserves no less protection."[5]
- When a goatee is worn by a black man as an expression of his heritage, culture, and racial pride, "its wearer also enjoys the protection of First Amendment rights."
- There were no written rules or policy in the school system regulating the discretion conferred upon each principal by the school board in matters of personal appearance. In the absence of such regulations, the action of the principal in requesting the removal of the goatee was "arbitrary, unreasonable and based on personal preference."
- Furthermore, the decision to recommend nonreappointment was racially motivated and tainted with "institutional racism," the effects of which were manifested in "an intolerance of ethnic diversity and racial pride."

Accordingly, the court ordered the school board to reappoint Booker Peek "on the same basis and with the same assignment which would have been made if the recommendation of his principal had been favorable."

THE BLANCHET CASE: CAN NECKTIES BE REQUIRED?

In September 1967 a Louisiana school board passed the following new policy:

Each teacher is expected to give proper attention to his personal appearance. A pleasing appearance in dress and manner influences the reaction of students to the teacher and to the general learning environment. A teacher also comes in daily contact with the public, a public which is sometimes very critical of the appropriateness and neatness of the teacher's dress. The teacher who is particular about personal appearances not only contributes to his own acceptance by others, but also influences the attitudes of students and adults toward the teaching profession. The matter of appropriate dress should be of equal concern to men and women teachers and should reflect accepted standards of good grooming. In the interest of enhancing the image of the teaching profession at school, in the classroom, and in the community, it shall be required that male teachers wear neckties in the official performance of their duties during the course of the school day. Teachers of physical education, industrial arts and vocational agriculture, when teaching outdoor or shop classes, may wear dress appropriate to the teaching of those activities.[6]

When teacher Edward Blanchet received word of the new policy, he requested the school board to reconsider it on the grounds that it was unreasonable and unconstitutional. Responding to the request, the board reconsidered and reaffirmed its policy. When Blanchet refused to comply with the necktie requirement, he was charged with "willful neglect of duty" and suspended until he agreed to comply. Blanchet then filled suit to enjoin the board from enforcing the resolution or from disciplining him for failure to obey it.

Questions to consider

1. Is it reasonable for a school board to be concerned with the public image of a teacher? If so, is it reasonable for school boards to require that teachers dress in accordance with "conventional professional

standards" in the community? Or does the regulation of a teacher's dress go beyond the authority of a school board?
2. If you were a member of a school board, would you institute a dress code for teachers? If so, what would the code require? Or would you allow complete freedom for teachers to dress as they wished? Would you require teachers to dress neatly? Would you allow dress that disrupted school activities?
3. Would you apply the same principles in judging the constitutionality of dress regulations as of grooming regulations? Is there a difference? If so, what is the basis of the difference?

The opinion of the court

The Louisiana Court of Appeals was impressed by Blanchet's character and conviction. Thus, Judge Tate wrote:

> *From motives all concede to be of the utmost sincerity, this dedicated teacher and father of seven felt the regulation so unreasonably interfered with his personal liberty that, on the strength of this conviction, he chanced his livelihood and the career to which he had dedicated most of his adult life.*
>
> *While we might lightly say that, after all, a necktie is only a piece of cloth, nevertheless for the same motives which impelled the Boston merchants not to pay that insignificant little tax on tea just before this nation's independence, Blanchet felt strongly that this regulation impinged on his personal liberty to dress as he wished, without having any reasonable relationship to any educational value.*[7]

Despite Blanchet's convictions, arguments, and evidence, the Court did not rule in his favor. Here is what happened and why.

Blanchet argued that the rule requiring male teachers to wear neckties during the school day was arbitrary, unreasonable, and unrelated to any educational aim. To support this argument he introduced evidence indicating that for years most male teachers in rural areas taught without ties, that wearing ties was uncomfortable in the hot spring and summer months in Louisiana, and that only a small minority of other school boards in the state required teachers to wear neckties. The evidence also indicated that during his eighteen years of teaching Blanchet had always dressed neatly, though he usually did not wear a tie. Furthermore evidence showed him to be "a dedicated and effective teacher, an assistant principal at his school, [and] a sober church-going family man."

In support of its position the school board argued that wearing neckties enhances the image of the teacher as a professional man, increasing the respect accorded him by community and students. Some educational witnesses testified that more formal dress enhances the teacher's authority in the eyes of the student. There was evidence that most leading citizens and professional men in the community usually wear ties, "representing a conventional attire for those in positions of leadership." And it was shown that several other school boards had adopted a similar necktie requirement "as furthering educational policies in their own parishes."

Thus, there was evidence both for and against the board's policy. The Court seemed to indicate that if it had been the school board it might not have passed the new policy. But it also indicated that it could not substitute its views for the judgment of the board.

This is based on legal principles providing that within the limits of their authority the wisdom or good judgment of school boards cannot be questioned by the courts. Member of school boards are presumably elected or appointed "because of their peculiar fitness for the post." In contrast, judges are chosen because of their legal knowledge, not for their experience in administering a public school system. Therefore, a "presumption of legality attaches to the action" of a school board. Only when evidence shows that the action of such a board is arbitrary or unreasonable is a court justified in interfering. Since in this case the Court found that there was a rational basis for the board's policy, it could not be overturned as arbitrary and unreasonable.

Blanchet also argued that the policy should be considered an unconstitutional infringement on his personal liberty to dress as he wished. He cited the Finot case to support his argument. The Court acknowledged that the "constitutional issue is not free from doubt," especially "in view of some of the more recent federal pronouncements." Nevertheless, it ruled that "the school board's necktie regulation may be held valid as not unreasonably restricting the personal liberty of the teacher-employee to dress as he wills."

Finally, the court decreed that Blanchet should be reinstated to his position "on his statement that he intends to comply with the policy requiring the wearing of neckties."

SUMMARY AND CONCLUSIONS

The Lucia case held that, even if wearing a beard is not a constitutional right, school officials cannot dismiss teachers for wearing beards unless pursuant to clear written rules that are published and communicated to teachers and are applied with reasonable due process.

The Finot case went further than Lucia and held that a beard is a form of personal expression or symbolic speech and is therefore entitled to the peripheral protection of the First Amendment. Thus, the court concluded that beards as such cannot be constitutionally prohibited. According to *Finot*, only if it can be proven that a beard has interfered with a teacher's effectiveness can a school take action against the teacher. The *Finot* court would presumably strike down similar rules prohibiting a teacher from wearing a mustache, a goatee, or long hair. Exceptions would probably be made in cases in which the controversial grooming was disruptive and distracting or posed a danger to health or safety. Otherwise it would be constitutionally protected.

The Blanchet case held that a school's dress policy for teachers is a matter of administrative discretion and is not subject to judicial review unless it is clearly unreasonable or arbitrary. (On the basis of this ruling, a school board could presumably require men to wear business suits and prohibit women from wearing pants suits.) Some courts would probably apply the principles of the Lucia case in these matters; that is, even if a teacher does not have the constitutional right to dress as he pleases, he cannot be dismissed for the way he dresses unless pursuant to clear written rules that are communicated to teachers and applied fairly.

Although the *Blanchet* decision might seem outdated to many teachers and administrators, it is doubtful whether the *Finot* court would have decided the case differently. This is because clothing can be changed to suit the occasion. As the *Finot* opinion pointed out, "A beard cannot be donned and doffed for work and play as wearing apparel generally can, and, therefore, the effect of a prohibition against wearing one extends beyond working hours."

The courts might, however be more likely to protect certain nonconforming clothing under special circumstances. Thus, they might protect a black teacher of African Studies who wears a dashiki as directly relevant to his job or as a matter of academic freedom and racial pride. But it is doubtful that any court would protect a math teacher who insists on coming to class in jeans, sandals, and a T-shirt because he does not approve of middle-class attire.

In the future, however, a teacher's dress may be considered in the same category as his beard or moustache: as a form of symbolic speech and personal expression. The way a teacher dressed would then be limited only if it directly interfered with his teaching. To prove "interference," the school administrators would have to show that the style of dress was distracting (as in the case of a well-endowed braless or miniskirted teacher in a class of adolescent boys) or might be detrimental to the health or safety of other teachers or students (as in the case of a shop teacher who insisted on wearing unconventional clothing that could easily get caught in dangerous machinery.)

In sum, a teacher's grooming is increasingly considered a protected form of symbolic speech, but his clothing is not. Courts consider it a more serious invasion of a teacher's rights to order him to shave his beard than to expect him to follow a dress code. One restriction is in effect only during the working day; the other is more permanent. Increasingly, however, schools are liberalizing their dress codes for teachers and students, and future courts may extend the same peripheral protection of the First Amendment to dress styles that beards receive today.

A NONLEGAL POSTSCRIPT

Readers often wonder about the human beings involved in court cases. The social and emotional conflicts generated by controversies that wind up in court often have consequences that overshadow the legal results. While a teacher may prevail in court, a negative community reaction may drive him out of town. We do not know what happened to most of the teachers in the cases we have discussed, since our work is based primarily on library research. We do know, however, that Mr. Lucia is still teaching successfully in Massachusetts. And the extent to which our culture has changed may be indicated by the fact that Paul Finot is now an administrator, wearing a beard, in the same school district that tried to discipline him a few years ago.

NOTES

[1]*Lucia* v. *Duggan,* 303 F. Supp. 112, 115 (1969).

[2]*Id.* at 118–119.

[3]*Finot* v. *Pasadena City Board of Education,* 250 C.A. 2d. 189, 191 (1967).

[4]*Id.* at 199.

[5]*Braxton* v. *Board of Public Instruction of Duval County, Florida,* 303 F. Supp. 958 (1969).

[6]*Blanchet* v. *Vermilion Parish School Board,* 220 S.2d 534, 541 (1969).

[7]*Id.* at 540.

6
Loyalty oaths

A teacher who is bereft of the essential quality of loyalty and devotion to his government and the fundamentals of our democratic society is lacking in a basic qualification for teaching.[1]

—*a New Jersey Court*

. . . Government should leave the mind and spirit of man absolutely free. Such a governmental policy encourages varied intellectual outlooks in the belief that the best views will prevail.[2]

—*Justice Hugo Black*

In 1956 Robert Hamilton, Dean of the University of Wyoming's College of Law, published a book entitled *Legal Rights and Liabilities of Teachers.* The book included a discussion of teachers' loyalty oaths, which had then been enacted by about half of the states. Professor Hamilton praised the legislatures that had passed loyalty oath laws for being "commendably concerned with the protection of the schools from the influence of subversive teachers."[3]

He then discussed two court opinions sustaining loyalty oaths that had been challenged by teachers. The first involved a suit by Oklahoma teachers. They objected to a part of the oath that prohibited them from advocating or becoming a member of any organization that advocates the overthrow of the government by force or other unlawful means. In upholding the constitutionality of the oath, the Supreme Court of Oklahoma pointed out that teachers and other public employees should expect to have their loyalty investigated by higher authorities. "Employees of the state," wrote the Court, "enter upon their duties with full knowledge and in these times, expectation, that the state will, if it has not already done so, make full investigation on the point, and if thought expedient require on oath disclosing the attitude of public officials and employees."[4]

The second case involved a challenge to the constitutionality of a similar oath by New Jersey teachers. In citing the case Professor Hamilton wrote that "the language of the court in sustaining the law is so important to teachers" that he would quote it at length. The court's opinion reflects the philosophy of loyalty oath proponents and the attitudes and beliefs of many legislators, administrators, and judges during the 1950's.

Freedom from belief in force and violence as a justifiable weapon for the destruction of government is the very essence of the teacher's qualifications. The apprehended danger is real and abiding. We have long had evidences of the pressure here of a Godless theology ruthlessly fostered by a foreign power which has for its aim the violent overthrow of government and free society. And one of its weapons is the debasement of teaching as a softening measure in the consummation of the subversive process. The school system affords the opportunity and means for subtle infiltration. There is no intrusion upon personal freedoms when the government intervenes, as here, to avert this peril to its very existence. A teacher who is bereft of the essential quality of loyalty and devotion to his government and the fundamentals of our democratic society is lacking in a basic qualification for teaching. . . . In the current struggle for men's minds, the state is well within its province in ensuring the integrity of the educational process against those who would pervert it to subversive ends.[5]

Thus, for many legislators and administrators the purpose of loyalty oaths was to ensure "the integrity of the educational process" against subversive teachers. Others believed teachers' oaths should serve additional purposes. These included requiring teachers to promote such values as "respect for the flag," "reverence for law and order," and "undivided allegiance" to the government. As the next case indicates, the Washington legislature wanted to use teachers' loyalty oaths to accomplish all of these purposes.

But are loyalty oaths a good way to insure loyal teachers? Or is their main effect to restrict free speech and inhibit academic freedom? Are "investigations by higher authority" a good way to eliminate disloyal teachers? Or are there better ways to achieve this purpose? These are some of the questions raised by the cases in this chapter.

THE BAGGETT CASE: A DANGER TO CONSCIENTIOUS TEACHERS

In 1931 legislation was passed in the State of Washington requiring teachers, upon applying for a licence to teach or renewing an existing contract, to subscribe to the following loyalty oath:

I solemnly swear (or affirm) that I will support the Constitution and laws of the United States of America and the State of Washington, and will by precept and example promote respect for the flag and institutions of the United States of America and the State of Washington, reverence for law and order, and undivided allegiance to the government of the United States.[6]

In 1955, another statute was passed requiring that each state employee also swear that he does not advise or teach others to commit any act intended to overthrow or alter the constitutional form of government by revolution or violence. In 1962, the president of the University of Washington notified all employees that they would be required to take the oath of allegiance as provided in the 1931 act and also swear that they were not subversive persons pursuant to the 1955 statute. Both oaths were made subject to the penalties of perjury.

In response, a group of Washington teachers, staff, and faculty brought a class action asking that the two statutes requiring these oaths be declared unconstitutional.* In 1964, the U.S. Supreme Court heard their arguments and ruled in their favor. The Court held that the oaths are invalid because their language is unduly vague, un-

*A class action is a suit brought on behalf of other persons similarly situated. Thus in this case the class action was probably brought on behalf of Wisconsin teachers and state employees who were required to take the oath.

certain, and broad. Here is some of the reasoning underlying its decision:

The 1955 oath

The Court said that teachers taking this oath disclaiming subversive activity may conclude that anyone who teaches or advises members of the Communist Party is subversive because such teaching or advice may aid the activities of the Party. Does the statute prohibit teachers from supporting a communist candidate for office? Does it reach anyone who supports any cause that is also supported by communists? If so, the statute requires "foreswearing of an undefined variety of guiltless . . . behavior."

Is it subversive to participate in international conventions with communist scholars? Is selecting scholars from communist countries as visiting professors and working with them at the University considered subversive if such scholars are members of the Communist Party, which by statutory definition is dedicated to the overthrow of the government? Because the answers to these questions are uncertain, the Court said that the oath disclaiming subversive activity goes beyond prohibiting the overthrow of the government by force or violence. It extends to altering the government by "revolution," which could include any rapid or fundamental change. By this definition any person supporting or teaching peaceful but far-reaching constitutional amendments might be engaged in subversive activity. Or, if a teacher supported U.S. participation in world government he might be considered subversive. Therefore, this part of the oath is unconstitutionally vague, broad, and uncertain.

The 1931 statute

This law exacts a promise that the teacher will "promote respect for the flag and institutions" of the United States and the State of Washington. The Court noted several problems.

How wide, for example, is the range of activities that might be deemed inconsistent with this promise? Would a teacher who refused to salute the flag because of his religious beliefs be accused of breaking his promise? Even criticism of the design or color of the state flag, or unfavorable comparison of it with that of another state could be deemed disrespectful and therefore in violation of the oath.

The Court also wondered about the national and state "institutions" for which the teacher is expected to "promote respect." Do they include every significant practice, law, and custom of our government or of our culture? Do they consist of those institutions to which the majority of Americans are loyal? If so, the oath might prevent a teacher from criticizing his state's judicial system, the Supreme Court, or the FBI. Or it might be interpreted as prohibiting a teacher from advocating the abolition of the Civil Rights Commission or the House Committee on Un-American Activities.

Moreover, it is difficult to know what can be done without transgressing the promise to "promote undivided allegiance" to the U.S. Government. "It would not be unreasonable," wrote Justice White, "for the serious-minded oath taker to conclude that he should dispense with lectures voicing far-reaching criticism of any old or new policy followed by the Government of the United States." He could hesitate to join special-interest group opposing any current national policy, for if he did he might be accused of placing loyalty to the group above allegiance to the United States.

The problem of unconstitutional vagueness is further aggravated because the 1931 statute inhibits the exercise of individual freedoms affirmatively protected by the First Amendment. As Justice White noted, the uncertain meanings of the oaths require teachers to "steer far wider of the unlawful zone" than if the boundaries of those zones were clearly marked. The result is that teachers with a conscientious regard for what they solemnly swear and sensitive to the dangers posed by the oaths' indefinite language can avoid risk "only by restricting their conduct to that which is unquestionably safe. Free speech may not be so inhibited."[7] Whenever statutes place limits on First Amendment freedoms, they must be "narrowly drawn to meet the precise evil the legislature seeks to curb," and the conduct prohibited must be "defined specifically" so that the persons affected remain secure in their rights to engage in activities not clearly prohibited.

Objection by the state

The attorney for the State of Washington labeled "wholly fanciful" some of the activities the Court suggested might be prohibited by the two oaths. This may be correct; but it only emphasizes the difficulties caused by the two statutes. If the oaths do not include the behavior suggested, what do they cover? "Where," Justice White wondered, "does fanciful possibility end and intended coverage begin?"

It is not enough to say that a prosecutor's sense of fairness would prevent a successful perjury prosecution for some of the activities apparently included within these sweeping oaths. The hazard of being prosecuted for guiltless behavior remains. "It would be blinking at reality," wrote the Court "not to acknowledge that there are some among us always ready to affix a Communist label upon those whose ideas they violently oppose. And experience teaches us that prosecutors too are human."[8]

This decision does not question the power of the state to safeguard the public service from disloyal conduct. But measures that define disloyalty must allow public employees to know what is considered disloyal and exactly what conduct is prohibited by the oath. Because the majority of the Court found both oaths unduly broad, vague, and uncertain, they were held to be unconstitutional.

A dissenting opinion

In a sharp and sometimes sarcastic rebuttal to the majority opinion, Justice Clark wrote:

It is, of course, absurd to say that, under the words of the Washington Act, a professor risks violation when he teaches German, English, history or any other subject included in the curriculum for a college degree, to a class in which a Communist Party member might sit. To so interpret the language of the Act is to extract more sunbeams from cucumbers than did Gulliver's mad scientist. And to conjure up such ridiculous questions, the answers to which we all know or should know are in the negative, is to build up a whimsical and farcical straw man which is not only grim but Grimm.[9]

THE WHITEHALL CASE: "NEGATIVE" OATHS AND ACADEMIC FREEDOM

Several years after the Baggett case, a "negative" loyalty oath aimed at eliminating "subversive" teachers came before the Supreme Court.[10] The majority opinion and the dissent further clarified the Court's position on this type of oath. The oath was prepared by the Attorney General of Maryland pursuant to a state law that included provisions for enforcement and penalties for violation.

Whitehill was a lecturer at the University of Maryland who refused to sign the oath stating that he was not "engaged in one way or another in the attempt to overthrow the Government . . . by force or violence."

The majority of the Court was concerned that Whitehill could not know, except by risking a perjury prosecution, whether as a member of a "subversive" group he would "in one way or another" be engaged in an attempt to overthrow the government. The law requiring the loyalty oath provided for the discharge of "subversive" persons and called for perjury action against those who violated the oath. Regarding these provisions, the Court commented that "the continuing surveillance which this type of law places on teachers is hostile to academic freedom." The Court held that the required oath was not precise or clear. Instead it found an "overbreadth that makes possible oppressive or capricious application as regimes change." That threat could inhibit academic freedom as much as successive suits for perjury. Here, concluded the Court, "we have another classic example of the need for 'narrowly drawn' legislation in this sensitive and important First Amendment area."

In a dissenting opinion Justice Harlan said he could not understand the reasoning of the majority. Whitehill was only asked "whether he is now in one way or another engaged in an attempt to overthrow the government by force or violence." References to academic freedom cannot disguise the fact that Whitehill was simply asked to disclaim present, actual treasonable conduct. In view of the Court's past decisions, it is not clear why the majority found the Maryland oath unconstitutional. "The only thing that does shine through the opinion of the majority," concluded Justice Harlan, "is that its members do not like loyalty oaths."

THE MONROE CASE: VINDICATING A VICTIM OF REPRESSION

Albert Monroe was a tenured professor at San Francisco State College in 1950, when a state loyalty oath was enacted.[11] When Monroe refused to sign the oath, he was dismissed. Since he believed the loyalty oath law was unconstitutional, he began to challenge it through state administrative channels. During this process the California Supreme Court upheld the constitutionality of the oath. Monroe therefore decided it would be futile to fight his dismissal in court, and he took another job.

Fourteen years later the California Supreme Court reversed itself. It concluded that the state loyalty oath was unconstitutional and, in the Vogel case, overruled its earlier decision.[12] On the basis of the *Vogel* ruling, Monroe petitioned the Trustees of the California State Colleges for reinstatement. The Trustees refused, and this time Monroe took his case to court.

On behalf of the California Supreme Court, Justice Tobriner wrote that failure to reinstate Monroe would have a number of negative consequences. Its effect would be to continue to punish Monroe for asserting his First Amendment rights, which had finally been vindicated. It might "chill" other teachers, preventing them from fully exercising their rights of freedom of speech and freedom of association. And the "pall of orthodoxy resulting from earlier exclusionary policies would continue to inhibit the present educational environment."[13]

On the other hand, Monroe's reinstatement would prevent any further injury that might flow from his "conscientious adherence to now-accepted constitutional principles." Furthermore, the reinstatement of Monroe and others like him would enrich the academic community "by reintroducing into that community individuals with conscientiously held beliefs and ideals, beliefs which in the past have been excluded from the public schools simply because of official disapproval."

In its opinion, the Court not only vindicated Monroe but also condemned the state loyalty oath. It criticized the oath because it denied to anyone who refused to take it the opportunity to explain his motives and reasons, and because the oath's assumption of guilt by association was automatic and irrefutable. "The state," wrote Justice Tobriner, "can no longer justify continued exclusion from the public university community of all those who chose to rebel against this form of 'guilt by association.' "

In conclusion, Justice Tobriner described Monroe as "a victim of the repressive political climate of the post-war era" who had been "forcibly separated by the state from his chosen profession of college teaching for more than 20 years." Thus, the Court ruled, "there now remains no constitutionally permissible grounds for continuing [Monroe's] exile from the state college system."[14]

THE OHLSON CASE: AFFIRMING PROFESSIONAL STANDARDS

A Colorado statute requires that no one may enter into or continue teaching in a state public school unless he takes this oath:

I solemnly swear (or affirm) that I will uphold the Constitution of the United States and the constitution of the State of Colorado, and I will faithfully perform the duties of the position upon which I am about to enter.[15]

A group of teachers from the Denver public schools and the state universities and colleges in Colorado went to court to have this oath declared unconstitutional. They argued that the oath is vague and violates the First Amendment rights of freedom of speech and association, that it deprives teachers of due process of law because it lacks procedural safeguards, and that it violates the Fourteenth Amendment because it does not apply to all public employees.

The U.S. District Court, however, did not agree. On behalf of the Court Judge William Doyle wrote that the oath in this case "is not unduly vague." The oath is simply a recognition of our system of constitutional law. It is not overly broad, and it does not constitute a sweeping and improper invasion of a teacher's rights of free association and expression. Respect for law does not preclude the right to dissent. Nor does it limit the right to seek, through lawful means, the repeal of laws with which the oath-taker disagrees. "Support for the constitutions and laws of the nation and state does not call for blind subservience."

The teachers' second argument—that swearing to "faithfully perform the duties" of their position is unconstitutionally vague—was also rejected by the Court. It held that a state can reasonably ask teachers in public schools to subscribe to professional competence and dedication. "It is certain," wrote Judge Doyle, "that there is no right to be unfaithful in the performance of duties."

The teachers' third argument was that the statute violated due process in not providing a hearing upon dismissal for refusal to take the oath. The Court, however, ruled that due process "does not demand a hearing in connection with every dismissal from public employment." A teacher who is dismissed for refusal to take the oath has no need to cross-examine his accuser, since no hearing can change the fact that he refused to take the oath. His reasons for refusal are irrelevant as long as the oath is simple, direct, and unambiguous.

Finally, the teachers claimed that the statute deprived them of equal protection under the Fourteenth Amendment by arbitrarily classifying teachers as a specific group of state employees and requiring them to take the oath. On the contrary, wrote Judge Doyle, the oath is "an almost universal requirement of all public officials, including lawyers and judges, and it cannot be truthfully said that teachers are being picked on." True, the oath does not apply to all state employees. But as long as the oath is reasonable as applied to teachers, who work in a sensitive and influential area, there is no constitutional requirement that it be applied to all public employees.

In conclusion Judge Doyle commented that he was "unable to fully discern" why teachers "find the taking of any oath so obnoxious." The oath has roots as deep as the Constitution. And that historic document clearly permits the requirement that government officials take oaths to uphold the Constitution. The writers of the Constitution thought the requirement of an oath of loyalty was worth whatever deprivation of individual freedom of conscience was involved.

Questions to consider

1. What factors distinguish constitutional oaths from unconstitutional ones?
2. What do you think are the advantages and disadvantages of loyalty oaths? during normal times? during times of national tension?
3. Do loyalty oaths offer assurance of loyal teachers? Are there any alternative ways of achieving this goal?
4. If you were a state legislator, would you vote for a bill that required teachers to take a clear and simple oath pledging to uphold the Constitution and maintain professional standards? Why or why not?

SUMMARY AND CONCLUSIONS

It appears from the cases cited in this chapter that clear, limited, and unambiguous loyalty oaths are upheld, while those that are vague, broad, and uncertain are declared unconstitutional. It would also appear that courts view some kinds of oaths differently than they do others. They seem to look favorably on general, positive oaths in support of the Constitution, as well as on those pledging to uphold a standard of professional competence. This type of oath, illustrated by the Colorado statute in the Ohlson case, has its origin in the Constitution and historically has been taken routinely by high government officials. Usually there is no established machinery to enforce the oath or penalize violators.

In contrast, other oaths (e.g., swearing that one does not belong to any subversive organization or promising "undivided allegiance" to the U.S. Government) tend to be scrutinized more closely by the courts. Such oaths (often referred to as "negative oaths") have frequently been devised by state legislatures for the purpose of eliminating teachers who belong to "subversive" political organizations. The statutes that require them often include provisions for their enforcement and provide for dismissal or other penalties for violation. They have sometimes been used to restrict political freedom and eliminate controversial teachers. The Baggett case provides several examples of this type of oath. These differences explain why some oaths (e.g., to "support the Constitution") that do not seem particularly clear or unambiguous are upheld, while others are declared unconstitutional (e.g., to "promote respect" for the flag of the United States).

The Whitehill and Baggett cases explained the reasons for the Supreme Court's apparent mistrust of loyalty oaths. The Court's critical examination of such oaths—especially those that placed teachers under surveillance—has helped protect academic freedom and maintain a healthier climate in American schools during the past decade.

However there is some evidence that the Supreme Court under Chief Justice Burger will not be as careful in examining loyalty oaths in the future. A 1972 opinion of the Court in the case of *Cole* v. *Richardson* would seem to support this conclusion.[16] A lower court had held that a Massachusetts statute requiring public employees to swear to "oppose the overthrow of the government" by force, violence, or illegal means was unconstitutionally vague. The Supreme Court disagreed. It ruled that the "oppose the overthrow" clause did not require any specific action but was only intended to assure that public employees were willing to live by the Constitution. Thus it appears that the Burger Court will not scrutinize loyalty oaths as carefully or take the exact wording of the oaths as seriously as did the Warren Court. Justice Burger even suggested that the oath in this case is really "no more than an amenity."

To those who fear that unconstitutional prosecutions and harassment might result from such oaths, Justice Burger emphasized that none had occurred since the oath was required in 1948 and none would occur "while this Court sits." Moreover, the Chief Justice himself indicated some personal doubts about whether such loyalty oaths were really in the public interest when he wrote: "The time may come when the value of oaths in routine public employment will be thought not 'worth the candle' for all the division of opinion they engender."

In sum, the attitude of most judges seems to have changed markedly since the days when a New Jersey court commended the state legislature for trying to protect our schools from the pressures of a "Godless theology" by passing a loyalty oath law. The California Supreme Court illustrated this change in its recent opinion in the Monroe case, which publicly condemned the excesses of loyalty oaths and vindicated teachers who were injured by them. In recent years, most courts have carefully scrutinized loyalty oaths, since they tend to inhibit the exercise of First Amendment rights. If oaths were too broad, uncertain, or vague (such as those broadly disclaiming membership in subversive organizations), they were held to be unconstitutional. Two types of oaths, however, have consistently been upheld by the courts: (1) loyalty oaths drawn with precision and prohibiting clearly unlawful conduct and (2) simple employment oaths affirming support for the Constitution or pledging to uphold professional standards. As for the future, the 1972 Cole case would seem to indicate that the Burger Court may not scrutinize loyalty oaths as carefully as most courts have done during the past decade.

NOTES

[1]As quoted in Robert R. Hamilton, *Legal Rights and Liabilities of Teachers*, Laramie, Wyo., School Law Publications, 1956, p. 84.

[2]*Adler* v. *Board of Education*, 342 U.S. 485, 479 (1952).

[3]Hamilton, *op. cit.*, p. 82.

[4]*Ibid.*, p. 83.

[5]*Ibid.*, pp. 84–85.

[6]*Baggett* v. *Bullitt*, 377 U.S. 360, 361–362 (1964).

[7]*Id.* at 372.

[8]*Id.* at 373.

[9]*Id.* at 382–383.

[10]*Whitehill* v. *Elkins*, 389 U.S. 54 (1967).

[11]The 1950 oath states in part: ". . . I do not advocate, nor am I a member of any party or organization, political or otherwise, that now advocates the overthrow of the Government of the United States or of the State of California by force or violence or other unlawful means; that within the five years immediately preceding the taking of this oath, I have not been a member of any party or organization, political or otherwise, that advocated the overthrow of the Government of the United States or of the State of California by force or violence. . ." *Monroe* v. *Trustees of the California State Colleges*, 6 C. 3d 399, 411 (1971).

[12]*Vogel* v. *County of California*, 434 p. 2d 961 (1969).

[13]*Monroe* at 412.

[14]*Id.* at 414.

[15]*Ohlson* v. *Phillips*, 304 F. Supp. 1152–1153 (1969).

[16]*Cole* v. *Richardson*, U.S. Supreme Court, April 18, 1972, as reported in 40 Law Week 4381, April 18, 1972.

7

Membership in controversial organizations

One's associates, past and present, as well as one's conduct, may properly be considered in determining fitness and loyalty. From time immemorial, one's reputation has been determined in part by the company he keeps.[1]

—*Mr. Justice Minton*

A law which applies to membership (in subversive organizations), without the specific intent to further the illegal aims of the organization, infringes unnecessarily on protected freedoms. It rests on the doctrine of guilt by association which has no place here.[2]

—*Mr. Justice Douglas*

Because of this policy (of intellectual freedom), public officials cannot be constitutionally vested with powers to . . . choose the persons or groups people can associate with. Public officials with such powers are not public servants; they are public masters.[3]

—*Mr. Justice Black*

Loyalty oaths are one way a community can try to exclude teachers who are considered disloyal. This chapter considers another way: disqualifying teachers who are members of revolutionary and subversive organizations.

Does the community have the right to exclude communists from the classroom? Can a school board prohibit members of revolutionary or subversive groups from becoming teachers? These are some of the questions considered in the Adler and Keyishian cases. These cases illustrate the competing views concerning teacher membership in controversial organizations. They also illustrate how the dissenting opinion of a minority can become the view of the majority within a decade. Although these cases focus primarily on excluding Communist Party members from the classroom, the same issues and problems arise concerning rules barring members of other extremist organizations. Thus, these questions and controversies are as much alive today as they were at the time of the Adler case (1952) and the Keyishian case (1962).

THE ADLER CASE: GUILT BY ASSOCIATION UPHELD

In 1949 the New York legislature passed the Feinberg Law, which was designed to eliminate members of the Communist Party and other revolutionary groups from the school systems. The preamble of that law made elaborate findings that members of revolutionary groups like the Communist Party have been "infiltrating" into the public schools. As a result, "propaganda can be disseminated among children by those who teach them and to whom they look for guidance, authority and leadership."[4] The legislature also found that members of such groups use their position to teach "a prescribed party line or group dogma or doctrine without regard to truth or free inquiry." This propaganda, the legislature declared, "is sufficiently subtle to escape detection in the classroom; thus the menace of such infiltration into the classroom is difficult to measure." To protect children from such influence, the legislature believed that "laws prohibiting members of such groups . . . from obtaining or retaining employment in public schools be rigorously enforced."[5]

In the Adler case the Feinberg Law was attacked as an abridgment of the rights of free speech and assembly of New York public school employees. The majority of the members of the Supreme Court, however, did not believe the law was unconstitutional, and the widely quoted opinion by Justice Minton has frequently been used to justify other restrictions on teachers' rights.

"It is clear," wrote Justice Minton, that citizens "have the right under our law to assemble, speak, think, and believe as they will.

It is equally clear that they have no right to work for the state in the school system on their own terms. They may work for the school system upon the reasonable terms laid down by the proper authorities of New York. If they do not choose to work on such terms, they are at liberty to retain their beliefs and associations and go elsewhere. Has the state thus deprived them of any right to free speech or assembly? We think not."[6]

Such persons may be denied the privilege of working for the school system either because they advocate overthrow of the government by force or because they are members of organizations known to have that purpose. For the classroom is a sensitive area. There, said Justice Minton, the teacher

> *shapes the attitude of young minds towards the society in which they live. In this, the state has a vital concern. It must preserve the integrity of the schools. That the school authorities have the right and the duty to screen the officials, teachers, and employees as to their fitness to maintain the integrity of the schools as a part of ordered society, cannot be doubted. One's associates, past and present, as well as one's conduct, may properly be considered in determining fitness and loyalty. From time immemorial, one's reputation has been determined in part by the company he keeps. In the employment of officials and teachers of the school system, the state may very properly inquire into the company they keep, and we know of no rule, constitutional or otherwise, that prevents the state, when determining the fitness and loyalty of such persons, from considering the organizations and persons with whom they associate.*[7]

If a teacher is disqualified from employment in the public school system by membership in a subversive organization, "he is not thereby denied the right of free speech and assembly! His freedom of choice between membership in the organization and employment in the school system might be limited, but not his freedom of speech or assembly, except in the remote sense that limitation is inherent in every choice. Certainly such limitation is one the state may make in the exercise of its police power to protect the schools from pollution and thereby to defend its own existence."[8] Therefore, the Court refused to declare the Feinberg Law unconstitutional.

The Douglas dissent

Three Justices wrote opinions dissenting from the majority of the Court. The strongest of these was that of Justice Douglas, who presents a disturbing picture of the way the Feinberg Law could destroy academic freedom, lead to guilt by association, and result in fear and orthodoxy pervading the schools. Because this opinion not only presents a powerful argument for freedom in the classroom but also foreshadows the future trend of judicial thinking, we quote from it extensively.

I cannot find in our constitutional scheme the power of a state to place its employees in the category of second-class citizens by denying them freedom of thought and expression. The Constitution guarantees freedom of thought and expression to everyone in our society. All are entitled to it; and none needs it more than the teacher.

The public school is in most respects the cradle of our democracy. The increasing role of the public school is seized upon by proponents of the type of legislation represented by New York's Feinberg Law as proof of the importance and need for keeping the schools free of "subversive influences." But that is to misconceive the effect of this type of legislation. Indeed the impact of this kind of censorship on the public school system illustrates the high purpose of the First Amendment in freeing speech and thought from censorship.

The present law proceeds on a principle repugnant to our society —guilt by association. A teacher is disqualified because of her membership in an organization found to be "subversive." The finding as to the "subversive" character of the organization is made in a proceeding to which the teacher is not a party and in which it is not clear that she may even be heard. . . . The very threat of such a procedure is certain to raise havoc with academic freedom. Youthful indiscretions, mistaken causes, misguided enthusiasms—all long forgotten—become the ghosts of a harrowing present. Any organization committed to a liberal cause, any group organized to revolt against an hysterical trend, any committee launched to sponsor an unpopular program becomes suspect. These are the organizations into which Communists often infiltrate. Their presence infects the whole, even though the project was not conceived in sin. A teacher caught in that mesh is almost certain to stand condemned. Fearing condemnation, she will tend to shrink from any association that stirs controversy. In that manner freedom of expression will be stifled.

But that is only part of it. . . . The law inevitably turns the school system into a spying project. Regular loyalty reports on the teachers must be made out. The principals become detectives; the students, the parents, the community become informers. Ears are cocked for telltale signs of disloyalty. The prejudices of the community come into play in searching out the disloyal. This is not the usual type of supervision which checks a teacher's competency; it is a system which searches for hidden meanings in a teacher's utterances.

What was the significance of the reference of the art teacher to socialism? Why was the history teacher so openly hostile to Franco Spain? Who heard overtones of revolution in the English teacher's discussion of The Grapes of Wrath? *What was behind the praise of Soviet progress in metallurgy in the chemistry class? Was it not "subversive" for the teacher to cast doubt on the wisdom of the venture in Korea?*

What happens under this law is typical of what happens in a police state. Teachers are under constant surveillance; their pasts are combed for signs of disloyalty; their utterances are watched for clues to dangerous thoughts. A pall is cast over the classroom. There can be no real academic freedom in that environment. Where suspicion fills the air and holds scholars in line for fear of their jobs, there can be no exercise of the free intellect. Supineness and dogmatism take the place of inquiry. A "party line"—as dangerous as the "party line" of the communists—lays hold. It is the "party line" of the orthodox view, of the conventional thought, of the accepted approach. A problem can no longer be pursued with impunity to its edges. Fear stalks the classroom. The teacher is no longer a stimulant to adventurous thinking; she becomes instead a pipeline for safe and sound information. A deadening dogma takes the place of free inquiry. Instruction tends to become sterile; pusuit of knowledge is discouraged; discussion often leaves off where it should begin.

This, I think, is what happens when a censor looks over a teacher's shoulder. This system of spying and surveillance with its accompanying reports and trials cannot go hand in hand with academic freedom. It produces standardized thought, not the pursuit of truth. Yet it was the pursuit of truth which the First Amendment was designed to protect. A system which directly or inevitably has that effect is alien to our system and should be struck down. Its survival is a threat to our way of life. We need be bold and adventuresome in our thinking to survive. A school system producing students trained as robots threatens to rob a generation of the versatility that has been perhaps our greatest distinction. The Framers knew the danger of dogmatism; they also knew the strength that comes when the mind is free, when ideas may be pursued wherever they lead. We forget these teachings of the First Amendment when we sustain this law.

Of course the school systems of the country need not become cells for communist activities; and the classrooms need not become forums for propagandizing the Marxist creed. But the guilt of the teacher should turn on overt acts. So long as she is a law-abiding citizen, so long as her performance within the public school system meets professional standards, her private life, her political philosophy, her social creed should not be the cause of reprisals against her.[9]

Despite the power of this dissent, a majority of the members of the Supreme Court in 1952 voted to uphold the Feinberg Law.

THE KEYISHIAN CASE: GUILT BY ASSOCIATION REJECTED

In 1962, Harry Keyishian was an English instructor at the Buffalo campus of the State University of New York. To comply with the state's Feinberg Law, Keyishian was asked to sign a certificate stating that he was not a Communist. The application of the Feinberg Law had been modified since the Adler case, but it still disqualified any teacher or administrator in New York's public educational system who advocated the overthrow of the government by unlawful means or joined any organization, particularly the Communist Party, advocating overthrow of the government.

Keyishian refused to sign the certificate, and as a result his contract was not renewed. He went to court to challenge the constitutionality of the law that led to the nonrenewal of his contract.[10]

Questions to Consider

1. What arguments could be used to support the Feinberg Law? Doesn't the community have a right to exclude revolutionaries from the classroom?
2. Should a community be able to exclude members of the John Birch Society or the American Nazi Party? What about members of the Black Panther Party or the Weatherman faction of Students for a Democratic Society?
3. What arguments could be used to support Keyishian's case? What constitutional provisions apply?
4. Can a teacher be a member of a political party without supporting all of its purposes? Could he be a member of a militant organization without supporting its unlawful activity? Should the law take these distinctions into account?

The argument for dismissing Keyishian

The Board of Regents of New York believed the *Adler* opinion should be followed and the Feinberg Law upheld for these reasons: The classroom is a sensitive area where the teacher shapes the attitude of young minds toward society. Therefore, school officials have the right and duty to screen teachers concerning their fitness to do the job. While individuals do not give up their rights by teaching in public schools, they are nevertheless obliged to answer questions concerning their fitness to serve as teachers. Teachers may be subject to reasonable terms of employment, such as not belonging to subversive organizations. If they do not choose to work on such terms, they are free to retain their beliefs and associations and go elsewhere. The intent of the Feinberg Law is simply to protect society's right of self-preservation and to preserve our democracy. Thus, a state should be permitted to disqualify a teacher who deliberately becomes a member of an organization that advocates the forcible overthrow of our government.[11]

The opinion of the Court

The majority of the justices of the Supreme Court disagreed. They held that it is unconstitutional to disqualify a teacher merely because he is a member of the Communist Party or any other subversive organization without also showing that the teacher has the specific intent of furthering the unlawful aims of that party or organization. These were some of the reasons for their decision:

- A law that bars employment of any person who "advises or teaches" the doctrine of forceful overthrow of the government is unconstitutionally vague. "This provision is plainly susceptible of sweeping and improper application." It could even prohibit the employment of a teacher who "merely advocates the doctrine in the abstract" without any attempt to incite others to unlawful action.
- "Our nation is deeply committed to safeguarding academic freedom, which is of transcendent value to all of us and not merely to the teachers concerned. That freedom is therefore a special concern of the First Amendment, which does not tolerate laws that cast a pall of orthodoxy over the classroom. . . . The nation's future depends upon leaders trained through wide exposure to that robust exchange of ideas which discovers truth out of a multitude of tongues rather than through any kind of authoritative selection."[12]
- "Scholarship cannot flourish in an atmosphere of suspicion and distrust. Teachers and students must always remain free to inquire, to study, and to evaluate, to gain new maturity and understanding; otherwise our civilization will stagnate and die."[13]
- While New York has a legitimate interest in protecting its educa-

tional system from subversion, that interest cannot be pursued by means that broadly stifle fundamental liberties when the end can be more narrowly achieved.

- "Under our traditions, beliefs are personal and not a matter of mere association, and men in adhering to a political party or other organization do not subscribe unqualifiedly to all of its platforms or asserted principles. A law which applies to membership, without the specific intent to further the illegal aims of the organization, infringes unnecessarily on protected freedoms. It rests on the doctrine of guilt by association which has no place here."[14]
- Even the Feinberg Law—applicable to public school teachers, who have young captive audiences—is subject to constitutional limitation in favor of freedom of expression and association, for the curtailment of these freedoms has a stifling effect on the academic mind.
- Those who join an organization but do not share its unlawful purposes and do not participate in its unlawful activities surely pose no threat, either as citizens or as public employees. Therefore, mere membership in the Communist Party, without a specific intent to further the unlawful aims of that organization, is not a constitutionally adequate basis for excluding Keyishian from his teaching position.

Because of these reasons, the Feinberg Law was set aside.

SUMMARY AND CONCLUSIONS

In the early 1950s many states passed laws to disqualify teachers who were members of the Communist Party and other subversive or revolutionary organizations. When these laws were challenged, school boards replied that they did not abridge the right of free speech; they were merely reasonable terms of employment. Teachers thus had the "free choice" of teaching on these terms or retaining their membership in revolutionary organizations and seeking other employment. This was the reasoning of the Supreme Court in the Adler case, and it set the tone for the decade.

During the ten years following the *Adler* decision, several things happened. First, the attitude of the public began to change. The widespread fear of a Communist conspiracy to infiltrate American public schools decreased. Second, the courts and the public began to reject the idea of guilt by association. Finally, the composition of the Supreme Court began to change. These factors led to increasing acceptance of Justice Douglas' dissenting opinion in the Adler case. Thus, when the Keyishian case came before the Court in 1962, the stage was set for the Court to move away from the *Adler* holding.

What is the law today concerning membership in controversial organizations? According to *Keyishian*, the Court: (1) took a strong stand in defense of academic freedom, (2) rejected the doctrine of guilt by association, (3) recognized that teachers can belong to controversial organizations without subscribing to all of their aims and actions, and (4) emphasized that teachers who join a revolutionary organization but do not share its unlawful purposes and do not participate in its unlawful activities pose no threat to the schools. While the Court recognized a community's interest in protecting its educational system from subversion, it held that this interest cannot be pusued by means that stifle constitutional rights when the purpose can be pursued more narrowly. In sum, schools cannot disqualify a teacher merely because he belongs to a revolutionary organization without specifically showing that he subscribes to the organization's illegal aims and activities.

The Keyishian case was decided in 1962. Since another decade has gone by, could the law change again? Although most Americans are less worried about communists today than in the 1950's, could they begin to pass laws disqualifying members of the Black Panther Party, militant student groups, or the American Nazi Party? Would these laws be upheld by a new Supreme Court?

We cannot know with certainty how a future Court would rule on different laws at a different time. And there is some indication that the Burger Court will be more conservative than the Warren Court and hence likely to give more weight to the rights of the community. We believe, however, that the law concerning teacher membership in controversial or revolutionary organizations is clear and that the holding of the Keyishian case would apply. This means that no school board or state legislature could disqualify teachers who are members of the Black Panther Party, the American Nazi Party, or any other revolutionary, extremist, or controversial organization unless it could show that the teacher specifically intended to pursue the organization's illegal aims and activities.

NOTES

[1] *Adler* v. *Board of Education*, 342 R.S. 485, 493 (1952).
[2] *Elfbrandt* v. *Russell*, 384 U.S. 11, 19 (1965).
[3] *Adler* v. *Board of Education*, 342 U.S. 485, 497 (1952).
[4] *Id.* at 490.
[5] *Ibid.*

[6] *Id.* at 492.

[7] *Id.* at 493.

[8] *Ibid.*

[9] *Id.* at 508–511.

[10] The New York laws and policies seeking to regulate subversive teachers are long and complex. However, this excerpt from Section 105 of the Civil Service Law is illustrative: No person shall be employed as superintendent, principal, or teacher in a public school or state college who "becomes a member of any society or group of persons which teaches or advocates that the Government of the United States or of any state or of any political subdivision thereof shall be overthrown by force or violence or by any unlawful means." Membership in the Communist Party shall constitute evidence of disqualification for appointment or retention in any position in the service of the state. *Keyishian* v. *Board of Regents of New York*, 385 U.S. 589, 645 (1967).

[11] *Id.* at 589. For further arguments supporting the Feinberg Law, see especially Justice Clark's dissent in the Keyishian case.

[12] *Id.* at 603.

[13] *Ibid.*

[14] *Id.* at 607.

8
Political activity

The generally accepted viewpoint has been that schools should divorce themselves from politics and that teachers should keep out of political activity. In 1956, teachers polled in a study by the NEA Research Division reflected in overwhelming numbers that they believed teachers should stay aloof from politics, except for the act of voting.[1]

T. M. Stinnet
—Professional Problems of Teachers

This disdain for the political profession in our schools and communities did not matter quite as much in the days when active participation in the political affairs of the nation was limited to a select few. But today the implications of national policy necessarily make politicians of us all![2]

—John F. Kennedy

Should teachers take an active part in politics? Should they be allowed to campaign for candidates, be active in political parties, or run for public office? In 1956, over 75 percent of the teachers questioned in a national survey answered negatively. They felt that teachers should not even work for a presidential candidate. Although more recent surveys have shown this figure to be dropping, it might still seem extraordinary that even a substantial minority of the teachers in the United States do not believe they should publicly support a presidential candidate—even away from school. Most educators and voters, however, believe that public school teachers must be more sensitive and careful about these issues than other professionals. Are they right? If so, should this limit their political rights? Can teachers, for example, be prohibited from participating in all partisan activity except voting? Can they be prohibited from active participation in nonpartisan political campaigns? Can they express their political views in school? Can they campaign for public office? These are some of the issues considered in this chapter.

THE JONES CASE: CAN A TEACHER RUN FOR OFFICE?

On 29 February 1960 a Florida lawyer, Thomas B. Jones, filed qualifying papers to seek nomination for the office of circuit judge in the spring primary. At the time, Jones was an associate professor of law at the University of Florida. The day after he filed Professor Jones was called to the office of the president of the university and informed of his dismissal because he had violated a university rule prohibiting employees from seeking election to public office. "Any employee," says the rule, "desiring to engage in a political campaign for public office shall first submit his resignation."[3]

Professor Jones believed that the prohibition against college professors seeking public office encroached on their rights as citizens and impinged on their right of academic freedom. Therefore, he went to court to have that prohibition declared unconstitutional.

The decision of the court

Jones claimed that "academic freedom" gives teachers the right to teach without being restricted concerning subject matter or related activity. On behalf of the Florida Supreme Court, Justice Thornal wrote that the position of Professor Jones would compel the courts to concede "that a license to teach in a public school system is subject to no regulations whatsoever regarding either the nature of the subject matter to be taught or the time and effort that may be required to be devoted to the classroom."

On the contrary, the Court argued that any right of an individual to work for the government or to seek public office must be subject to reasonable government regulation in the public interest. The question is whether the rule against political campaigning by university employees unreasonably intereferes with their constitutional rights. If not, the Court said, the rule must be upheld.

Justice Thornal then explained that the right to teach or to seek public office is not a constitutional absolute. Each of these "privileges" is subject to reasonable restraint. The test of reasonableness involves the nature of the right asserted by the individual and the extent to which it is necessary to restrict that right in the public interest.

The Court held that the rule prohibiting teachers from campaigning for elected office was reasonable because:

- It prohibits no one from teaching, and it does not prohibit a teacher from running for office. It merely says he cannot do both simultaneously.
- The demands on the time and energies of a candidate in a "warmly contested" political campaign would necessarily affect his efficiency as a teacher.
- Campaigning can have a detrimental effect on the students, not only because of the teacher's inefficiency but also because of the political influences that might be brought to bear on them.
- The potential political involvement of a state university, which depends on public support from all political elements, is a major consideration supporting the reasonableness of the prohibition against teachers running for office.

Jones, however, argued that he could campaign in the evening and on week-ends so as not to interfere with his professional duties. To this, Judge Thornal responded with extreme scepticism:

Anyone who has ever been associated with a heated political campaign will know that it involves hand shaking, speech making, telephone calling, letter writing, and door to door campaigning from morning well into the night. To anyone familiar with the practical aspects of American politics, it is asking too much to expect him to agree that success in a strenuous political campaign can be achieved merely by appearances at Saturday afternoon fish fries or early evening precinct rallies. The result simply is that it would be extremely difficult for a university professor to conduct his classroom courses with efficiency over a period of eight to ten weeks while simultaneously "beating the bushes" in search of votes to elevate him to the position of a circuit judge.[4]

Finally, the Court emphasized that its conclusion was "clearly supported by the opinion of the Supreme Court of the United States" in the Mitchell case, which sustained the constitutionality of the Hatch Act prohibiting U.S. civil service employees from seeking public office. The Hatch Act, enacted in 1940, states:

No officer or employee in the executive branch of the Federal Government or any agency or department thereof . . . shall take any active part in political management or in political campaigns. All such persons shall retain the right to vote as they shall choose and to express their opinions on all political subjects and candidates. Any person violating the provisions of this section shall be immediately removed from the position or office held by him. . .[5]

Questions to Consider

1. Should teachers be active in politics? Do they have a right to participate in partisan political activity?
2. Should they be allowed to actively support candidates for President, Congress, or mayor? Should they be permitted to support candidates for some offices but not others?
3. Are there any constitutional provisions that protect a teacher's right to be active in the political process? Do these rights conflict with others?
4. What are the probable consequences of allowing teachers to be active in politics? What are the probable consequences of prohibiting such activity?

THE MITCHELL CASE: A DISSENTING OPINION

In the 1947 Mitchell case the U.S. Supreme Court upheld the Hatch Act against a charge that it violated the First Amendment. In response to the majority of the Court, Justice Hugo Black wrote a forceful dissenting opinion supporting wider political freedom for public employees.* After pointing out that the Hatch Act bars millions of federal employees from political action as well as thousands of state employees who work for agencies financed by federal grants, he wrote:

*The Hatch Act does not specifically apply to teachers. But the Supreme Court decision to uphold the Hatch Act in the Mitchell case has been used to uphold similar state restrictions against teachers. And Justice Black's dissent presents the argument against broadly restricting the political activity of teachers and other public employees.

No one of all these millions of citizens can, without violating this law, "take any active part" in any campaign for a cause or for a candidate if the cause or candidate is "specifically identified with any national or state political party." Since under our common political practices most causes and candidates are espoused by political parties, the result is that, because they are paid out of the public treasury, all these citizens who engage in public work can take no really effective part in campaigns that may bring about changes in their lives, their fortunes, and their happiness. . . .[6]

The result is that the political privilege left to public employees is this: They may vote in silence, they may carefully and quietly express a political view, and they may be spectators at campaign gatherings, though it may be dangerous for them to agree or disagree with a speaker.

Justice Black argued that popular government must permit and encourage wide political activity by all the people. The right to vote and express private political opinions is not adequate. Popular government means that men may speak openly on matters vital to them and that falsehoods may be exposed through the processes of education and discussion. Legislation that muzzles citizens threatens popular government, not only because it injures the individuals silenced but also because it harms the community by depriving it of citizen participation.

It is said that the Hatch Act is intended to prohibit public employees from being forced to contribute money and influence to political campaigns and to prevent government employees from using their positions to coerce other citizens. But are such possibilities, asked Justice Black, limited to governmental employer-employee relationships? The same quality of argument would support a law restricting the political freedom of all private employees, particularly of corporations that do business with the government. If the possibility exists that some public employees might coerce citizens or other employees, laws can be drawn to punish the coercers. Justice Black noted that it is inconsistent with our system of equal justice for all to suppress the political freedom of large numbers of public employees because a few might engage in coercion.

Laws that restrict the liberties guaranteed by the First Amendment should be narrowly drawn to meet the evil aimed at and to affect only the minimum number of people necessary to prevent a grave danger to the public. The Hatch Act does much more. According to Justice

Black it prevents large numbers of citizens from contributing their arguments, complaints, and suggestions to the political debates that form the essence of our democracy. Such a limitation on the right of people to take political action is inconsistent with the First Amendment's guarantee of freedom of speech, assembly, and petition.

> *There is nothing about public employees,* [wrote Justice Black] *which justifies depriving them or society of the benefits of their participation. They, like other citizens, pay taxes and serve their country in peace and in war. The taxes they pay and the wars in which they fight are determined by the elected spokesmen of all the people. . . . I think the Constitution guarantees to them the same right that other groups of good citizens have to engage in activities which decide who their elected representatives shall be.*

Our political system rests on the foundation of a belief "in rule by the people—not some but all the people." Education has been fostered to prepare people for self-expression and good citizenship. In a country whose people elect their leaders, no voice should be suppressed—at least such is the assumption of the First Amendment. "That Amendment," wrote Black, "includes a command that the Government must, in order to promote its own interest, leave the people at liberty to speak their own thoughts about government, advocate their own favored governmental causes, and work for their own political candidates and parties."

The Hatch Act, which the majority held valid, reduces the constitionally protected liberty of millions of public employees "to less than a shadow of its substance." It relegates them to the role of "mere spectators of events upon which hinge the safety and welfare of all the people, including public employees." Finally, wrote Justice Black, "it makes honest participation in essential political activities an offense punishable by proscription from public employment. . . . Laudable as its purpose may be, it seems to me to hack at the roots of a Government by the people themselves."[7]

In 1947 a majority of the Supreme Court was not persuaded by Justice Black's argument. The Court ruled that a citizen's right to participate in the political process was not absolute and that this right must be balanced against the possible evil of political partisanship on the part of public employees. The Court noted that the Hatch Act did not restrict expression at the ballot box or in public affairs; it only prohibited a government employee from directing his efforts toward party success and partisan activity. Thus, the Court upheld the Hatch Act as a reasonable regulation to promote the efficiency and integrity of public service.

Some states have "little Hatch Acts" that restrict the political activities of civil service employees. Although these laws do not pertain specifically to teachers, courts might in some cases construe them as applicable to teachers. In addition, there are "solicitation" statutes in over a dozen states that are both restrictive and protective. They prohibit teachers and other public employees from soliciting either funds or services for political purposes. At the same time they also protect these employees from such solicitations.[8]

The Jones case and Justice Black's dissent outline the main arguments for and against teacher participation in partisan politics. In the past it was clearly the *Jones* and *Mitchell* opinions, and not that of Justice Black, that predominated. During the past two decades, however, the trend has changed. The following cases and comments provide evidence that Black's arguments are gaining general acceptance.

THE MONTGOMERY CASE: CAN TEACHERS BE BARRED FROM POLITICS?

The Tatum Independent School District is in eastern Texas. In April 1968 the Tatum School Board did not rehire Billy Montgomery, partly because of his political activity. The board's action was taken under a regulation prohibiting "all political activity except voting."[9] As a result, Montgomery sued the school board in the U.S. District Court for violating his constitutional rights.

The opinion of the Court by Judge Justice explained that the state may protect its educational system from undue political activity that may "materially and substantially interfere" with the operation of the school. On the other hand, the First Amendment to the Constitution guarantees the right of citizens to participate in political affairs. The problem is to arrive at a balance between the interest of the teacher as a citizen in participating in the political process and the interest of the state in promoting the efficiency of the public schools.

Judge Justice then ruled that the regulation enforced by the school board prohibiting teachers from engaging in all political activity except voting was inconsistent with the First Amendment guarantees of freedom of speech, press, assembly, and petition. To support its decision the Court cited the arguments of Justice Black in his dissent in the Mitchell case. The school board prohibition threatens popular government, wrote Judge Justice, not only "because it injures the individuals muzzled, but also because of its harmful affect on the community" in depriving it of the political participation of its teachers.

The following items are additional indications of the changing trend concerning teacher participation in political activity.

■ Excerpts from statements by the chairmen of the Republican and Democratic national committees:

As a nation we can ill afford either the voluntary or the enforced disenfranchisement of large groups of responsible citizens. This is particularly true of our teachers. . . . Teachers have a responsibility, yes a duty, to set an example of mature citizenship by participating fully in politics. . . .

The power of example is the teacher's greatest influence. The teacher who runs for office at any level involves his students inevitably in the political process. Any sensitive teacher who becomes a candidate (and we want no insensitive people either in teaching or in politics) does not have to involve his students in any partisan way. But the very fact of his candidacy both enlivens student interest and makes him much more aware of community views about schools. This in turn should make him a better teacher.[10]

■ The Texas Civil Statutes of 1969 states that "no school district . . . shall directly or indirectly coerce any teacher to refrain from participating in political affairs in his community, state or nation. . . ."[11]

■ In 1957 the Supreme Court of Oregon ruled that under the state constitution a teacher could not hold his position in the public schools while he was a member of the state legislature. In response, the electorate adopted a constitutional amendment in 1958 providing that an employee of any school board "shall be eligible to a seat in the Legislative Assembly and such membership in the Legislative Assembly shall not prevent such person from being employed as a teacher."[12]

■ In Hawaii, where there had been a prohibition against teachers participating in politics, citizens won a ten-year campaign in 1956, when the Board of Commissioners adopted a new ruling saying teachers "are permitted to exercise those political rights and responsibilities which they share in common with other citizens, such as electioneering for candidates, accepting positions in political campaigns, holding office in political party organizations, and serving as delegates to political party conventions."[13]

THE MINIELLY CASE: THE FIRST AMENDMENT AND POLITICAL ACTIVITY

In this case an Oregon law prohibiting public employees from running for public office was declared unconstitutional. Although Minielly was a deputy sheriff, the reasoning of the court also applies to teachers.

After citing a number of early cases indicating that "political rights of public employees may constitutionally be severely inhibited," the court noted that in the early 1950s "the trend began to move the other way."[14] Moreover, statutes that restrict First Amendment rights do not have a strong presumption of validity; to be constitutional they have to be justified by a clear public interest that is directly threatened.

The court recognized that a state has the right to make reasonable regulations for the promotion of efficiency and discipline in the public service. It saw nothing unconstitutional, for example, in preventing a public employee from running for office against his superior, since this would clearly be disruptive to the public service. The problem with the Oregon law, however, was that it went much further than necessary to achieve its goal. Furthermore, it is clear that "running for public office is one of the means of political expression which is protected by the First Amendment. The right to engage in political activity is implicit in the rights of association and free speech guaranteed by the Amendment."[15]

The court then discussed a number of recent First Amendment cases. "It is apparent from these cases," wrote the court, "that a revolution has occurred in the law relative to the state's power to limit federal First Amendment rights. Thirty years ago the statutes now under consideration would have been held to be constitutional. . . ." But in this case the court declared the law prohibiting public employees from running for state, federal, or nonpartisan office "unconstitutional because of overbreadth" and suggested that the legislature pass more narrowly drawn laws. "It cannot be demonstrated," concluded the court, "that the good of the public service requires all of the prohibitions of the present statute."[16]

THE LETTER CARRIER'S CASE: IS THE HATCH ACT UNCONSTITUTIONAL?

On 31 July 1972, a U.S. District Court held that the Hatch Act's prohibition against active participation in political management or political campaigns was unconstitutionally ambiguous.[17] The Court did not quarrel with the objectives of the Hatch Act, but with the difficulty in defining what conduct was prohibited.

If the Supreme Court had upheld the Hatch Act in the 1947 Mitchell case, how could a lower court rule differently? The District Court pointed out that subsequent Supreme Court decisions have gone further in protecting First Amendment freedoms against government incursions, that the public service has changed in size and complexity and that the *Mitchell* opinion therefore may have become outmoded by the passage of time.

What will be the impact of this decision? Since the opinion was handed down just as we completed this manuscript, it is too early to tell. We can predict, however, that the case will be appealed to the U.S. Supreme Court. If the Court upholds the decision, Congress would probably enact a clearer and perhaps narrower version of the Hatch Act. Even if the District Court's decision is overturned, the Mail Carrier's case will stand as one more indication of the trend toward greater protection of the First Amendment freedoms of public employees.

THE RACKLEY CASE: NONPARTISAN POLITICAL ACTIVITY

Gloria Rackley was a capable and qualified school teacher in Orangeburg, South Carolina. She was also an active member of the National Association for the Advancement of Colored People and a leader in the civil rights movement in her county. She engaged in peaceful picketing and demonstrations to end segregated practices in places of public accommodation such as hospitals, lunch counters, and public restrooms. In the fall of 1961 she was arrested for refusing to leave a "white" hospital waiting room. The following spring the superintendent explained to her that her civil rights activities were embarrassing to the school system and particularly to the teaching profession. While she continued to be an excellent classroom teacher, she also increased her participation in civil rights activities during the following two years. In September 1963 she was discharged by the school board after leading a group of 200 civil rights demonstrators, some of whom were encouraged to "break the law, jeer at policemen, and disturb good order."[18] Rackley sued to require the school district to reinstate her.

In considering this case the court pointed out that school boards have the right to consider a broad range of factors other than classroom conduct in determining whether to hire or discharge school teachers. This right, however, may not be exercised in an arbitrary or discriminatory manner to deprive a teacher of personal liberties secured by the Constitution. Therefore, the discretion exercised by school boards must be within reasonable limits so as not to curtail the constitutionally protected freedom of political expression and association.

Since the Constitution "does not permit a state to make criminal the peaceful expression of unpopular views," Rackley's participation in the September 1963 demonstration was an exercise of her constitutional rights. Thus, her civil rights activity could not provide a valid basis for her discharge. The court therefore ordered the board to reinstate Rackley and to continue her employment without regard to her "exercise of constitutionally protected activities in the civil rights field."

In similar cases in which competent teachers were dismissed for civil rights activity, the courts have reinstated the teachers. These cases clearly show a pattern of judicial protection for such nonpartisan political activity.[19]

THE GOLDSMITH CASE: PROMOTING A CANDIDATE IN CLASS

An early California case provides an example of a teacher who went too far in expressing his political views in class. In September 1922 a Sacramento high school teacher, A. L. Goldsmith, made the following remarks in class in support of a candidate for school superintendent:

> *Many of you know Mr. Golway, what a fine man he is, and what his hopes are to be elected soon. I think he would be more helpful to our department than a lady, and we need more men in our schools. Sometimes your parents do not know one candidate from another; so they might be glad to be informed. Of course, if any of you have relatives or friends trying for the same office, be sure and vote for them.*[20]

As a result of these comments, Goldsmith was charged with "unprofessional conduct" and suspended by the school board. Goldsmith went to court to seek reinstatement on the grounds that he had been a regular teacher for a number of years and had violated no specific law. Moreover, he argued that the statement he made resulting in his suspension really involved "minor matters."

The court disagreed and supported the action of the board. In its opinion, Judge Hart observed that a teacher's "advocacy" of the election of a particular candidate before students in a public school and attempting to influence students and their parents "introduces into the school questions wholly foreign to its purposes and objectives." Such conduct can "stir up strife" among students over a political contest, and the results would disrupt the discipline of the public school. Such conduct is contrary to "the spirit of the laws governing the public school system."[21]

Questions to Consider

1. To what degree can teachers express their political views in the classroom? Should there be greater freedom for teachers to express nonpartisan political views in school?
2. What, if any, partisan expression should be protected? Can a teacher wear a political button to class? Can teachers express their personal views about national, state, or local candidates if asked about them by their students during class? before or after class?
3. Can a social studies teacher assign partisan political readings? Can he express partisan opinions in class if he gives equal time to other views? Can he put political bumper stickers on his car if he parks it in the school parking lot? What about campaign posters in his car-windows?
4. Can a teacher wear a button or arm band protesting controversial political policies such as the Vietnam War?

THE ARM BAND CASE: WHAT IS PARTISAN POLITICS?

In November 1969, Charles James a high school English teacher in New York, wore a black arm band to class on Vietnam Moratorium Day. He was briefly suspended but told he could return to teaching with the understanding that he "engage in no political activity while within the school." But on 12 December 1969, another Vietnam Moratorium Day, James again went to class wearing a black arm band. As a result, he was dismissed by the board of education. Since he believed his dismissal was a violation of his constitutional rights, he appealed the board's decision to the Commissioner of Education. But the Commissioner supported the board.

Although the Supreme Court had ruled in the Tinker case that students have a right to wear arm bands to class,[22] the Commissioner said that a teacher is in a very different category. Teachers have a responsibility to present a wide range of views on a subject being considered. If the subject involves conflicting opinions, the teacher must present a fair summary of the entire range of opinions so that students may have access to all facets of the subject. By wearing the arm band the teacher in this case "was presenting only one point of view on an important public issue on which a wide range of deeply held opinion and conviction exists."[23]

The Commissioner then cited the New York Teachers' Association Code of Ethics, which considers it unethical for teachers to "promote personal views on religion, race, or partisan politics." The term *partisan politics*, wrote the Commissioner, is not limited to party politics but "embraces any political subject on which differing views exist."[24]

Despite the Commissioner's ruling, James, a practicing Quaker, believed he had a constitutional right to wear his arm band, and he took his case to court. In May 1972 the Second U.S. Circuit Court of Appeals ruled in his favor. The Court pointed out that there was no evidence in this case indicating any incidents or threats to school discipline or that any student, parent, or teacher had complained about James' arm band or were offended by his symbolic expression.

In making this decision Judge Kaufman relied on the Supreme Court opinion in the Tinker case, which noted that neither students nor teachers "shed their constitutional rights to freedom of speech or expression at the school-house gate."[25] Furthermore, the Court held that any limitation on the exercise of constitutional rights can be justified only by the conclusion, based on concrete facts, "that the interests of discipline or sound education are materially and substantially jeopardized, whether the danger stems initially from the conduct of students or teachers."[26] The Court acknowledged that the views of a teacher may carry more influence than the views of one's peers. But that factor alone, said Judge Kaufman, "does not relieve the school of the necessity to show a reasonable basis for its regulatory policies."

The Court did not hold that schools must wait "until disruption is on the doorstep" before they may take protective action. But the Court did emphasize that "freedom of expression demands breathing room." To preserve democracy, wrote Judge Kaufman, "we must be willing to assume the risk of argument and lawful disagreement."

The school board argued that the assumptions of the "free marketplace of ideas" on which freedom of speech rests do not apply to a captive group of children where the word of the teacher may carry great authority. Because students may have no choice concerning school attendance, the Court agreed that there must be some restraint on the free expression of a teacher's views. Thus when a teacher tries to persuade his students that his values should be their values, "then it is not unreasonable to expect the state to protect impressionable children from such dogmatism."

The James case, however, is different. Here the teacher's wearing of an arm band did not interfere with his classroom performance, was not coercive, and there was no attempt to proselytize or indoctrinate. Moreover recent Supreme Court decisions leave no doubt that we cannot allow school authorities to arbitrarily censor "a teacher's speech merely because they do not agree with the teacher's political philosophies."

In conclusion, Judge Kaufman commented that it would be foolhardy to shield sixteen or seventeen-year-old students from political issues until they walk into the voting booth after their eighteenth birthday. On the contrary, "schools must play a central role in preparing their students to think and analyze and to recognize the demagogue." Thus the Court concluded that under the circumstances present here, there was a greater danger that the school, by power of example, would appear to the students to be sanctioning that very "pall of orthodoxy" that has been condemned by the Supreme Court and that "chokes freedom of dissent."

SUMMARY AND CONCLUSIONS

The cases and comments considered in this chapter illustrate the conflicting and changing views concerning teacher participation in American politics. Despite these conflicts and changes, however, much of the law on the subject is clear.

In the past courts generally upheld laws and regulations prohibiting teachers from actively participating in partisan politics or seeking elective office. Thus, the Jones case ruled that a university regulation requiring teachers to resign before campaigning for office was constitutional.

In recent decades the trend of judicial thinking has changed. Courts are striking down rules that broadly prohibit teachers from becoming actively involved in politics or from seeking public office. Thus, the Minielly case ruled that a state law prohibiting all public employees from running for any political office was unconstitutional, and the Montgomery case held that school boards could not prohibit teachers from participating in "all political activity except voting."

Rather, the court ruled that communities could bar teachers from political activity only when such activity might "materially and substantially" interfere with the operation of the school.

A school board cannot discharge a teacher because she exercises her constitutionally protected civil right of political expression out of school. As the Rackley case illustrates, the teacher is protected even if she leads public demonstrations about a political issue that is highly controversial in her community.

During the past twenty years rules and statutes in a number of states (as diverse as Texas, Oregon, and Hawaii) have been changed to permit teachers to exercise those political rights which they share with other citizens, such as "electioneering for candidates, accepting positions in political campaigns," and holding elective office. And we have noted that national political leaders have even argued that teachers have a "duty" to "participate fully" in American politics.

In public schools a teacher is not permitted to indoctrinate students with his political views, nor is he allowed to urge students or parents to support a particular candidate or party. Thus, the dismissal of a California teacher was upheld when he tried to use the classroom to influence the election of a candidate for school superintendent. On the other hand, the James case indicated that a school board cannot prohibit a teacher from symbolic expression of a political opinion (such as wearing an arm band) when there is no evidence that the expression is either disruptive or coercive.

In conclusion it would appear that the trend of judicial decision is shifting away from the Supreme Court's holding in the Mitchell case. The Hatch Act is again being challenged, the arguments of Justice Black are being given greater weight, and we expect that in the next few years statutes and regulations limiting the rights of teachers to participate in partisan politics and prohibiting them from running for public office may be declared unconstitutional.

We do not believe that a school board should never restrict the rights of teachers to participate in politics. Rather, we argue that the principles of the Montgomery case should be applied: that teachers, like other citizens, should have the right to participate actively in the political process, unless such activity might "materially and substantially" interfere with the operation of the school. When there is evidence that political campaigning would probably interfere with his job, a teacher might be required to take a temporary leave of absence. If a teacher wishes to hold a time-consuming, paid political office, it might also be reasonable to require him to take a leave during his term of office.

NOTES

[1]Of those questioned, 77 percent felt that a teacher should not make speeches or give other services in behalf of a candidate in a presidential election, even outside of school hours. In 1960, another poll revealed that this percentage had apparently dropped to 50. T. M. Stinnet, *Professional Problems of Teachers*, New York, Macmillan, 1968, p. 264.

[2]*Id.* at 266.

[3]*Jones* v. *Board of Control*, 131 So. 2d. 713, 715 (1961).

[4]*Id.* at 718.

[5]The Hatch Act, 18 U.S.C. Sec. 61 h, 1940.

[6]*United Public Workers* v. *Mitchell*, 330 U.S. 75, 106–107 (1947).

[7]*Id.* at 105–115.

[8]NEA Research Memo, Washington, D.C., 1961, pp. 2–4.

[9]*Montgomery* v. *White*, 320 F. Supp. 303, 304 (1969).

[10]As quoted in Stinnet, *op. cit.*, pp. 266–267.

[11]Art. 2922–21a, Texas Civil Statutes, 1969.

[12]NEA Research Memo, Washington, D.C., August 1961, p. 5.

[13]Stinnet, *op. cit.*, p. 268.

[14]*Minielly* v. *State*, 411 P. 2d 69, 71 (1966).

[15]*Id.* at 73.

[16]*Id.* at 78.

[17]*Nat'l Assn of Letter Carriers, AFL-CIO* v. *U.S. Civil Service Comm.*, USDC Dist. Col. 7/31/72, as reported in 41 Law Week 2069, 8/8/72.

[18]*Rackley* v. *School District*, 258 F. Supp. 676, 678 (1966).

[19]E.g., *Johnson* v. *Branch*, 364 F. 2d. 177 (1966) and *Williams* v. *Sumter School District*, 255 F. Supp. 397 (1966).

[20]*Goldsmith* v. *Board of Education*, 225 pp. 783–784, (1924).

[21]*Id.* at 789.

[22]See *Tinker* v. *Des Moines*, 393 U.S. 503 (1969) reprinted in the appendix.

[23]*School Law Reporter, XI*, no. 3, National Organization on Legal Problems of Education, December 1970, p. 4.

[24]*Ibid.*

[25]*Tinker*, *op. cit.*, p. 506.

[26]*Charles James* v. *Board of Education of Central Dist. No. 1*, 461 F. 2d 566 (2d Cir. 1972).

9

Membership in teacher organizations

We are unanimous in the view that strikes by teachers are illegal. . . .

—Max J. Rubin, President
New York City Board of Education
New York Times, *April 12, 1962*

The Strike [in Washington, D.C.] started Tuesday with school officials estimating about 70 percent of the city's 7,500 teachers were refusing to come to work. The striking teachers returned to work Wednesday under a tentative agreement, but then renewed their strike Thursday after rejecting the proposed settlement.

Meanwhile, teacher strikes continued in Philadelphia and in eleven western Pennsylvania school districts.

—The Christian Science Monitor
September 23, 1972

■ Students at a large teacher education institution in California are wise not to have recommendations from professors *X*, *Y*, and Z in their placement files. These professors are known to be sympathetic to the American Federation of Teachers and the college placement officer, formerly a school administrator, is very hostile toward the organization. It is clear that students recommended by these professors receive prejudicial treatment from the placement service.

- When a person applies for a teaching position in the elementary schools of school district Alpha, one of the questions he faces pertains to membership in teacher organizations. Applicants who have been very active in either the National Educational Association or the AFT or their affiliates are systematically screened out and do not receive offers of employment.
- In school district Beta, administrative positions are usually filled from within the school system. Analysis of the pattern of appointments over the years discloses that teachers who have been members of the AFT never become administrators within the system.
- Dozens of grievances or court actions are begun each year claiming that activities on behalf of the AFT or NEA have been used by administrators or school boards as grounds for disciplinary action, suspension, dismissal, or demotion of teachers.
- In Sierra Monte School District the teacher organization brought the attention of the board to overcrowding in the schools, the inadequacy of books and instructional materials, and the low pay scale that made it impossible to attract well-qualified teachers. The board repeatedly turned down any request that would lead to new bond issues or higher tax rates. As a last resort the teacher organizations called for a strike.

Questions to consider

1. Why do so many school board members, administrators, and parents object to teachers joining teacher organizations? Why do they object more vigorously to membership in teachers' unions?
2. Are these objections merely expressions of personal preferences, or are there legitimate reasons why teachers as public employees should not organize? If the latter, what are the reasons?
3. Is there a right to strike, guaranteed by the Bill of Rights? Is such a right guaranteed by any other provision in the Constitution?
4. Is it unprofessional for teachers to organize? Is it unprofessional for them to strike?

RELEVANT CASES AND LEGAL PRINCIPLES

Since administrators and school boards have great discretion in the management of the schools, can such discretion be used to minimize or eliminate teacher organizations? Can a teacher be dismissed or otherwise disciplined for active participation in union or association causes? (We use the term *organization* to refer to both AFT and NEA affiliates; the word *union* refers to the AFT and its subunits.) How is the Constitution relevant to teacher organizations?

The first major case focusing on these issues arose in Chicago a little over fifty years ago.[1] In 1915 the Chicago Board of Education adopted a rule, parts of which follow.

1. *Membership by teachers in labor unions or in organizations of teachers affiliated with a trade union or a federation or association of trade unions, is inimical to proper discipline, prejudicial to the efficiency of the teaching force and detrimental to the welfare of the public school system, therefore such membership or affiliation is hereby prohibited. . . .*
3. *No person shall be employed hereafter in any capacity in the education department until such person shall state in writing that he or she is not a member, and will not, while employed in the education department become a member of any such prohibited organization. . . .*
5. *Any member of the education department who shall be found guilty of any violation of any provisions of this rule shall be liable to dismissal from the service or to such lesser disciplining as this board, in its discretion, in each case shall determine.*[2]

Suit was brought in the lower court of Cook County, Illinois, to prevent (enjoin) the board of education from enforcing this rule. The injunction was granted, the city appealed, and the appeals court reversed the decision, saying:

The board has the absolute right to decline to employ or to reemploy any applicant for any reason whatever or for no reason at all. The board is responsible for its actions only to the people of the city, from whom, through the mayor, the members have received their appointments. It is no infringement upon the constitutional rights of anyone for the board to decline to employ him as a teacher in the schools, and it is immaterial whether the reason for the refusal to employ him is because of the applicant being married or unmarried, is of fair complexion or dark, is or is not a member of a trades union, or whether no reason is given for such refusal. The board is not bound to give any reason for its action. It is free to contract with whomsoever it chooses.[3]

Various courts have cited with approval the Chicago case, including one in the State of Washington[4] that upheld the right of the board to force a teacher to sign a "yellow dog contract." (A yellow dog contract is one in which an employee agrees, as a condition of employment, not to join a union.) These cases have upheld the school boards on the ground that the boards have wide powers of discretion to run the schools. They are charged with operating efficient and effective school systems for the welfare of the children and of the state, and the courts are reluctant to substitute their judgment of what is in the best interest of the public for that of the boards. The early cases did not extend constitutional protection to unionization.

Law, however, changes with changing conditions. It has often been said that the U.S. Constitution would be merely a historic artifact if its provisions were not reinterpreted in light of changing cultural conditions. So it was in this area of the law, where growing acceptance of organizational membership in many walks of life led to new conclusions on the rights of teachers to organize and join associations. With the growing acceptance of unionization of public employees there has come increasing recognition that teachers too have a right to organize.

A circuit court of appeals held that teachers have a constitutionally protected right "of free association, and unjustified interference with teachers' associational freedom violates the Due Process clause of the Fourteenth Amendment."[5] It further noted that "There is nothing anomalous in protecting teachers' rights to join unions. Other employees have long been similarly protected by the National Labor Relations Act."

The Seventh Circuit Court of Appeals phrased the currently accepted view in clear and precise terms.

> *There is no question that the right of teachers to associate for the purpose of collective bargaining is a right protected by the First and Fourteenth Amendments to the Constitution.*[6]

Many other cases came to similar conclusions. For example, a federal court in Indiana held that the school board violated teachers' First Amendment rights to free association when it failed to renew their contracts in retaliation for union activities.[7]

We must distinguish, however, between the right to join an organization and the right to strike. In general, public employees are prohibited by law from striking, and at this writing only the states of Hawaii and Pennsylvania permit strikes by teachers and Alaska,

Vermont and Michigan have no legal penalties for strikes. Courts have repeatedly upheld laws that prohibit strikes by teachers and other public employees, and such laws have been found constitutional.[8] Thus, the right to join the NEA or AFT does not include the right to strike in most states, where such strikes are against the law. Merely because hundreds of strikes by teachers have occurred in recent years does not legalize such strikes. A teacher who takes part in an illegal strike may be appropriately disciplined by the board, while others in the same organization who did not take part in the strike must not suffer merely for membership in a legitimate organization. In the words of the court,

> *Those who join an organization but do not share its unlawful purposes and who do not participate in its unlawful activities surely pose no threat either as citizens or as public employees.* Elfbrandt *v.* Russell, *384 U.S. 11. Even if this record disclosed that the union was connected with unlawful activity, the bare fact that [sic] membership does not justify charging members with their organization's misdeeds.*

Furthermore,

> *A contrary rule would bite more deeply into associational freedom than is necessary to achieve legitimate state interests, thereby violating the First Amendment.*[9]

Just as business and industry did not want its foremen and minor executives involved in employee organizations, school districts have at times passed rules to prevent supervisors, deans, and other administrators from joining teacher organizations. A classic example of this was the Florida statute that prohibited "all persons employed in the Palm Beach County Public School System whose primary employment is in the capacity of administrator or supervisor . . . from participation or membership in any organization or affiliate of any organization the activities of which includes the collective representation of members of the teaching profession with regard to terms, tenure or conditions of employment. . . ."[10]

The District Court in declaring the statute null and void said that

> *This is a classical example of a Fourteenth Amendment denial of equal protection claim. . . . The defendants have made no effort to demonstrate that Palm Beach County is in any way unique so as to justify placing its educational employees in a class apart from those*

of other Florida Counties. . . . Similarly . . . (the statute) impinges upon the basic freedoms of expression and association protected by the First and Fourteenth Amendments.[11]

It is clear, then, that teachers and other educators have a constitutionally protected right to join associations and to affiliate with the NEA, the AFT, or other employee associations. Whether or not they should do so is not a question for the courts but for the political and educational judgment of teachers themselves. But while the legal right is firmly established, it would be a mistake to conclude that this is no longer a controversial area in our culture. There are still many communities where school boards and administrators view the organizational activities of teachers with great disfavor. It is probable that many a nontenured teacher is not reappointed because of his vigorous participation in organizational activities, but the grounds stated, if any, relate to his teaching effectiveness, his classroom control, or some other acceptable basis for nonreappointment. Without proof of the real ground for dismissal, the courts can do nothing. Boards and administrators should realize, however, that such actions violate the spirit of our Constitution, eroding everyone's civil rights, including their own.

In recent years the right to bargain collectively and the right to strike have become the significant issues related to organizational membership. Although many legal questions were raised concerning collective negotiations in public employment when it first appeared in the education field, most states have now accepted it and specifically authorize it by statutes.

Although the right to form teacher associations and to bargain collectively is clearly established, we can still anticipate new problems. Over the next several years litigation will center on more technical issues such as what matters are included and excluded from collective negotiations, what is "inherently managerial policy," and interpretation of state statutes and specific contracts.[12] Questions about the right to strike are also treated by state law. It is a generally accepted legal doctrine that public employees do not have a right to strike unless specifically authorized by state law. As mentioned earlier, to date only the states of Hawaii and Pennsylvania have enacted legislation that removes statutory barriers to strikes by teachers.

Educators tend to disfavor the term *strike* because of its historic association with blue-collar labor organizations. The terms *sanctions* or *withholding of services* are less objectionable to teachers, though the behavior and its consequences might be identical with those of strikes. But the courts are not impressed by the labels used. They cut through verbal camouflage and reach to the heart of an issue or controversy. Recent examples come from New Jersey and Florida.

In New Jersey, "sanctions" were brought by a teachers' organization against a school system. The "sanctions" constituted collective, concerted action, including massive resignations, blacklisting of the school district, and a campaign to discourage teachers from accepting employment there. The court, in placing a ban on "sanctions," concluded that the net effect of such a practice is the same as that of a strike. It would "accomplish a shutdown, a thrust at the vitality of government, and comes within the same policy which denounces a concerted strike . . . or slowdown or other obstruction of the performance of official duties."[13] The Supreme Court of Florida similarly reaffirmed the widely accepted prohibition against strikes by teachers in a direct statement that "a strike against government (is one) which all authorities agree cannot be tolerated in the absence of consent by the government."[14]

The right to engage in organizational activity, whether in unions or associations, does not confer immunity for incompetence. A teacher who is not acceptable to a school system on other legitimate grounds cannot hide behind vigorous organizational activity. This principle is analogous to that of the proposed dismissal of a black teacher on probationary status. If a black teacher is incompetent a claim of racial discrimination does not protect his teaching position.

This principle is illustrated in the New York case of a probationary teacher who was told by the board that the quality of her work was not up to the standard the district was trying to achieve. The teacher countered with the charge that her dismissal was in retaliation for activities in behalf of the teacher's union. This claim required that the matter go to trial to determine whether the action of the board was based on constitutionally impermissible grounds, namely organizational activity, or whether it was a legitimate exercise of administrative discretion. The court made it clear that "If the petitioner possesses all the attributes of an excellent teacher, but additionally arouses the displeasure of the School Board merely because she is a union activist, she may not be denied tenure on that ground. On the other hand, we are not to be understood to hold and we do not hold that union activity provides a shelter for a teacher whom the Board decides not to retain for *bona fide*, legitimate reasons. Thus, it will be for the trial court to decide whether to give credence to the Board's claim that it was not motivated by a desire to punish the petitioner for her union activities and that it found her wanting for legitimate cognizable reasons."[15] The same result was reached in another case, in which a teacher was dismissed for his lack of "self-direction and cooperation," though he was active in organizing teachers.[16]

SUMMARY AND CONCLUSIONS

The right of teachers to organize and to associate for purposes of collective bargaining is now clearly established. During the first half of the twentieth century this right was generally denied to teachers, but the courts now hold that the First and Fourteenth Amendments secure and guarantee such associations and activities.

The right to join organizations, however, does not entail the right to strike. Teachers and other public employees do not have the right to strike or to engage in similar activities such as sanctions unless the legislature specifically grants such authority. At this time only the states of Hawaii and Pennsylvania have legislation enabling teachers to strike. The many policy questions dealing with the right of teachers to strike are questions for legislative bodies, not for the courts. Courts will interpret contracts, collective bargaining agreements, and related statutes. However, the wisdom of collective action as well as philosophic views influencing public policy related to the right of teachers to strike are not appropriate matters for courts to decide.

In the years ahead we expect many controversies over the application and interpretation of collective bargaining agreements and their proper scope and meaning, as well as disagreements concerning the right to strike. There will be significant controversy about the desirability of tenure laws and whether collective negotiation agreements might not in fact provide a more fair and expeditious way of protecting competent teachers.[17] Clearly major gains have been made by teachers in establishing their right to organize and to freely associate with fellow professionals to pursue matters of mutual interest. It is equally clear, however, that the courts will not protect teachers who are incompetent, immoral, or uncooperative merely because they are also engaged in protected organizational activities.

A disclaimer

There are interesting and difficult problems related to teacher organizations, collective bargaining, and strikes that we do not discuss in this volume. We have restricted our presentation of cases and analysis to civil rights and have excluded other aspects of labor law as well as the law of contracts and torts, all of which is important for teachers. There is extensive literature on these areas in college libraries throughout the nation.[18]

NOTES

[1]*People ex rel Fursman* v. *City of Chicago*, 278 Ill., 318, 116 N.E. 158 (1917).

[2]*Id.*, p. 158.

[3]*Id.*, p. 160.

[4]*Seattle High School Chapter No. 200, of the American Federation of Teachers* v. *Sharples et al.*, 293 Pac. 994 (1930).

[5]*McLaughlin* v. *Tilendis*, 398 F.2d 287 (1968).

[6]*Indianapolis Education Association* v. *Lewallen* (U.S. Court of Appeals, 7th Circuit, 13 August 1969).

[7]*Hanover Township Federation of Teachers* v. *Hanover Common School Corporation*, 318 F. Supp. 757 (1970). U.S.D.C., N.D. Indiana, Hammond Division.

[8]*Lawson* v. *Board of Education of Vestal Cent. Sch. Dist. No. 1*, 315 N.Y.S. 2d 877 (1970), and *Trustees of California State College* v. *Local 1352, San Francisco State College Federation of Teachers*, 92 Cal. Rptr. 134 (1970).

[9]*McLaughlin* v. *Tilendis*, *op. cit.*, p. 289.

[10]Florida Laws 1969, ch. 69–1424.

[11]*Orr* v. *Thorp*, 308 F. Supp. 1369 (1969).

[12]See for example *The Pennsylvania Labor Relations Board* v. *State College Area School District, The Board of Directors*, case no. PERA-C-929-C (1971). The controversy centered around conflicting interpretations of Pennsylvania's Public Employee Relations Act, illustrating a shift from basic constitutional questions to questions of interpreting statutes and contracts.

[13]*Board of Education* v. *New Jersey Education Association*, 247 A 2d 867 (1968).

[14]*Pinellas County Classroom Teachers Association* v. *Board of Public Instruction*, 214 So. 2d 34 (1968).

[15]*Tischler* v. *Board of Education*, 323 N.Y.S. 2d 508 (1971).

[16]*Simcox* v. *Board of Education Lockport Tp.*, 443 F. 2d 40 (1971).

[17]For a brief but interesting discussion and prediction for the 1970s, see Myron Lieberman, "Why Teachers Will Oppose Tenure Laws," *Saturday Review*, 4 March 1972, pp. 55–56.

[18]See, for example, Lieberman, Myron, and Moskow, Michael H., *Collective Negotiations for Teachers; An Approach to School Administration*, Chicago, Rand McNally, 1966; Stinnet, Timothy M., *Turmoil in Teaching; A History of the Organizational Struggle for America's Teachers*, New York, Macmillan, 1968; Edwards, Newton, *The Courts and the Public*

Schools, rev. ed., University of Chicago Press, 1955; Remmlein, Madeline K., *School Law,* 2d ed., Danville, Ill., Interstate Printers and Publishers, 1962; Garber, Lee D., and Reutter, Edmund E., Jr., *The Yearbook of School Law,* Danville, Ill., Interstate Printers and Publishers, published annually.

10
Arbitrary action, discrimination, and fair procedures

. . . N*or shall any state deprive any person of life, liberty, or property, without due process of law; nor deny any person within its jurisdiction the equal protection of the laws.*

—*Fourteenth Amendment to the Constitution*

▪ A woman teacher is directed by the school board to take a leave of absence at the end of her fourth month of pregnancy. She and her physician claim that she is in good health and perfectly fit to continue her work. When the Board forces her to take a leave, she alleges a violation of her constitutional right to equal protection.
▪ When School District Alpha integrates its schools, Mr. X is dismissed from his teaching position. The board claims that there is now an oversupply of teachers in the district and that Mr. X is being discharged because he is less competent than other available teachers. Mr. X claims that his dismissal is racially motivated and alleges a violation of due process of law.
▪ When Ms. A, a probationary teacher, is not reappointed for the next school year, she claims that her vigorous union activities are the reason for the board's action and alleges a violation of due process of law.
▪ Mr. X, a probationary teacher, is advised to seek a position

elsewhere for the next school year. He is told that the quality of his work is "not up to district standards." When he asks for a formal hearing with more specific charges, he is denied it. Mr. X files suit claiming a denial of due process.

The items just cited illustrate the wide range of cases in which teachers claim that their Fourteenth Amendment rights have been violated. These rights are among the most important yet most complicated ones guaranteed by our federal Constitution. The right to due process, for example, appears in both the Fifth and the Fourteenth Amendments, the former providing that "no person shall . . . be deprived of life, liberty, or property, without due process of law," while the latter specifies that "nor shall any State deprive any person of life, liberty, or property, without due process of law."

"Due process of law" has never been precisely defined. Although it is a generally accepted and powerful legal doctrine, its meaning varies according to the situation, and no general definition of it is applicable to all cases and circumstances. Courts, for example, have said that fair play is the essence of due process[1] or that due process requires only that there be no violation of traditional notions of "fair play" and "substantial justice." While the exact meaning of "due process of law" cannot be specified in an abstract definition, the courts agree that the phrase has the same meaning in both the Fifth and the Fourteenth Amendments.

There is a large body of law related to the due process clauses of the Constitution. In our brief treatment we focus only on matters related to the civil rights of teachers. Yet we hope the reader will gain some insight into the general principles of this important doctrine and its relevance to the lives of students and the public as well as teachers. Due process (or the ideal of fairness) applies not only to judicial proceedings, or acts of the legislature, but also to acts of local agencies or extensions of the state such as school boards, superintendents, principals, and even teachers.

Popular notions of due process come from the mass media, particularly television, and relate to celebrated criminal cases. The cases involving the civil rights of teachers are not criminal matters but civil proceedings. There are various differences between criminal and civil proceedings. The degree of proof is one important difference. Also, a crime is a wrong against society, whereas a civil action involves the assertion of an individual or group right. Therefore, not all of the procedural safeguards of criminal proceedings apply to the civil rights of teachers.

As courts have interpreted the Fourteenth Amendment through the years, several important principles have emerged. States and other arms of government must provide equal treatment, fair procedures, and must not be arbitrary, unreasonable or discriminatory in their policies and practices. In order to have these principles applied to teachers, the courts first had to determine whether teaching was a privilege that governments could grant and withdraw at will or whether "life, liberty, or property" was involved in the occupation of teaching.

IS TEACHING A RIGHT OR A PRIVILEGE?

At one point in history public employment, including teaching, was considered a privilege, not a right. As such it was subject to conditions that could not be attached to the exercise of a right. To illustrate this principle, here is an extreme example. It is a privilege for a civic group to use your living room for a meeting. You may require, as a condition of receiving such a privilege, that the group begin its meeting with a prayer. You as a private individual may attach such conditions to a privilege you have the power to grant, but a public school that is available for meetings to various civic groups could not attach such a condition to the use of the facilities because it would violate the First Amendment provision separating church and state.

In the field of public employment, no one has a right to a public position, but unconstitutional conditions may not be attached to such a privilege. In other words, teaching as public employment may not be made conditional on giving up such rights as free speech or assembly.

The question arises as to whether there is a right to any kind of employment. The Constitution does not expressly grant such a right. However, the courts by implication have derived a right to work from the Fourteenth Amendment. In 1923 the Supreme Court declared that the concept of liberty in the Fourteenth Amendment "denotes not merely freedom from bodily restraint but also the right of the individual . . . to engage in the common occupations of life."[2] And if a state denies a person a license or the opportunity to practice his chosen profession, due process requires that he be given a hearing and a chance to respond to charges against him.[3]

However, since there is no constitutionally protected right to *public* employment, due process is not required when the only thing at stake is a *specific* job.[4] For example, if Mr. X, an outspoken campus activist, wishes to be certified as a teacher, the state certification agency may not deny him the opportunity or discriminate against him because of his vigorous, peaceful exercise of his right to speak freely and to organize fellow students. Mr. X, however, does not have a right to a teaching position at Hillside School. Hillside School has wide discretion to select its teachers, though this discretion should not be exercised in violation of constitutional rights.

While courts have never said that there is a right to public employment, they have recognized the right to "practice a chosen profession," including teaching. Within the meaning of "liberty" one may choose an occupational goal and, if otherwise qualified, pursue it on an equal basis with anyone else. Some courts assert that upon entering an occupation one acquires a "property" right in that occupation that is protected by constitutional provisions against arbitrary or discriminatory action by government officials. At times courts speak of the "expectancy of continued employment" as a right to be protected.

The Supreme Court cut to the heart of the matter when it proclaimed that "We need not pause to consider whether an abstract right to public employment exists. It is sufficient to say that constitutional protection does extend to the public servant whose exclusion pursuant to a statute is patently arbitrary or discriminatory."[5]

Arbitrary action

But when is an action arbitrary or discriminatory? Since there is a tendency for each of us to consider any law, rule, or action we dislike as somehow arbitrary or discriminatory, let us turn to some of the cases that have interpreted these terms.

In the Wieman case, for example, a loyalty oath of the State of Oklahoma was declared unconstitutional under the due process clause. The oath was based on membership in certain organizations, some of whose members may have been loyal while others were disloyal. The court indicated that membership in a subversive organization may be innocent, since some people join proscribed organizations while unaware of their activities and purposes. In fact, testimony of J. Edgar Hoover was cited to support this opinion. Consequently, to classify everyone on the basis of mere membership is unreasonable. In the words of the Court, "Indiscriminate classification of innocent with knowing activity must fall as an assertion of arbitrary power. The oath offends due process." In other words, the state may classify people for certain purposes, but the classification must be reasonable and must be related to a legitimate governmental aim.

One obvious example of legitimate classification would be to separate shower facilities for males and females in schools. An illegitimate and therefore arbitrary classification would be to allow only males to vote in school elections or to provide that school administrators will be selected from among the male members of the faculty.

Discrimination

Sex. School policies and practices that classify on the basis of sex are increasingly being reexamined. When are they arbitrary; when are they reasonable and thus legitimate? At one point in history it was a common practice for school boards to dismiss women teachers when they married. From today's perspective it seems almost unbelievable that court cases were necessary to declare that marriage is not a reasonable ground for dismissing a woman teacher. Oddly enough, even today some state laws allow individual school districts to provide for such dismissal in their contracts with teachers.[6]

Similarly, most cases hold that it is arbitrary to dismiss a woman teacher who was absent for childbirth, yet even this is not a uniformly accepted principle. There have been cases as recently as 1945[7] that ruled that pregnancy and childbirth constitute "incompetency" or "neglect of duty," justifying dismissal because they render the teacher incapable of carrying on her job. Other courts have dismissed such reasons as absurd.[8]

Recent court rulings have treated marriage and pregnancy as normal events among teachers; state laws typically require pregnant women to take a leave of absence at the fourth or fifth month of pregnancy. Are such rules arbitrary and thus a violation of due process? Or is there a reasonable connection between the rule and some legitimate concern of the state? Courts have held both ways, depending on the circumstances. When a school board demonstrated that before it instituted a maternity leave policy "the teachers suffered many indignities as a result of pregnancy which consisted of children pointing, giggling, laughing and making snide remarks causing interruption and interference with the classroom program of study," the court upheld the leave policy as a reasonable one. In this case[9] the Cleveland, Ohio, Board could show that prior to the leave policy teachers tended to stay on the job far too long. ". . . And although no child was born in the classroom, a few times it was very close. The evidence showed that in one instance where the teacher's pregnancy was advanced, children in a Cleveland junior high school were taking bets on whether the baby would be born in the classroom or in the hall!" Testimony showed that the purpose of the regulation was to protect the teacher and to maintain the continuity of the classroom program and prevent disruption.

The Cleveland Board also presented evidence that the incidence of violence was steadily increasing in the schools and that physical assaults upon teachers by pupils were increasing significantly. The court further considered the weight changes that occur during normal pregnancies and the fact that frequency of urination increases, agility is impaired, sudden physical exertion is forbidden, and the incidence of toxemia is as high as ten percent. Other possible complications were discussed, leading the court to conclude that a maternity leave policy is grounded in reason.

The district court explained the well-known principle that the equal protection clause of the Fourteenth Amendment does not exclude all classifications but only those that are without some reasonable basis and are therefore arbitrary. A classification might be reasonable even though in practice it results in some hardships and some inequality. Moreover, if the reasonableness of such a policy is called into question the burden of showing that it is unreasonable and thus arbitrary rests on the party challenging it.

Other courts, however, have struck down the typical maternity rule as being arbitrary. An example is the Virginia case of *Cohen* v. *Chesterfield County School Board and Dr. Robert F. Kelly.*[10] The relevant portion of the school district maternity policy reads as follows:

> *Termination of employment of an expectant mother shall become effective at least four (4) months prior to the expected birth of the child. Termination of employment may be extended if the superintendent receives written recommendation from the expectant mother's physician and her principal, and if the superintendent feels that an extension will be in the best interest of the pupils and school involved.*

On 2 November 1970 Ms. Cohen informed the board that she expected a child on 28 April 1971. She requested maternity leave commencing on 1 April 1971, at the end of her eighth month of pregnancy. The board granted the leave as of 18 December 1970, denying her request for the later date. When Cohen's appeal to the board was denied, she went to court claiming that her constitutional rights under the Fourteenth Amendment had been violated.

The court found neither medical nor psychological reasons for a pregnant teacher to be forced to take a mandatory leave of absence. It found the policy to be arbitrary, discriminatory, and a denial of equal protection. In the words of the court,

> *It is sufficient to say that constitutional protection does extend to the public servant whose exclusion pursuant to a statute (or regulation) is patently arbitrary or discriminatory. The maternity policy of the School Board denies pregnant women such as Mrs. Cohen equal protection of the laws because it treats pregnancy differently than other medical disabilities. Because pregnancy, though unique to women, is like other medical conditions, failure to treat it as such amounts to discrimination which is without rational basis, and therefore is violative of the equal protection clause of the Fourteenth Amendment.*

It is difficult to reconcile the La Fleur and Cohen cases. They were litigated at the same time, so neither court knew of the decision and reasoning of the other. Perhaps the distinguishing factor might be the extent of violence and assaults on teachers cited in the Ohio case as posing extra danger for pregnant teachers. No such problems were in evidence in the Virginia case. However, the language of the court in the Ohio case leads us to believe that the ruling would have been the same even if no evidence of violence had been introduced. More authoritative rulings will come from higher courts, legislation, or a constitutional amendment. In the meantime we view these two cases as largely contradictory. In an area of rapid social change such as the emerging rights of women, courts often reflect current social, cultural, and philosophic disagreements. The apparently contradictory holdings of these cases can also be used to illustrate some of the difficulties courts find in applying the constitutional prohibitions against the denial of equal protection of the laws. (The distinction may very well be the judge. In spite of the idea that we are supposed to be "governed by law rather than by men," the unfortunate fact is that the result sometimes depends on which judge hears the case.)

A different aspect of sexism is visible in a Georgia policy denying maternity leave to probationary teachers. The court found the policy repugnant to the equal protection clause of the Fourteenth Amendment. The board argued that if untenured teachers were granted maternity leaves it would be impossible to evaluate them for tenure. The court rejected this argument, saying that "the board may extend the probationary period if it desires. Moreover, untenured teachers are permitted to go on study leave, which may be taken for as long as one year, and military leave, which commonly lasts two years."[11] It would be aribtrary and discriminatory to deny equal leave privileges to pregnant probationary teachers.

Although it does not involve teachers, the case of *Kirstein* v. *The Rectors and Visitors of the University of Virginia* is relevant by analogy.[12] Upon a challenge by four women, the court struck down the all-male admission policy of the University of Virginia.

> *The Commonwealth of Virginia may not now deny to women, on the basis of sex, educational opportunities at the [University] . . . Plaintiffs have been . . . denied their constitutionl rights to an education equal with that offered men . . . and . . . such discrimination on the basis of sex violates the Equal Protection Clause of the Fourteenth Amendment.*

We can expect many new developments related to this area, where educators and the courts will repeatedly face the question of the legitimacy of classification. Granted that some classification is reasonable, the issue for the courts to decide is whether the particular grouping in dispute is arbitrary or discriminatory. Bold and well-conceived legal action in behalf of equality for women has already achieved significant results, with more to come.

Race. A decision is arbitrary or capricious if it is unsupported by facts or is not grounded in reason, or is based on impermissible grounds like race or religion, or the denial of free speech. Only such broad, general outlines can be laid down; the principle then must be applied to each situation. A U.S. Circuit Court so held in *Johnson* v. *Branch*.[13]

Ms. Johnson had taught in the same high school in Enfield, North Carolina, for twelve years. Throughout this period she had been rated by her principal as excellent in both teaching and extracurricular duties. North Carolina has no tenure; all teachers work on annual contracts, renewable at the discretion of the board of education upon the recommendation of the principal. During her thirteenth year of teaching, Johnson took part in civil rights and political activities in town. She received warnings from her principal concerning some minor infractions at school, though none related directly to her classroom work. "Instead they covered such matters as being 15 minutes late to supervise an evening athletic contest; arriving at the school building a few minutes after the prescribed sign-in time but before any class was due to commence; failure to furnish written explanation for not attending a P.T.A. meeting; failure to stand in the door of the classroom to supervise pupils as the classes changed, and failure to see that the cabinets in her room were clean and free of fire hazard."[14]

Johnson improved her performance after the notice, and the principal acknowledged the improvement and urged her to continue in this vein. It was clear, looking at the total situation, that the subsequent nonrenewal of Johnson's contract was based on matters other than the minor infractions, yet those infractions were offered by the board as the reasons for her dismissal. The District Court upheld the board and its exercise of discretion, but the Circuit Court reversed this decision and ordered the board to renew Johnson's contract and pay her damages. This does not mean that a school board has no discretion in disciplining or dismissing a teacher. "The statute gives discretion to the school board in deciding whether or not to continue the employment of a teacher. Discretion means the exercise of judgement, not bias or capriciousness. Thus it must be based on fact and supported by reasoned analysis."[15] In this case the court found that racial discrimination was the reason for the nonrenewal of the contract.

While affirming this principle, the same court decided in another case that the board's dismissal of a teacher was not arbitrary if the teacher had been convicted of public drunkenness and assaulting an officer.[16]

School boards have an important responsibility and with it the corresponding authority and discretion to manage the schools. As the Supreme Court said, it "cannot be doubted" that

School authorities have the right and the duty to screen the officials, teachers, and employees as to their fitness to maintain the integrity of the schools as a part of ordered society.[17]

The same Court has also ruled that fitness for teaching depends on a broad range of factors and that there is no requirement in the federal Constitution that classroom conduct be the sole basis for fitness.[18] There is, however, the general due process requirement that the actions of school officials not be capricious, arbitrary, or unreasonable.

Certain kinds of arbitrary actions are also discriminatory. Sex has recently been added to the impermissible bases for discrimination, joining race, religion, ethnicity, and national origin. Most of the legal developments in the area of discrimination arose in the aftermath of the landmark desegregation decision of *Brown* v. *Board of Education of Topeka.*[19]

Although the *Brown* decision did not relate directly to faculty segregation, its implementation in school district reorganizations led to the dismissal or demotion of many black educators. Discriminatory faculty personnel policies based on race reached appellate courts several years after the *Brown* decision. In 1965 the Supreme Court ruled that faculty allocation on a nonracial basis must be an integral part of any desegregation plan.[20] Other cases have followed, reaffirming the principle that faculty and staff desegregation is an important aspect of the basic task of achieving a public school system wholly free of racial discrimination.[21] When school systems failed to respond to the general requirement that faculty and staff be desegregated, the courts became increasingly specific in their expectations and orders. A leading example of this development came from the Fifth Circuit in Mississippi:

Staff members who work directly with children, and professional staff who work on the administrative level will be hired, assigned, promoted, paid, demoted, dismissed and otherwise treated without regard to race, color, or national origin.

If there is to be a reduction in the number of principals, teachers, teacher aides, or other professional staff employed by the school district which will result in a dismissal or demotion of any staff members, the staff member to be dismissed or demoted must be selected on the basis of objective and reasonable non-discriminatory standards from among all the staff of the school district. In addition if there is any such dismissal or demotion, no staff vacancy may be filled through recruitment of a person of a race, color or national origin different from that of the individual dismissed or demoted, until each displaced staff member who is qualified has had an opportunity to fill the vacancy and has failed to accept an offer to do so.

Prior to such a reduction, the school board will develop or require the development of nonracial objective criteria to be used in selecting the staff member who is to be dismissed or demoted. These criteria shall be available for public inspection and shall be retained by the school district. The school district also shall record and preserve the evaluation of staff members under the criteria. Such evaluation shall be made available upon request to the dismissed or demoted employee."[22]

This case is an example of the way courts have promulgated more specific guidelines and directives when the schools have not responded to earlier findings of discrimination. Other cases became still more specific in their requirements, thereby reducing administrative discretion. Conversely, the more honestly and diligently educators carry out the spirit of the law, the less need for judicial interference in the administration of the schools. When a school system continues to follow racially discriminatory personnel policies, the courts will strike them down. There are many examples of black teachers being reinstated with back pay after having been terminated in violation of legal principles providing for faculty desegregation.[23]

The courts recognize that school boards and administrators must have discretion to manage the schools. They must make decisions about teacher placement, promotion, and demotion. Although such discretion is necessary its exercise must not be influenced by race, religion, ethnic background, national origin, or sex. Under our Constitution classification based on these characteristics is discriminatory and is therefore a violation of the equal protection clause of the Fourteenth Amendment. In sum, the constitution requires that *a teacher may not be suspended, dismissed, reduced in rank or pay, or otherwise deprived of any professional benefit for arbitrary or discriminatory reasons.*

FAIR PROCEDURES

Lawyers recognize that a right without a process to defend it is no right at all. The basic purpose of procedural due process is to provide fair and useful processes for asserting and protecting whatever rights the laws otherwise provide. The procedures required by due process usually include the right to a hearing, the opportunity to be represented, to present evidence, to question witnesses, and an impartial judge.

Keep in mind that the Fourteenth Amendment does not impose uniform procedures on all of the states. It requires that we follow the Constitution plus the laws of the particular state in which we are located. Thus, what procedural due process requires in Texas is not necessarily identical with the due process provisions of Vermont or Ohio. There are alternative reasonable and fair processes that the states may create and follow, and still meet the requirements of the

Fourteenth Amendment. This is illustrated by the different rules concerning dismissal of tenured and nontenured teachers.

Tenured teachers

The laws, rules, or contracts that provide for tenure also specify the process whereby a tenured teacher may be suspended, dismissed, or otherwise disciplined. The courts are strict in their insistence that procedural safeguards provided in the tenure law be meticulously observed. The case of a Michigan teacher illustrates this principle. Mr. Kumph taught successfully in the same school system for nine years. He received a sabbatical year to travel and study abroad, with the requirement that he submit an interim report to the superintendent while on leave. When he failed to meet this condition, he was not offered a contract for the ensuing year. The school system and the lower court agreed that the teacher terminated his relationship with the school district by breaking a requirement of his leave of absence. The Circuit Court of Appeals, however, reversed the decision and protected the teacher. The Court insisted that a tenured teacher can be dismissed only by careful compliance with the procedural safeguards of the tenure legislation, including, for example, a sixty-day written notice before the end of the school year.[24] This the board had failed to observe.

There is no constitutional provision for tenure. Tenure is granted either by state law or by contract within a school district. There is no civil right that guarantees tenure. In cases of alleged violations one must examine the state laws that provide for tenure and the conditions under which it may be broken. The typical state law provides that incompetence or immorality are grounds for dismissing a tenured teacher. What constitutes incompetence or immorality is a mixed question of fact, community standards, and professional judgment and must be examined in the trial courts. However, neither incompetence nor immorality may be defined in a way that would violate constitutional principles. A school board, for example, may not declare a teacher immoral or incompetent for teaching Darwinian evolution to high school students. Conversely, the assignment of Darwin's original works to a typical fourth-grade class would be a piece of evidence of incompetence; additional evidence would have to be introduced. In any event it is clear that some kind of procedural due process is available to tenured teachers whose positions are in jeopardy.

There are those who argue that contracts between teacher organizations and school boards should replace tenure laws. It is argued that such contracts would be more efficient and less expensive to enforce than complex legal procedures.[25] While some states are reexamining their tenure laws, about three-fourths of them currently have such laws. In states that have no tenure laws, some schools or school districts provide tenure by contract and some by administrative rule.[26] Although many private institutions also grant tenure by contract, our discussion includes only public institutions. With respect to the rights of nontenured teachers, many due process questions are as yet unsettled.

Untenured teachers

In recent years some states have enacted laws providing some procedural rights for probationary teachers. In Alaska, Connecticut, Rhode Island, and California, for example, suspension or dismissal may not take place without some elements of due process.[27] In most states there are no such laws. In such states, unless a teachers' contract provides for fair process, we must look to the national Constitution. Courts in some of these states, even in the 1970s, seem to follow the ringing declaration made by a judge over fifty years ago that:

> *The board has the absolute right to decline to employ or to reemploy any applicant for any reason whatever or for no reason at all. The board is responsible for its actions only to the people of the City, from whom, through the Mayor, the members have received their appointments.*
>
> *It is no infringement on the constitutional rights of anyone for the board to decline to employ him as a teacher in the schools, and it is immaterial whether the reason for the refusal to employ him is because the applicant is married or unmarried, is of fair complexion or dark, is or is not a member of a trades union, or whether no reason is given for such refusal. The board is not bound to give any reason for its action.*[28]

This language is so clear and so all-inclusive that further discussion might seem superfluous. But is the case still good law? Look at it in the light of what happened to two teachers in 1969.

Eleanor Pred and Stanley Eteresque were English and mathematics teachers, respectively, in the Miami-Dade County, Florida, Junior College. Each was in his third year of teaching and, if reappointed, would have acquired tenure according to Florida law. The board of Public Instruction of Dade County refused to grant them fourth-year contracts, thereby denying them tenure. The probationary teachers claimed that the action of the board was in retaliation for active participation in the local teachers' association and because Ms. Pred was advancing the "new demands for campus freedom" in her classroom.

Members of the board claimed that the teachers were not being discharged, only that their contracts were not being extended beyond the end of the year. They further claimed that it is essential for the board to have discretionary power over probationary teachers in order to manage the schools properly. The teachers, on the other hand, alleged that they were competent in all respects and that the board was punishing them "solely for the purpose of destroying the Plaintiff's rights of freedom of speech and assembly and for the purpose of curtailing and restricting academic freedom."

The District Court upheld the board, and the teachers appealed to the Fifth Circuit Court of appeals, which reversed the lower court in a powerful opinion. The Court was angered by the long delay before the facts of the dispute were established.

This is another monument to the needless waste of lawyer and judge time and, perhaps more important, client money. For now, 14 months later, the case must go back to start the normal process of discovery leading to the production of facts or the demonstrated lack of them on which, either before or after the conventional trial, the real merits of the case will be determined.[29]

John R. Brown, Chief Judge of the Circuit Court, quoted extensively from various decisions of the Supreme Court of the United States in explaining his reasons for reversing the lower court. To the argument that there is no right to public employment, he replied: "Equally unpersuasive is the argument that since there is no constitutional right to public employment, school officials only allowed these teacher contracts to expire. . . . The right sought to be vindicated is *not* a contractual one, nor could it be since no right to reemployment existed. What is at stake is the vindication of constitutional rights—the right not to be punished by the state or to suffer retaliation at its hand because a public employee persists in the exercise of first amendment rights."[30]

He further quoted with approval from three leading cases: "To state that a person does not have a constitutional right to government employment is only to say that he must comply with reasonable, lawful, and non-discriminatory terms laid down by the proper authorities . . ."[31] ". . . constitutional protection does extend to the public servant whose exclusion pursuant to a statute is patently arbitrary or discriminatory."[32] "The theory that public employment which may be denied altogether may be subjected to any conditions, regardless of how unreasonable, has been uniformly rejected. The protections of the First Amendment have been given special meaning when teachers have been involved. Simply because teachers are on the public payroll does not make them second class citizens in regard to their constitutional rights. Our nation is deeply committed to safeguarding academic freedom . . . and to impose any strait jacket upon the intellectual leaders in our colleges and universities would imperil the future of our nation."[33]

The Court recognized that untenured teachers also have constitutional rights. If the probationary teacher asserts that his dismissal, or nonrenewal of contract, is in retaliation for his exercise of a constitutionally protected right rather than a matter of teaching competence, a fair procedure must be available to determine the facts. If the facts indicate that the dismissal was prompted by the exercise of a right, the courts will apply the "balancing of interests" tests. As the Court explained in a First Amendment case (the Pickering case), "The problem in any case is to arrive at a balance between the interests of the teacher, as a citizen, in commenting upon matters of public concern and the interests of the State, as an employer, in promoting the efficiency of the public services it performs through its employees." The board of education cannot merely speculate that a teacher's activities will be harmful or disruptive to the efficient operation of the school. Administrators may not at their discretion forbid the exercise of a constitutional right. As the Tinker case clearly stated, "Certainly where there is no finding and no showing that the exercise of the forbidden right would materially and substantially interfere with the requirements of appropriate discipline in the operation of the school, the prohibition cannot be sustained."[34]

Thus, the case of Ms. Pred and her fellow teacher was sent back to the lower court for trial to determine the facts and to apply the balance of interests test to the specific situation. The same result was reached in the case of *Lucia* v. *Duggan*, discussed earlier, dealing with personal appearance. This case was particularly significant in Massachusetts, since it was commonly understood that untenured teachers had no right to due process. Under Massachusetts law they were subject to arbitrary, unilateral suspension or dismissal. The Lucia case made it clear that procedural due process applies to untenured teachers *if a constitutionally protected right is being threatened.*

Lucia v. *Duggan,* as well as many other cases of due process, are often brought to court under the Civil Rights Act of 1871.[35] This law states:

Every person, who under color of any statute, ordinance, regulation, custom, or usage, of any State or Territory, subjects, or causes to be subjected, any citizen of the United States or other person within the jurisdiction thereof to the deprivation of any rights, privileges, or immunities secured by the Constitution and laws, shall be liable to the party injured in an action at law, suit in equity, or other proper proceeding for redress.

One of the first cases applying the Civil Rights Act of 1871 to the case of an untenured teacher was that of *Bomar* v. *Keyes.*[36] In this case Ms. Bomar was dismissed by the board of education because she chose to serve for four weeks on a federal grand jury. When she appealed to the New York Commissioner of Education, her appeal was dismissed on the ground that she had "not secured permanent tenure. Having been dismissed by the Board of Education during her probitionary period, such a dismissal is not subject to review." In other words, the Commissioner assumed that a probationary teacher had no right to procedural due process. Bomar pursued her case in court, alleging a violation of the Civil Right Act of 1871. It was in the U.S. Circuit Court of Appeals that she finally won her case. Judge Learned Hand held that if she had been discharged for having exercised her right to serve on the jury, the decision could not stand and she had a right to a trial to determine the cause of her dismissal. The Civil Rights Act of 1871 is thus used to enforce a variety of constitutional rights.

Organizational activities

In the face of rising union activity among teachers, administrators and school boards have often reacted with dismissals and other sanctions. For a variety of reasons administrators (and many teachers) have looked with disfavor on unionization of teachers. As we have seen, teachers have a right to free association, which includes forming and joining unions. If there is such a right, can an untenured teacher be discharged for exercising such a right? The answer is no.[37] In the McLaughlin case, for example, the court stated

It is settled that teachers have the right of free association, and unjustified interference with teachers' associational freedom violates the Due Process clause of the Fourteenth Amendment. Public employment may not be subjected to unreasonable conditions, and the assertion of First Amendment rights by teachers will usually not warrant their dismissal.

Even though the individual plaintiffs did not have tenure, the Civil Rights Act of 1871 gives them a remedy if their contracts were not renewed because of their exercise of constitutional rights.

Untenured teachers do not have a right to procedural due process in all controversies. A denial of a constitutional right must be alleged for this right to accrue. If a teacher is dismissed during his probationary year, or not rehired, because he cannot control his class or is ineffective in teaching math, he cannot claim that a constitutional right has been violated.

The case of Mr. Wilson clearly illustrates this point.[38] Wilson, a probationary teacher, alleged that the only reason for the nonrenewal of his contract was his active participation in the local teachers' association. The board cited two reasons: (1) "effectiveness as a teacher is declining rather than improving"; and (2) "employment was not recommended by the school administration." In its response the court said:

Plaintiffs . . . protest that the Board must accord due process, both substantive and procedural, in all of its operative procedures. If this were so, we would have little need of tenure or merit laws as there could only be, as argued by the plaintiffs, a discharge for cause, with the school board carrying the burden of showing that the discharge was for a permissible reason. We do not believe this to be the law, as there are many public employees who are separated from their employment by a purely arbitrary decision, upon a change of administration or even a change of factual control where the appointments are not protected by civil service or some type of tenure, statutory or contractual.

Further, the court indicated that

Absent statutory or contractual requirements, persons discharged for inefficiency, incompetency, or insubordination have no constitutional right to a hearing with rights of cross-examination of witnesses.

The Orr case

The case of Thomas Justin Orr, a high school teacher in Ohio, illustrates the dominant trend on the question of procedural due process for nontenured teachers.[39] Orr, a probationary teacher, was told that his contract would not be renewed for the 1970–1971 school year. He was given a chance to resign in order to keep a clean record and thus enhance his possibilities for employment elsewhere. When he refused to resign he received written notice that his contract would not be renewed. Orr requested a written statement from the board specifying the reason for the nonrenewal of his contract. When there were no responses to his requests, he filed suit.

The District Court ruled in Orr's favor, but the Sixth Circuit Court of Appeals reversed the ruling. The appeals court correctly noted that there is no Supreme Court ruling on the issue of the right of a probationary teacher to due process when faced with nonrenewal of a teaching contract. Circuit courts are split, as are district courts. The First Circuit Court, for example, has held that a probationary teacher is entitled to a "written explanation, in some detail, of the reasons for non-retention" but "that a hearing is not constitutionally compelled."[40] However, the Fifth Circuit ruled that no reasons or hearing need be given.[41]

The Ohio Court clearly recognizes that there are impermissible grounds for nonrenewal of a contract. These are First, Fifth, and Fourteenth Amendment rights. However, when such rights are not involved and the only question is one of right to employment, the Court accepts earlier statements that "the Fourteenth Amendment only protects against the State depriving one of life, liberty, or property without due process of law. 'It has been held repeatedly and consistently that Government employment is not 'property'. . . . We are unable to perceive how it could be held to be 'liberty'; certainly is not 'life.' "

In concluding that a probationary teacher does not have a right to due process, the Ohio case reflects commonly stated reasons: "In the unique situation of a probationary school teacher, the failure to give reasons for the refusal to rehire is not arbitrary and capricious action on the part of the Board since the very reason for the probationary period is to give the Board a chance to evaluate the teacher without making a commitment to rehire him. A non-tenured teacher's interest in knowing the reasons for the non-renewal of his contract and in confronting the Board on those reasons is not sufficient to outweigh the interest of the Board in free and independent action with respect to the employment of probationary teachers. The Board is not a legal tribunal. It is an employer, and when it decides to hire or not to hire a particular teacher, it is acting 'as proprietor, to manage the internal operations' of the public schools. . . . We hold that the failure to give a reason for the refusal to rehire, or to grant a hearing in connection therewith, standing alone, is not constitutionally impermissible conduct on the part of the Board of Education."[42]

Cases to consider

In the cases that follow consider whether or not there is a constitutional principle involved:

1. In state W there is a tenure law. Teacher A is not yet tenured, and during his probationary period his supervisor and principal are concerned about his teaching effectiveness. Toward the end of his second year, he is notified that he will not be rehired for the following year.

In this example there is no constitutional question involved. The untenured teacher does not have a right to procedural due process unless his state (like Connecticut or California) specifically provides such process by statute.

2. In state X there is no tenure law, but school district Alpha grants teachers tenure by contract after a probationary period. During his probationary period teacher B is notified that he will not be rehired for the next year.

Here again there is no constitutional question involved, and the teacher does not have a right to due process.

3. In state Y there is a tenure law. Teacher A, a probationary teacher, is told repeatedly by his supervisor and his principal that he is not effective in his classroom. Mr. A is also very active in a controversial civil rights movement in the community. He is notified that his contract will not be renewed.

A does not have the right to a hearing on the issue of his teaching competence unless his state so provides by statute. But A may claim that he is being discharged because of his civil rights activities. On that issue he has a right to a fair hearing.

4. In state Z there is a tenure law. Teacher B has been repeatedly praised by her supervisor and principal for her excellent teaching. Near her tenure-granting period she makes some controversial speeches on a local radio station, advocating world government. Shortly thereafter she is notified that her contract will not be renewed.

Although Ms. B would have no right to a hearing on the question of her competence, these facts indicate that the real reason for non-renewal of her contract is displeasure with her controversial radio speeches. Since her freedom of speech is involved, she has a right to a fair hearing. On the facts as given Ms. B would prevail and gain tenure.

To summarize:

- All state laws, school rules, and policies are subject to the Constitution of the United States.
- A state or a school may not deny the constitutional rights of either tenured or untenured teachers.
- While the state has the right to operate its schools, the Civil Rights Act of 1871 prohibits the state or school officials from depriving any teacher of his constitutional rights.
- The courts will constantly weigh the conflicting interests in each situation. The facts of each situation will determine which way the balance of interests test will be resolved.

What is a fair process?

We have discussed various situations and principles related to procedural due process. We have also indicated that the several states do not have to provide identical procedural safeguards to satisfy the Constitution. One of the most complete statements as to what constitutes fair procedure is to be found in the Supreme Court decision in *Goldberg* v. *Kelly*.[43] This case did not involve teachers, but we believe the principles would apply to teachers. The Court indicated that "the minimum procedural safeguards . . . demanded by rudimentary due process" would include:

- The opportunity to be heard at a reasonable time and place.
- Timely and adequate notice giving details of the reasons for the proposed suspension or dismissal.
- An effective opportunity to defend oneself, including oral presentation of evidence and arguments.
- An opportunity to confront and cross-examine witnesses.
- The right to retain an attorney.
- A decision resting solely on the legal rules and evidence adduced at the hearing.

- A statement of the reasons for the determination and the evidence relied on.
- An impartial decision maker.

There seems to be a trend toward according due process to all teachers. For example, courts in Minnesota[44] and Arizona[45] have held that the summary dismissal of an untenured teacher is invalid. Cases in Virginia,[46] Wisconsin,[47] and Massachusetts[48] have reached similar conclusions. But due process for all teachers is certainly not a uniform practice. Thus, cases in Massachusetts,[49] New Jersey,[50] New Hampshire,[51] Minnesota,[52] and Ohio[53] have denied probationary teachers the right to due process. The law on this issue is not settled. The several states have arrived at different conclusions, and the only rule that applies to all jurisdictions is that all teachers, tenured and untenured, have a right to procedural due process if they are dismissed or not reemployed on constitutionally impermissible grounds such as race, religion, sex, or exercise of free speech, assembly, or association.

In view of inconsistent lower-court rulings, the Supreme Court agreed to consider appeals involving questions of due process for probationary teachers and on 29 June 1972 handed down decisions in the Roth and Sinderman cases.[54] While both of these cases involved college professors in public institutions, the decisions are likely to set precedents for public elementary and secondary schools as well. The majority of the Court ruled in the Roth case that an untenured teacher does not have "a constitutional right to a statement of reasons and a hearing on the University's decision not to rehire him for another year." The Court (a majority of five with three dissents and one abstention) emphasized its view that the nontenured teacher does not have a property right to continued employment and he cannot claim that his "liberty" was violated without due process "when he is simply not rehired in one job but remains as free as before to seek another."

The Roth case is likely to influence lower courts to rule in the future that untenured teachers do not have a *constitutional* right to due process unless their respective states by *statute* provide such a right. An interesting distinction, however, arose in the Sinderman case at Odessa College, Texas. There, certain informal practices and the official faculty guide led professors to believe that informal tenure existed even though the college had no official tenure system. Under such circumstances the Court distinguished this case from Roth and ruled that it was reasonable for the teacher to anticipate continued employment absent sufficient cause for termination. A reasonably based expectancy of continued employment is enough of a property interest that it cannot be denied without fair procedures, including a hearing, a statement of the "grounds for his nonretention and opportunity to challenge their sufficiency."

Internal procedures

Schools and school boards often provide their own internal procedures for handling disciplinary matters among teachers. This is often referred to as "academic due process." The courts tend to respect these internal procedures but will nonetheless scrutinize them for adequacy. While the courts may impose higher standards of due process, failure by a board to follow its own rules and procedures provides the teacher with a strong claim that his rights have been violated. The same principle applies when collective bargaining contracts provide for procedural safeguards.

The requirement that a school board must follow its procedures applies to both tenured and untenured teachers, even where a board has not officially approved such rules and regulations. For example, in a case in which the board members were aware of a booklet setting forth rules and regulations and a tenured teacher was dismissed without the rules being followed, the court reversed the board and reinstated the teacher.

> *It is the court's opinion that the Board should have complied with the procedures set out in the . . . booklet. Even though the booklet may never have had official approval by formal Board action, the members were well aware of its contents.*
>
> *The promulgation and distribution of the . . . booklet, with the apparent acquiescence and approval of the School Board, without informing those to whom it was distributed that it was not a binding document, when coupled with reliance on it, made the booklet one which should have been followed in terminating the contract. . . .*[55]

Concerning procedural due process we can set forth three general rules:

1. A teacher may not be suspended, dismissed, demoted, reduced in compensation, or otherwise deprived of any professional benefit without a fair and open process if the action against him is brought because of his exercise of a constitutional right.

2. In the case of untenured teachers, when a question of professional competence and not a constitutional right is involved, some states by law grant the right to a fair process, while others allow the school boards to act unilaterally at their discretion.
3. In the case of untenured teachers, when only the question of nonrenewal of contract is involved, the Supreme Court has ruled that there is no constitutional right to procedural due process.

NOTES

[1]*Galvan* v. *Press*, 74 S.Ct. 737, 742, 347 U.S. 522 (1954).
[2]*Meyer* v. *Nebraska*, 262 U.S. 390, 399 (1923).
[3]*Greene* v. *McElroy*, 360 U.S. 474, 79 S. Ct. 1400 (1959).
[4]*Cafeteria Restaurant Workers Union, Local 473* v. *McElroy*, 367 U.S. 886, 81 S.Ct. 1743 (1961).
[5]*Wieman* v. *Updegraff*, 344 U.S. 183, 192 (1952).
[6]See *Corpus Juris Secundum*, Vol. 78, pp. 1086–1087.
[7]*West Mahonoy Tp. School Dist.* v. *Kelly*, 41 A. 2d 344 (1945).
[8]*Corpus Juris Secundum*, *op. cit.*, p. 1087.
[9]*La Fleur* v. *Cleveland Board of Education*, 326 F. Supp. 1208 (1971).
[10]326 F. Supp. 1159 (1971).
[11]*Junks* v. *Mays*, 40 Law Week 2193 (1972), cited in *NOLPE Notes*, *7*, no. 1, January 1972.
[12]Civil Action No. L20-69-R, Slip Op. (U.S.D.C.E.D. Va., 9 February 1970).
[13]364 F. 2d 177 (1966).
[14]*Id.* at 178.
[15]*Id.* at 181.
[16]*Bradford* v. *School District No. 20, Charleston, South Carolina*, 364 F. 2d 185 (1966).
[17]*Adler* v. *Board of Education*, 342 U.S. 485, 72 S. Ct. 380 (1952).
[18]*Beilan* v. *Board of Education*, 357 U.S. 485, 72 Ct. 380 (1952).
[19]374 U.S. 483 (1954). This case is often referred to as Brown I, while 349 U.S. 294 (1955) is called Brown II.
[20]*Bradley* v. *School Board of the City of Richmond*, 382 U.S. 103 (1965).
[21]*United States* v. *Montgomery County Board of Education et al.*, 395 U.S. 225 (1969), and *Singleton* v. *Jackson Municipal Separate School District*, 419 F. 2d 1211 (1970).
[22]*En Banc School Cases*, No. 28349, Slip Op. at 12–14 (U.S. Ct. of App. 5th Cir. Dec. 1969).
[23]See, for example, *Rauls* v. *Baker County, Georgia, Board of Education*, 445 F. 2d 825 (1971).
[24]*Kumph* v. *Wayne Community School District*, 188 N.W. 2d 71 (1971).
[25]See Myron Lieberman, "Why Teachers Will Oppose Tenure Laws," *Saturday Review*, 4 March 1972, pp. 55–56.

[26]For an excellent discussion of the advantages and disadvantages of the tenure system see Byse, "Tenure and Academic Freedom," in *Challenge and Change in American Education*, S. Harris, ed., 1965, p. 313–327.

[27]See Frakt, "Non-Tenure Teachers and the Constitution," 1811, Kan. L. Rev. 27, 50–53 (1969).

[28]*People ex rel. Fursman* v. *City of Chicago*, 278 Ill. 318, 116 N.E. 158 (1917), p. 325.

[29]*Pred* v. *Board of Public Instruction*, 415 F. 2d 851, 852 (5th Cir. 1969).

[30]*Id.* at 865.

[31]*Slochower* v. *Board of Higher Education*, 350 U.S. 551, 555 (1956).

[32]*Wiemann* v. *Updegraff*, 344 U.S. 183, 191 (1956).

[33]*Keyishian* v. *Board of Regents*, 385 U.S. 589, 603 (1967).

[34]*Tinker* v. *Des Moines School District*, 393 U.S. 511, 89 S.Ct. 739, 21 (1969).

[35]Title 42 United States Code, Section 1983.

[36]162 F. 2d 136 (1947).

[37]*McLaughlin* v. *Tilendis*, 398 F. 2d 287 (1968).

[38]*Wilson* v. *Pleasant Hill School District, R-111 et al.*, U.S.D.C., W.D. of Missouri (case no. 18,501-4, 1 March 1971).

[39]*Orr* v. *Trinter*, 444 F.2d 128 (1971).

[40]*Drown* v. *Portsmouth School District*, 435 F. 2d 1182, 1185 (1970).

[41]*Thaw* v. *Board of Public Instruction*, 432 F.2d 98 (1970).

[42]*Orr*, *op. cit.*, p. 135.

[43]38 U.S. L. Week 4223, 24 March 1970.

[44]*Kuehn* v. *School District No. 70*, 22 N.W. 2d 220 (1946).

[45]*Johnson* v. *Board of Education*, 419 P.2d 52 (1966).

[46]*Thaw* v. *Board of Public Instruction of Dade County*, 432 F.2d 98 (1970).

[47]*Gouge* v. *Joint School District No. 1*, 310 F. Supp. 984 (W.D. Wisc. 1970).

[48]*Lucia* v. *Duggan*, 303 F. Supp. 112 (1969).

[49]*De Canto* v. *School Committee of Boston*, 260 NE 2d 676 (1970).

[50]*Wharton Teachers' Association* v. *Board of Education of the Borough of Wharton*, Decision of the New Jersey Commissioner of Education, 1971.

[51]*Drown* v. *Portsmouth School District*, 435 F.2d 1182 (1970).

[52]*Pearson* v. *Independent School District No. 716*, Minnesota Supreme Court, Case no. 190, 25 June 1971.

[53]*Orr* v. *Trinter*, 444 F. 2d 128 (1971).

[54]*Board of Regents of State Colleges et al.*, v. *Roth*, 92 S.Ct. 2701 (1972), and *Perry et al.* v. *Sinderman*, 92 S.Ct. 2701 (1972).

[55]*Johnson* v. *Angle*, U.S.D.C., Nebraska, no. 71-L-222, 5 November 1971.

11

Conclusions, trends, and cautions

It is fashionable in many circles today to focus on the negative, to criticize life in the United States of America as oppressive, fascistic, racist, sexist, bureaucratic, materialistic, and impersonal. While much of this criticism is overstatement, it is equally blind to ignore the shortcomings of our complex culture.[1] Any fair appraisal of the civil rights of teachers will discern that significant changes have occurred in directions favorable to the exercise of such rights. Although day-to-day changes are difficult to recognize, the long-range gains are clear. Recognizing such gains should lead no one to smug satisfaction, for in no other occupation is there more need for vigilance and cooperative effort to protect gains made while striving for more complete attainment of all civil rights.

One need only read the daily newspapers to become aware of how fragile these rights are and how ready some communities, some parents, and a variety of organizations are to force teachers into a docile, conforming, noncontroversial mold. Eternal vigilance is nowhere more needed, but such vigilance must be based on knowledge of the constitutional principles involved as well as their application to the sensitive area of schooling.

Out of our frontier background, and through the era of "boarding 'round," when teachers had no private lives, a new occupational group has emerged. Today's teachers are generally better educated, more organized, and more willing to claim the rights accorded their fellow citizens. There are, however, powerful arguments for traditional restrictions, which we ignore at our peril. As we survey the areas of civil rights controversy, we can identify a clash of interests in each. We must examine these competing interests and the ways courts have resolved them to know where we now stand and possibly to predict the course of future developments. The following section briefly presents the conclusions we derive.

FREEDOM OF EXPRESSION

In this area of First Amendment rights, teachers have made major gains. There are distinctions drawn, and properly so, between a teacher's right to speak freely or express himself in writing away from school and in school. In the past, a teacher's right to free expression was severely curtailed both in and out of school, and open criticisms of public figures, national policies, school boards, or school policies jeopardized one's teaching certificate, his job, or both.

Out of school

Teaching is a unique occupation in various ways. One feature we must keep in mind is that "much of what students learn is caught, not taught." This is a popular way of saying that teachers are adult models who, in the eyes of the community, represent certain ideals for children to emulate. Whether or not this is a defensible role in which to cast teachers is an interesting philosophical question. As a matter of fact millions of parents as well as many laws and court rulings cling to the idea of the teacher as an adult model for the young. And since we are all concerned about the proper upbringing of our children, we tend to be very concerned about the adult models we provide for our students.

While the courts recognize that behavior away from school cannot be completely ignored in determining a teacher's competence, *generally a teacher's right to free expression away from school is the same as that of anyone else.* A teacher is no longer a teacher twenty-four hours a day; he also has a life as a private citizen. As such, he has the same right to freedom of expression as anyone else, subject to the ordinary rules of libel and slander, and the general principles of criminal law. His rights and restrictions are summarized as follows:

1. A teacher cannot be compelled to give up his First Amendment right to comment on matters of public interest in connection with the operation of the schools. An exception to this rule might be made if a school board can show a compelling need for confidentiality or demonstrate that the teacher's working relationship with his superiors would be seriously impaired by public criticism.
2. Even if public criticism by a teacher is incorrect the erroneous statements cannot be the basis of dismissal unless they were made knowingly or recklessly.
3. A teacher cannot be discharged for exercising his First Amendment right to speak or write outside of school on controversial issues that are not related to education.
4. The First Amendment also protects a teacher's right to circulate controversial petitions on school premises during her free time unless such activity poses a serious and imminent threat to order and efficiency in the schools.

In school

Academic freedom is the phrase generally used to refer to a teacher's right of free expression inside the schools. The concept embodies her right not only to speak and write but also to select books, teaching materials, and teaching techniques she deems appropriate to gain her objectives.

Controversy in this area takes a variety of forms and reflects general cultural developments as well as regional and local variations. For example, not too long ago controversies raged over the use of books written by communist "and other left-wing" authors.[2] *Catcher in the Rye* was another target of self-appointed guardians of public morality, and some extreme groups even objected to the reading of Tarzan books because "there was no clear evidence in the books that Tarzan and Jane were legally married." Although some controversies related to the schools seem to be perennial, as our culture changes so do our disagreements about academic freedom.

In recent years a variety of "dirty word" cases have reached the courts in which the central issue was the limits of academic freedom as applied to the particular situation. It is clear that freedom of speech is not absolute. However, the courts are concerned that teachers not be intimidated and thus made cautious, fearful, and timid in the face of controversial ideas and teaching methods. In the past one would hear about academic freedom only at the college level. Such freedom now extends to high schools and may be extended to elementary schools, with appropriate considerations for the age and experience of the students.

The exact limits of academic freedom are not established, and it is doubtful that they can be. The courts, however, have given us some guidelines that show the enormous gains made by teachers in the cause of freedom of speech in the schools. *As a general rule, the teacher's use of controversial material or language will be protected by the First Amendment unless it can be shown that it is irrelevant to her teaching objective, inappropriate to the age and maturity of her students, or disruptive of school discipline.*

While referring to such general rules, each situation must also be considered on its unique facts. Although the layman wants to know exactly "what the law is," in most areas of civil rights controversy there are no fixed or absolute rules. In these areas one can identify "rights in conflict," or competing interests that need to be balanced and resolved. With regard to freedom of expression, whether away from school or in school, competing interests are identifiable. On the one hand, the teacher has an interest in maximizing his freedom to speak, to write, and to use materials he considers effective in his teaching. On the other hand, parents and society (and administrators on behalf of society) want their schools to nurture their ideas, and they want to employ teachers who represent certain kinds of adult models for their children. Both interests are legitimate. The balance of interests test weighs the competing rights in light of the facts of each situation. However, because freedom of speech is regarded as a powerful right, courts tend to go a long way in its protection. It has often been said that this right is so fundamental that it is a necessary condition of all our other rights. Consequently, we can understand why it has come to be so jealously guarded against restrictions on a teacher's right to free expression away from school or inside the classroom.

A note of caution

A sizable gap exists between what the law is and what communities practice. It would be both naive and misleading to suggest that teachers have as much freedom of expression in practice as the courts allow them. Teachers tend to avoid public controversy, and this makes it possible for local pressure to control their behavior. A particularly invidious practice occurs when an administrator or school board prohibits a teacher from a legitimate exercise of free speech, knowing that she would rather submit to illegitimate restrictions than use her money, time, and energy to fight for her rights.

It is our belief that most administrators and school boards will follow the law if they know what it is. We also believe that teachers are more likely to claim their rights if they know what they are. We hope this volume will add to the knowledge of teachers, administrators, and school boards and thus help keep our civil rights alive in the schools and, through the schools, in the rest of society.

THE TEACHER AS A PERSON

Recognizing that teachers influence their students by the kind of human beings they are, beyond the lessons of the classroom, communities often attempt to control a teacher's moral life, his leisure pursuits, and his personal appearance. In the first chapter we presented a brief catalog of restrictions commonly found in our culture as recently as the beginning of this century. Most of these restrictions are gone today, though some small communities still want to hire teachers who will be paragons of virtue twenty-four hours a day.

When controversies reach our courts, the rights of teachers to pursue a normal life consistent with others in the community receives legal protection. Unusual situations arise, however, that are difficult to resolve. For example, does a teacher have a right to work during weekends or vacations as a go-go dancer in a local night club? May he work as a bartender in a low-class saloon? Should summer attendance at a nudist camp, living in a commune, wearing bizarre clothes, smoking marijuana, or openly and indiscriminately flirting cost a teacher his job?

Teacher morality

There is a clear trend in the decisions of our courts to separate a teacher's professional life from his private, away-from-school conduct. As long as his effectiveness as a teacher is not impaired, his personal behavior away from school cannot be restricted by the public or by the school administration. Conduct away from school that involves breaking the law, however, is a different matter. No one has a civil right to break a law, whether it's drunken driving, burglary, or public homosexual behavior. Teachers involved in illegal conduct may lose their jobs as well as their teaching certificates. The courts will decide whether a particular act constitutes immorality of sufficient magnitude to make one unfit to teach.

While the circumstances of each case must be carefully considered, certain general principles can be distilled from the cases that have reached the courts.

Personal and private activity. Courts increasingly hold that if a teacher's job is not affected, her private acts are her own business and should not be the basis of disciplinary action. Activity that is considered immoral is not in itself grounds for dismissal. Thus, a teacher's use of vulgar language in private or personal correspondence, excessive drinking or use of marijuana, and even homosexual activity carried on with a consenting adult in private have been held to be insufficient grounds for dismissal.

Public immorality. Courts tend to support disciplinary action taken against teachers whose immorality becomes public through their own indiscretion or negligence.

Immoral conduct with students. Courts uphold disciplinary action taken against teachers involved in immoral conduct with students. It should come as no surprise that communities and administrators also tend to be most concerned about such cases. Whether such conduct is in public or private, at or away from school, with or without the consent of students only affects the severity with which the courts view that behavior. The public and the courts view the teacher-student relationship as one laden with trust and not to be abused by a teacher. Consequently, teachers have been dismissed or disciplined for drinking or having sexual relations with students, for encouraging the use of marijuana, and even for using excessive obscene language with teenage boys and girls.

Personal appearance

In the popular mind as well as in the opinion of many school administrators, a teacher's personal appearance is often associated with "morality" or with "professional conduct." Efforts to control personal appearance have stemmed from the conviction that teachers should be adult models for students and that the schools must be able to regulate a teacher's appearance in order to maintain "grooming codes" for students. Over the years, however, significant gains have been achieved by teachers through the courts and through organizational strength. Despite these gains, the gaps between what courts say and what people do often remain, and controversies still rage over the personal appearance of teachers. The most common disagreements can be categorized under "grooming" and "dress codes."

Grooming. Although grooming has a broader meaning in common discourse, we use it here to refer to beards, mustaches, and hair length and style, since recent controversies have centered on efforts to control and regulate these aspects of grooming.

While there is no reference to grooming in the Constitution, courts have extended civil rights protection against undue state regulations in different ways. Beards, mustaches, and hair styles have received protection under the First Amendment as "symbolic speech," and, if kept clean and neat, teachers have a right to wear them. Courts have not been impressed by the argument that in order to regulate students' personal grooming the schools must apply the same rules to teachers. There is some question as to whether schools should be able to regulate student grooming. Courts, however, hold that there are legitimate bases for differentiating teachers from students when it comes to beards, mustaches, and hair styles.

Some courts protect grooming under the First Amendment as symbolic speech and under the due process clause of the Fourteenth Amendment. In addition, the concept of "liberty" in the Fourteenth Amendment can be interpreted to include grooming, and unless it can be shown that beards or hair styles interfere with the operation of the school it is arbitrary to prohibit them. Schools can, however, expect beards and hair to be clean and neat, and worn in a manner that does not invite or encourage disruption of the learning process. Thus, bizarre practices can probably be controlled.

Attire. The law related to a teacher's dress is somewhat different. Generally the courts uphold a school district's right to impose reasonable regulations. The distinction between hair grooming and clothing is reasonable if one considers the fact that after school hours and away from school a teacher is free to follow his personal taste in clothing. Beards cannot be removed for school hours and replaced at 5:00 p.m. the way dashikis, sandals, miniskirts, or capri pants can. Consequently, when courts apply the balancing test and consider a teacher's interests in wearing what he wishes on the one hand and a community's interest in having adult models in the schools and minimizing possible interference with the functioning of the schools, the courts tend to hold in favor of the school system. Courts consider this limitation of teachers' rights temporary and not of fundamental interest.

Community trends. Increasingly our public schools stay away from formal, specific regulations of teachers' grooming and attire. At times we find very general policies that give leeway to teachers as long as health considerations are observed. If a particular practice is disruptive and actually interferes with classroom performance, however, informal methods are typically used to alter it. While schools still tend to have grooming codes for students, they have generally abandoned such codes for teachers, and contracts tend to be silent on this matter. In the future collective negotiation contracts will tend to handle these matters, typically by means of binding arbitration. For example, a recent controversy over the appropriateness of a pants suit was resolved by an arbitrator in a Michigan school system. Such arbitration can consider situational variables, the age and maturity of children, the subject taught, and the health and safety dimensions of the situations. It is also less expensive than going to court.

LOYALTY AND FREEDOM

Every nation is concerned about the loyalty of its teachers. The most extreme examples of such concern can be found in communist and fascist nations, where the schools are explicitly used for centrally determined national purposes. In our own nation preoccupation with teachers' loyalty usually reflects international conflicts, threats, and tensions. However, some degree of public concern is visible even in calm times. Controversies in this area can be analyzed in terms of the tension between loyalty and freedom, and organized under the headings of: (1) loyalty oaths for teachers, (2) membership in controversial organizations, (3) political activities, and (4) membership in teacher organizations.

Loyalty oaths for teachers

Loyalty oaths have had a complex history in our federal and state courts. When one realizes that fifty different state legislatures have created oaths of their own, in addition to those of the federal government, one is more likely to understand the troublesome legal history of these oaths. We must distinguish between the wisdom and usefulness of such oaths and the civil rights questions involved.

Loyalty oaths have been challenged mainly under the First and Fourteenth Amendments. Under the First, the claim has been made that such oaths tend to restrict a teacher's speech and association to "that which is unquestionably safe." The Fourteenth Amendment attacks on the oaths have questioned their vagueness, their breadth, and their unequal application to teachers over other public employees.

Briefly, courts tend to act as follows: (1) Loyalty oaths will be upheld if drawn with precision to prohibit clearly unlawful conduct. (2) Affirmative oaths pledging support for the Constitution or pledging to uphold professional standards tend to be upheld. (3) Oaths that are overly broad or vague, such as the "disclaimer oaths" aimed at membership in subversive organizations, are likely to be held unconstitutional.

Membership in controversial organizations

Keep in mind that teachers not too long ago were dismissed for membership in any organization the local community considered controversial. Although controversial organizations are legion, in this section the conclusions come from leading decisions of the Supreme Court related to membership in the Communist Party. The Court rulings and its reasoning, of course, are applicable to membership in other controversial organizations such as the American Nazi Party, the John Birch Society, the Black Panther Party, the SDS, or the KKK.

The Supreme Court has ruled that the First Amendment protects a teacher's right to belong to controversial organizations. This right is protected even in the case of revolutionary organizations unless it is specifically shown that the teacher subscribes to the illegal aims and activities of the group. Mere membership, or guilt by association, is not ground for dismissing a teacher. The community has a legitimate interest in having loyal teachers who do not violate the law, but teachers have powerful First Amendment rights in freedom of association and assembly. In striking a balance in favor of First Amendment freedoms, the Court emphasized that a teacher who joins a revolutionary organization but does not share its unlawful purposes and does not participate in its unlawful activities poses no threat to the schools.

Political activities of teachers

This is another area of civil rights in which impressive changes have taken place during recent decades. Earlier injunctions against teacher participation in politics have been lifted, at times by court rulings and at times by state law.

There are still many people who urge that teachers be politically silent both in and out of school. The leading cases do not support this view, however. State laws prohibiting teacher participation in politics have been declared unconstitutional. The judicial trend will probably reflect the recent holding that a teacher can be barred from political activity only if it materially and substantially interferes with the operation of the school. Such freedom extends to partisan politics as well as controversial nonpartisan political issues.

Inside the schools, however, teachers may not use their special influence in behalf of political causes. Where relevant to course objectives they may help the class inquire into alternative political positions, candidates, and issues. But the courts will not protect the teacher who uses the school to advance her partisan political beliefs. Furthermore, when a teacher's political activity is likely to interfere with the operation of the school or she wants to hold a paid political office, it is reasonable to require her to take a leave of absence.

Teacher organizations

Historically communities have frowned on teacher organizations and courts have upheld laws and rules prohibiting them. Today, however, the right of teachers to organize and to bargain collectively is clearly established. The courts hold that the First and Fourteenth Amendments protect such associations and activities.

The right to associate with others in an occupational organization does not entail the right to strike or to engage in activities similar to strikes, such as "sanctions." It is a widely accepted principle that government employees, including teachers, may strike only if they are so authorized by state law. At this writing only the states of Hawaii and Pennsylvania have laws enabling teachers to strike; however, Alaska, Vermont and Michigan have no legal penalties for strikes, either. Legal activity in the years ahead will relate to the scope of negotiated agreements, their meaning, and the laws regulating them. It is quite possible that tenure laws will be replaced by negotiated contracts that will clearly specify the conditions of employment and termination, and the specific steps to be observed in disciplinary procedures.

A note of caution

Despite teachers' right to organize, there are conservative communities and school administrators who continue to be resentful of teacher organizations, particularly militant ones. A variety of subtle means are used to discourage teacher participation in such organizations, such as less favorable evaluation reports, transfer to less desirable teaching situations, and assignment to more difficult classes. A clever administrator who does not respect the legal rights of teachers to join organizations can express his displeasure in many hidden ways. He should realize, however, that such behavior shows disrespect for the law and even teaches ways of undermining the democratic processes.

ARBITRARY ACTION, DISCRIMINATION, AND FAIR PROCEDURES

Education in our nation is the responsibility of each state. States may delegate power over schooling to units within the state, such as regions, counties, or municipalities. The ultimate responsibility rests with the state, however, even when such power is delegated to local units. This is why the action of public school officials is state action within the meaning of the law. Courts recognize that school officials, whether board members, superintendents, or principals, must have discretion to manage the schools. But this discretion may not be used in an arbitrary, unreasonable, or discriminatory manner. When it is so used, the action violates the Fourteenth Amendment.

An act by a school official is arbitrary when there is no rational connection between the means used and some legitimate educational goal or when less damaging means are available to attain the same goal. Courts have declared many actions of school officials arbitrary or discriminatory and therefore unconstitutional. It is arbitrary, for example, to dismiss a teacher for belonging to an unpopular, controversial organization. Indiscriminate classification or "guilt by association" are also unreasonable actions. Similarly, it is arbitrary to propose penalizing a teacher for lawful, militant civil rights activities away from school. Classifications based on race or sex are often discriminatory and therefore unconstitutional.

Schools as well as courts are rethinking earlier assumptions that led to many unreasonable practices based on sex. Today there are conflicting court rulings on mandatory maternity leaves. Some courts leave the decision in the hands of the teacher and her physician; others uphold school policies despite medical advice. We believe that the trend of judicial decision is toward declaring rigid maternity leave policies arbitrary and discriminatory action and that the courts will increasingly respect the right to continue working as long as there is no interference with teaching efficiency and effectiveness. New developments in this area will result from increased awareness of sexism, from the work of women's groups, and from the proposed Equal Rights Amendment.

Racism is another major area of discriminatory action. The courts have long held that race is not a legitimate basis for classification. Although the courts have been firm in upholding this principle, schools and communities have found many ways to frustrate the spirit of the law.

Recent controversies related to the civil rights of teachers have centered on discriminatory dismissal and promotion practices. The law is clear that racial discrimination in school personnel policies is unconstitutional. As a general rule a teacher may not be suspended, dismissed, reduced in rank or pay, or otherwise deprived of any professional benefit for arbitrary or discriminatory reasons. Since many racist practices were maintained anyway, the courts issued specific guidelines and directives to force more objectivity and fairness on the schools.

Fair procedures

This aspect of the Fourteenth Amendment requires that no official action be taken to deprive anyone of life, liberty, or property without a fair procedure. Tenured teachers are provided such procedures by the state laws that grant them tenure or, where no such laws exist, by their contracts. But procedural due process is a crucial problem for probationary teachers.

Historically a probationary teacher could be dismissed for any cause or even for no cause at all. In some states this practice continues today, and the courts are divided on how much due process to require in cases involving probationary teachers. The courts realize that it would put a heavy burden on the schools if untenured teachers received all the procedural safeguards accorded tenured ones. They respect administrative discretion and the need for efficiency in the operation of the schools. Extensive procedural safeguards for untenured teachers would add a sizable burden in money, time, and energy. On the other hand, the courts are also aware of the probationary teacher's interest in continued employment and his desire for a fair hearing when his employment is threatened. Hence the dilemma of conflicting interests.

Some states (e.g., Connecticut and California) resolve the dilemma through legislative action providing some degree of due process for probationary teachers. In other states, where there are no statutes on the subject, courts have reached conflicting conclusions. Some uphold the earlier tradition and deny that untenured teachers have any right to fair process; others extend the Fourteenth Amendment to such teachers and require at least a hearing, a statement of the reasons for the proposed action, and an opportunity to answer the charges. If the reason for the dismissal or contract nonrenewal has to do with the exercise of a constitutional right, even a probationary teacher has a right to a fair hearing. The Supreme Court ruled that if the only issue is the nonrenewal of the contract of a probationary teacher, there is no right to a hearing or statement of the reasons for the nonrenewal.

It is probable that collective negotiation contracts will provide the means for evaluating probationary teachers in the future. There is growing pressure for some extension of fair process to such teachers, since it does not seem right that they be completely at the mercy of school administrators. However, there will still be differences between tenured and untenured teachers; the procedures for safeguarding probationary teachers will be less stringent, and the administration will have more discretion in judging their competence. Another probable development will be increased participation by teachers in decisions affecting their professional lives.

Distinguishing educational from legal matters

Not all conflicts involving teachers, schools, administrators, and communities are appropriate matters for the courts. Although many problems, such as those presented in this volume, have significant legal dimensions, it is a serious error to expect the courts and the law to resolve all, or even most, educational problems. Legal institutions are neither appropriate nor competent to handle many of them. After all, school boards were created to determine educational policy. The responsibility and the commensurate authority to administer the schools includes discretionary powers over such diverse matters as the planning and construction of physical facilities; operation and maintenance; curriculum; policies and procedures related to students, faculty, staff, and auxiliary personnel; fiscal matters; public relations; and so on. Within each of these areas disagreements arise, and the board must have broad discretionary powers if it is to work effectively. Such power is either explicitly granted by statute or implied as necessary to carry out a legally imposed function.

It is well to keep in mind that the courts do not as a general rule interfere with the exercise of discretionary power by a board even when a board's decision seems to lack wisdom. The courts will intervene—if someone brings a lawsuit—only if the action of the board is flagrantly or entirely unreasonable (a clear abuse of discretion), or violates state law or a constitutional provision.

To distinguish between an educational and a legal question, here are some examples.

Example 1. School districts A and B are contiguous elementary school districts within the same state. District A uses letter grade report cards in its schools, while district B reports to parents only in conferences. Several parents in district B complain about this practice and demand report cards. This matter is one for educators and the board to decide and not for the courts.

Example 2. School districts X and Y are located in the same state. X offers a variety of foreign languages in its schools, while Y offers only one. Parents complain that this is unequal treatment. The courts will not interfere in this dispute.

Example 3. Riverside School District will not renew the contract of Mr. Frank, a probationary teacher, because in the judgment of the principal and the supervisor Frank has very poor rapport with students. The courts will not interfere with this judgment unless Frank can show that other impermissible grounds such as race, religion, or union activity are the real reasons for the nonrenewal of his contract.

Example 4. Seaside School District is converting its old "egg-crate" schools to "open-structure" buildings in which all classes will be team-taught. Several teachers bring suit to prevent this change because they have succeeded for many years in self-contained classrooms in traditional structures. The courts will respect administrative discretion in this matter and will not substitute their judgment in what is properly an administrative matter.

Many more examples could be given. Educational matters are for educators to decide. The courts neither approve nor disapprove of educational decisions when they respect the discretion of the board, administrators, and teachers. When the courts protect teachers' rights to negotiate collectively, they are not recommending such activity any more than protecting Paul Finot's right to wear a beard is a recommendation by the courts that male teachers grow beards. Textbook selection, transfer of personnel, and millions of other decisions are educational matters that fall outside the purview of the courts. However, under unique circumstances almost any educational decision could become grist for the legal mill. If a teacher is transferred to another school for racial or political reasons, if textbook selection is tainted by special considerations that amount to preferential treatment, if the selection of principals is based on sexist criteria, civil rights concerns intrude into educational deliberations. In such circumstances, which are always questions of fact, the lines separating legal from educational matters have been breached, and the courts will act.

Can you contract away your rights?

Constitutional rights that cannot be taken away by official order or policy cannot be given away in a contract. Thus, if the initial contract of employment in a school district provides that a teacher who accepts a position will not make public speeches criticizing school policy, join a subversive organization, or grow a beard, the contract provision is not binding. The reason for this is that civil rights protect a significant public interest as well as the interests of a particular individual. Moreover, there is pressure on the applicant who needs a job to sign away his civil rights, and as the courts have noted, if the state can make a person give up one of his rights in exchange for its favor, it can make him give up all of them.

CIVIL RIGHTS AND PRIVATE SCHOOLS

During the spring of 1972, when certain students at Stanford University prevented a controversial professor from conducting his classes, it was said that the First Amendment does not apply to Stanford. It comes as a surprise to many people that the civil rights provisions of the Constitution do not apply to private schools, since no state or congressional action is involved. Just how far this principle can be carried is not clear. Its limits have not been tested in courts except in cases of racial discrimination involving schools supported by public funds.

There is at least one legal theory that could be argued to extend constitutional rights beyond the doors of private schools and certainly to the teachers away from school. This theory is that when a private organization performs a state function it has to satisfy constitutional principles just as a public organization would. For example, where a private political party (Democratic or Republican) conducts primary elections, it is performing a state function and cannot discriminate on a racial basis. In the same way, since education is a state function, if a private school performs that function why should it not be subject to constitutional principles? The analogy makes some sense, but it can't be carried to its logical extreme because it would disallow private parochial schools. It could be argued, however, that religion is also a First Amendment right. Thus, private schools could be religious but would have to abide by the other civil rights guarantees of the Constitution.

No court has accepted this line of reasoning as yet, and one can only speculate as to whether or not it will ever become law. Although our analysis should be viewed strictly within the context of the public schools, we hope private schools will also respect the constitutional rights of teachers and students.

A FINAL NOTE

Many commentators view our culture-conflicts, disagreements, and large numbers of lawsuits with alarm. They are particularly unhappy when teachers assert their civil rights through court action or through organizational power. "Would it not be more professional," it is often asked, "if teachers waited for communities to grant them their full rights?"

Our view is to the contrary, and we believe we are consistent with the holdings of the highest court of the land. No other occupational group needs and deserves the full range of civil rights more than teachers. Our concern is not only with teachers as individuals but also their students and the future citizens of our country. We also believe that unless teachers *have* civil rights and *use* them, they are not likely to respect the rights of their students. We have based our efforts on the hope that some understanding of the principles of civil rights can be gained through the use of this book and that such an understanding will lead to increasing realization of these rights in our daily living, in and out of school.

NOTES

[1]For a refreshingly optimistic view, see Jean-Francois Revel, *Without Marx or Jesus,* J. F. Bernard, trans., Garden City, New York, Doubleday, 1971.

[2]The reader will gain some valuable insights from Maryanne Raywid, *The Axe Grinders,* New York, Macmillan, 1962, and Jack Nelson and Gene Roberts, Jr., *The Censors and the Schools,* Boston, Little, Brown, 1963.

Appendix 1
How does the system work?

In this section we consider some questions laymen often ask about our legal system. Among others, we consider why local school officials are responsible to the national Constitution; how the federal and state judicial systems are organized; and how to find the law. There are other matters that lawyers must know in order to understand how the system works. For example, they must know about many administrative agencies, differences in jurisdiction among them and among the various courts. These matters, however, are too technical for inclusion in this volume.

EDUCATION AS A STATE FUNCTION

In a recent discussion with the dean of the school of education of a large public university, we were amazed to hear him assert that the federal Constitution expressly delegates power over education to the various states. The dean is clearly mistaken. Our national Constitution is strangely silent on schooling. Scholars have speculated through the years about the reasons for this omission and tend to agree that, were the Constitution to be reframed today, education would occupy a prominent place in it.[1]

By implication the federal government could move into the field of public education under several provisions of the Constitution. Prominent among these is Article I, Section 8:

"The Congress shall have power to lay and collect taxes, duties, imports and excises, to pay the debts and provide for the common defense and general welfare of the United States. . . ." The "welfare clause" could be used without difficulty or distortion to imply congressional power to legislate in school matters. As a matter of fact, as many as fourteen different parts of the Constitution have influenced educational development in the United States.[2]

While it is arguable that under the implied powers embodied in the Constitution our federal government could have developed a system of schools, as a matter of fact it did not do so. Instead, another provision of the Constitution has been relied on to establish the principle that education is primarily a state function. The Tenth Amendment, ratified in 1791, stipulates that "the powers not delegated to the United States by the Constitution, nor prohibited by it to the States, are reserved to the States respectively, or to the people." Consistent with this principle, every state constitution makes provision for a system of state-supported schools. These provisions vary from state to state, some being quite general while others are more specific and include such matters as the minimum length of the school year and the age range between which schooling must be freely provided.[3]

The courts have accepted the general principle that power over the schools is among those reserved to the states. In the words of Supreme Court Justice Jackson,

> *A Federal Court may interfere with local school authorities only when they invade either a personal liberty or a property right protected by the Federal Constitution. . . .*
>
> *We must have some flexibility to meet local conditions, some chance to progress by trial and error. . . .*

Justice Jackson further warned that adoption by the Court of "an unchanging standard for countless school boards . . . is to allow zeal for our own ideas of what is good in public instruction to induce us to accept the role of a super board of education for every school district in the Nation.[4]

It is quite clear, then, that education is primarily a state function to be carried out pursuant to the constitutions, legislative enactments, and administrative agencies of the several states. All of these, of course, are subject to the principles of the federal Constitution as interpreted by the Supreme Court of the United States. That Court itself has spoken to this matter as follows:

The Fourteenth Amendment, as now applied to the states, protects the citizen against the State itself and all of its creatures—Boards of Education are not excepted. These have, of course, important delicate and highly discretionary functions, but none that they may not perform within the limits of the Bill of Rights. That they are educating the young for citizenship is reason for scrupulous protection of Constitutional freedoms of the individual, if we are not to strangle the free mind at its source and teach youth to discount important principles of our Government as mere platitudes.[5]

This point has often become blurred by our historic emphasis on local control of schools. It is true that states may delegate certain powers over schooling to regions within the states such as counties, cities, towns, or other political subdivisions. However, the basic authority and responsibility, in principle, remains with the states. Local school boards, superintendents, principals, and teachers perform state functions when they act in their professional capacities. This is a most important concept to understand because it links the actions of school officials to the Fourteenth Amendment of the federal Constitution. Remember the wording of that amendment?

All persons born or naturalized in the United States, and subject to the jurisdiction thereof, are citizens of the United States and of the State wherein they reside. No State shall make or enforce any law which shall abridge the privileges or immunities of citizens of the United States; nor shall any State deprive any person of life, liberty, or property, without due process of law; nor deny to any person within its jurisdiction the equal protection of the laws.

One must understand this relationship of the schools to their respective states to realize that when a school official acts it is a state action within the meaning of constitutional law. For example, when the school board of a town in Massachusetts prescribes that each school day begin with a prayer, it is a state action that violates the "separation of church and state" doctrine. When a school psychologist in California, using a standardized test written in English, determines that Chicano children are mentally retarded and therefore must be placed in separate classes, he is acting as a state official and is violating the equal protection and due process clauses of the Fourteenth Amendment. And when teachers or principals systematically treat some children differently from others because of the color of their skin or their national origin, their actions are state actions for civil rights purposes.

This is often overlooked in the ordinary life of the schools, when a principal orders a teacher to remove a beard, when teachers frisk students' briefcases and lockers, or when a counselor systematically "guides" black and brown students into vocational classes. Their actions are state actions.

Another important principle of constitutional law must be understood by educators. It is the principle that the basic liberties of our Bill of Rights apply to state actions through the Fourteenth Amendment. This was a highly controversial development at one point in American history. However, today it is widely accepted by scholars and certainly by the courts that the adoption of the Fourteenth Amendment made ". . . national citizenship primary and state citizenship derivative therefrom."[6] Consistent with this principle, for example, is the pronouncement of the Supreme Court that "The fundamental concept of liberty embodied in the Fourteenth Amendment embraces the liberties guaranteed by the First Amendment. . . ."[7] Thus, while the words of the first ten amendments restrained only the Federal Government, after the Fourteenth Amendment was adopted in 1868 it became possible to apply some of these restraints to the states. This was accomplished by the courts' interpretation that the Fourteenth Amendment incorporated the basic protections of the First and specifically applied them to all state actions. In practice this means that all of the civil rights protections of the First Amendment apply to the actions of all public school officials just as much as those of the Fourteenth Amendment.

THE STRUCTURE OF THE SYSTEM

Perhaps a more accurate heading for this section would be "The Structure of the Systems," for in actuality we have a system of federal courts and fifty systems of state courts. For our purposes general descriptions of the federal system and the state system will suffice.

The federal courts

The Supreme Court was specifically created by the Constitution,[8] but the other federal courts are established by Congress. Congress also has the power to alter the federal court system, creating new courts and abolishing existing ones to meet the needs of our changing culture. Currently, except for some special courts like the Court of Claims, Court of Customs and Patent Appeals, and Tax Court, we have a hierarchic system of three levels. The first level, the trial court, is the U.S. District Court. Each state has at least one district court, and some large and populous states have as many as four. Cases from these courts, as a general rule, are reviewable by the U.S. Court of Appeals, of which there are eleven, including one in the District of Columbia. (See map, p. 167) The top level, of course, is the Supreme Court of the United States. This three-level hierarchy is depicted in the chart on p. 168.

Except for the Supreme Court, whose jurisdiction is specified in the Constitution,[9] Congress determines which cases shall be tried where,* the route each type of case will follow, and the relationship between the courts and the many administrative agencies of the government.

The state courts

Since state courts are created by state constitutions and legislative bodies, they vary considerably in titles, authority, and procedures. Nevertheless, there are commonalities among them that make an intelligible general description and schematic presentation possible.

The hierarchic court systems of the states can be organized on four levels. At the lowest level are the small claims, traffic, and police courts, justices of the peace, and magistrates' courts. Cases heard at this level usually cannot be appealed to higher courts. At the next higher level we find probate, municipal, and superior courts, as well as special trial courts such as traffic and juvenile courts. From this level appeal is possible to the next, the intermediate appellate courts variously named in the different states. At the zenith of the state court hierarchy is the state supreme court: in Massachusetts, the Supreme Judicial Court; in Kentucky, the Court of Appeals; in Connecticut, the Supreme Court of Errors. The chart on p. 168 depicts the general pattern of state court hierarchies.

The appellate courts within a state also have power to review the decisions of state administrative agencies. Since states vary in their provisions for appeal from both courts and administrative agencies, one must check the laws of the particular state involved. One final

*This is where disagreements arose between Congress and President Nixon during the spring of 1972, when the President proposed to limit the jurisdiction of the courts over desegregation cases.

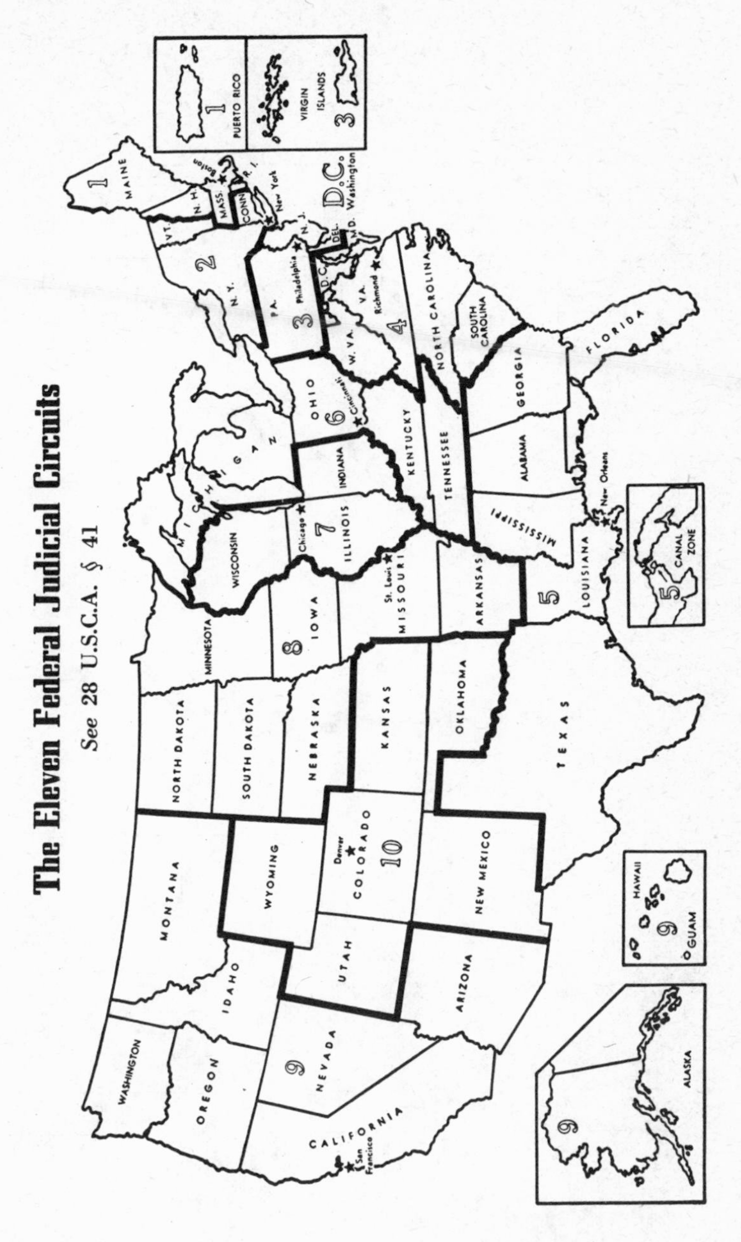

SOURCE: Courtesy of West Publishing Company, St. Paul, Minnesota.

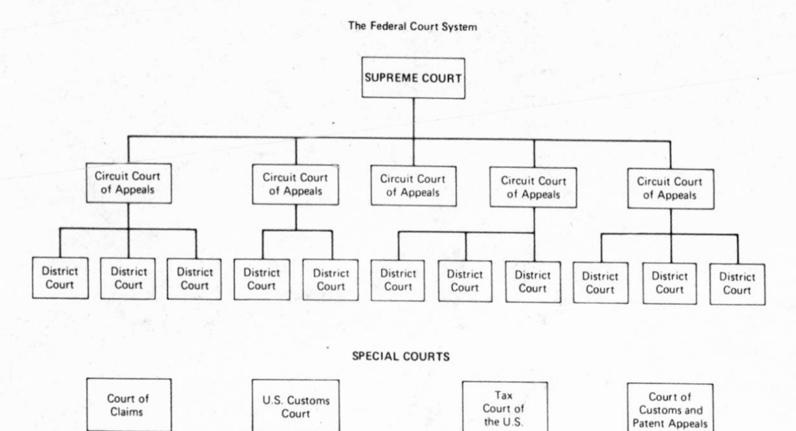

*There are currently 11 Circuit Courts of Appeals including one in the District of Columbia. Several judges may serve on any of these courts, on District Courts as well as other courts.
**There are currently 89 District Courts, including one in the District of Columbia.

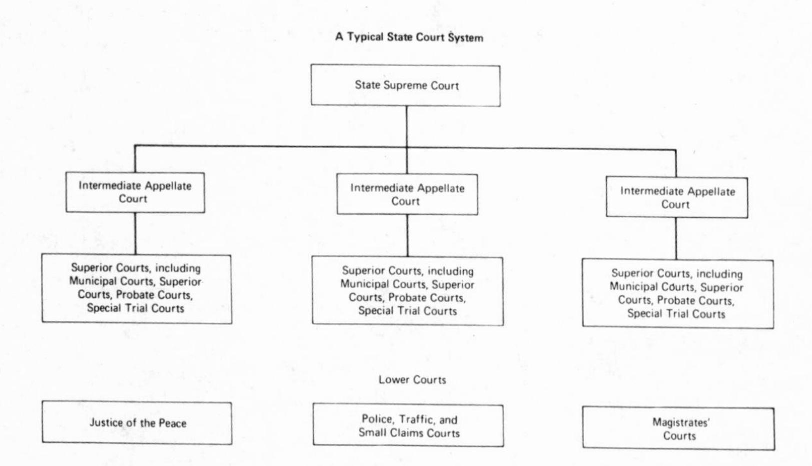

but significant point must be noted in this brief sketch of our legal structures. While it appears that the state and federal systems are completely parallel, the Supreme Court of the United States has final authority on all questions of federal law. Consequently, cases litigated in the state courts that involve questions related to the U.S. Constitution or to federal laws may be appealed from the state supreme courts to the highest court of the land.

HOW TO FIND THE LAW

With many governmental units creating law and with the various courts adjudicating cases, the task of "finding the law" can be very complicated. A little knowledge in this case may indeed be dangerous, for when one is faced with a real problem a thorough search of the law library is necessary. Short of a good course in legal research, or its equivalent in experience, one cannot master the tools of legal research. Consequently, it is wise to seek legal advice either through one of the teacher organizations or through private counsel. Thus the following explanations are merely introductory and should enable the reader to understand references we have used and to look up cases we have cited.

Decisions of appellate courts, state and federal, are published both as official reports and by private publishing houses. The decisions of the Supreme Court of the United States, for example, are published officially as the *United States Reports* (cited "U.S.") by the West Publishing Company, the best known private publishing firm in this field, and in the *Supreme Court Reporter* (cited "Sup. Ct."). These decisions are also published by Lawyers Cooperative Publishing Company, as the *United States Supreme Court Reports* or *Lawyers Edition* (cited "L.Ed."). Thus, the same case may be followed by three separate citations—e.g., *Brown* v. *Board of Education of Topeka*, 349 U.S. 294, 75 Sup. Ct. 753, 99 L.Ed., 1083 (1955). This means that the *Brown* case can be found in volume 349 of the *United States Reports* at page 294, in volume 75 of the *Supreme Court Reporter* at page 753, or in volume 99 of the *Lawyers Edition* at page 1083, and that the decision was handed down in 1955.

The *National Reporter System* of the West Publishing Company includes both federal and state courts in a comprehensive regional reporting system. It is advisable that anyone interested in doing legal research become aquainted with these reporters and practice using them. Librarians specifically trained in the search for legal materials can be found in most libraries that have such holdings, and they are quite helpful.

The cases adjudicated by the appellate courts of the various states are reported by the *National Reporter System* in nine regional units as follows:

Title	*States Included*	*Cited*
The Pacific Reporter	Montana, Wyoming, Idaho, Kansas, Colorado, Oklahoma, New Mexico, Utah, Arizona, Nevada, Washington, Oregon, California, Alaska, and Hawaii	"Pac." or "P. (2d)"
The South Western Reporter	Kentucky, Tennessee, Missouri, Arkansas, and Texas	"S.W." or "S.W. (2d)"
The North Western Reporter	Michigan, Wisconsin, Iowa, Minnesota, North Dakota, South Dakota, and Nebraska	"N.W." or "N.W. (2d)"
The Southern Reporter	Florida, Alabama, Mississippi, and Louisiana	"So." or "So. (2d)"
The South Eastern Reporter	Virginia, West Virginia, North Carolina, South Carolina, and Georgia	"S.E." or "S.E. (2d)"
The Atlantic Reporter	Maine, New Hampshire, Vermont, Connecticut, New Jersey, Pennsylvania, Maryland, and Delaware	"Atl." or "Atl. (2d)"
The North Eastern Reporter	Massachusetts, Rhode Island, New York, Ohio, Indiana, and Illinois	"N.E." or "N.E. (2d)
The New York Supplement	New York	"N.Y. Supp."
The California Reporter	California	"Cal. Rptr."

The reader will notice that while all of the states are included in regional reporters, New York and California have separate series in addition. This was a pragmatic publishing move based on the volume of cases reported in the courts of the two most populous states. A case is reported by its official state citation, followed by the regional reporter citation together with the year of the decision—for example, *Morse* v. *San Diego High*, 34 Cal. App. 134, 166 Pac. 839 (1917).

Notice that as the regional reporters climb to high numbers owing to the many volumes of cases reported, the publisher begins a second series. For example, in the Pacific Reporter series "P.2d" is a continuation of "Pac.," as in *School District* v. *Bruck,* 255 Ore. 496, 358 P.2d 283 (1960).

A further important tool in legal research is the *American Digest System,* an index of cases to the *National Reporter System.* A publication of the West Publishing Company, it consists of the Century Digest, spanning cases from 1658 to 1896, the *Decennials* for cases in each ten-year period from 1897 to 1956, and the *General Digest,* third series, covering cases since 1957.

For the beginner or for anyone interested in an overview of a particular topic, a variety of legal encyclopedias are available. Among these perhaps the best known are *Corpus Juris Secundum,* cited as "C.J.S.," and *American Jurisprudence,* "Am. Jr." Note, however, that while the materials cited should suffice to introduce educators into the highly organized mysteries of legal research, the sources of law as well as the research tools necessary to find them are much more extensive than indicated here.[10]

Warning

The brief descriptions and explanations we have provided should lead no one to believe that he can now act as his own legal counselor. As a matter of fact, even among trained lawyers there is a widely accepted saying that "He who is his own lawyer has a fool for a client." It might be of interest to the reader that when Clarence Darrow, one of the country's great criminal lawyers, was accused of tampering with a jury, he hired a lawyer to defend him.

We do mean to sensitize educators to the range of civil rights problems that surround and permeate public school teaching. We want to inform them of overall principles as well as some problem areas and unanswered questions. Our constant advice, however, to anyone who suspects that he is involved in a civil rights violation is that he discuss the situation with a lawyer. In most communities today we find organizations of teachers, one of whose functions is to render advice on these matters. These organizations, whether affiliated with the NEA or the AFT, are concerned with any action against a teacher that has actual or potential consequences for other teachers or for the schools.[11] In addition, advice and help is often available from the American Civil Liberties Union (ACLU), a nonpartisan organization long active on behalf of the civil rights of all Americans. Since the enforcement of one's constitutional rights is often an expensive, prolonged, and technical process, it is highly recommended that an aggrieved individual seek the help and support of interested organizations.

NOTES

[1]See, for example, Ellwood P. Cubberley, *Public Education in the United States*, Chicago, Houghton Mifflin, 1934, pp. 84–85. Also, Edward S. Corwin, *The Constitution and What It Means Today*, New York, Atheneum, 1963.

[2]*Federal Relations to Education*, Part II: Basic Facts, Report of the National Advisory Committee on Education, Washington, D.C., National Advisory Committee on Education, 1931, pp. 4–9.

[3]See Ellwood P. Cubberley, *op. cit.*, and Edward C. Bolmeier, *The School in the Legal Structure*, Cincinnati, W. H. Anderson, 1968, pp. 65–77.

[4]*McCollum* v. *Board of Education*, 69 S. Ct. 461 (1948).

[5]*West Virginia State Board of Education* v. *Barnette*, 319 U.S. 624 (1943).

[6]Corwin, *op. cit.*, p. 248.

[7]*Cantwell* v. *Connecticut*, 310 U.S. 296, 84 L.Ed. 1213, 60 S. Ct. 900 (1940).

[8]See Article 3, Section 2.

[9]Article 3, Section 2, Clause 1.

[10]A useful little volume we recommend is *A Schoolman in the Law Library*, by Arthur A. Rezny and Madeline Kinter Remlein, Danville, Ill., Interstate Printers and Publishers, 1962.

[11]If no local organizations are available, contact the national offices: National Education Association, 1201 16th St., N.W., Washington, D.C. 20036; American Federation of Teachers, 1012 14th St., N.W., Washington, D.C. 20005.

Appendix 2
Two sample cases

Here we present two school-related civil rights cases in their totality, since most people who read this book have never seen a completely reported Supreme Court case, though they have seen headlines, brief excerpts, and elegant quotes. A complete case will provide some insight into the careful work of the Court as it examines related cases, precedents, alternative arguments, and the reasoning of lower courts. Perhaps some insight will also be gained into the changing, growing process that keeps the Constitution vital and relevant to life today.*

Epperson is an interesting example of a Supreme Court case in which the judges agree on the outcome but disagree on the constitutional bases of the decision. The concurring opinions are written by judges who agree with the result reached by the majority but not with its reasoning; therefore, they present their own reasons in separate opinions.

Tinker is an example of a Supreme Court case that extends the First and Fourteenth Amendments into a new area. It is a significant case for the future of schooling. Partly because of its potential impact on schools, Justice Black presents a powerful dissenting opinion.

*A highly readable, moving account of an actual case that will give the reader valuable insight into the workings of the Court is *Gideon's Trumpet*, by Anthony Lewis, Vintage Books, New York, 1966.

EPPERSON *v.* ARKANSAS.

Syllabus.

EPPERSON ET AL. *v.* ARKANSAS.

APPEAL FROM THE SUPREME COURT OF ARKANSAS.

No. 7. Argued October 16, 1968.—Decided November 12, 1968.

Appellant Epperson, an Arkansas public school teacher, brought this action for declaratory and injunctive relief challenging the constitutionality of Arkansas' "anti-evolution" statute. That statute makes it unlawful for a teacher in any state-supported school or university to teach or to use a textbook that teaches "that mankind ascended or descended from a lower order of animals." The State Chancery Court held the statute an abridgment of free speech violating the First and Fourteenth Amendments. The State Supreme Court, expressing no opinion as to whether the statute prohibits "explanation" of the theory or only teaching that the theory is true, reversed the Chancery Court. In a two-sentence opinion it sustained the statute as within the State's power to specify the public school curriculum. *Held:* The statute violates the Fourteenth Amendment, which embraces the First Amendment's prohibition of state laws respecting an establishment of religion. Pp. 102–109.

(a) The Court does not decide whether the statute is unconstitutionally vague, since, whether it is construed to prohibit explaining the Darwinian theory or teaching that it is true, the law conflicts with the Establishment Clause. Pp. 102–103.

(b) The sole reason for the Arkansas law is that a particular religious group considers the evolution theory to conflict with the account of the origin of man set forth in the Book of Genesis. pp. 103, 107–109.

(c) The First Amendment mandates government neutrality between religion and religion, and between religion and nonreligion. Pp. 103–107.

(d) A State's right to prescribe the public school curriculum does not include the right to prohibit teaching a scientific theory or doctrine for reasons that run counter to the principles of the First Amendment. P. 107.

(e) The Arkansas law is not a manifestation of religious neutrality. P. 109.

242 Ark. 922 416 S. W. 2d 322, reversed.

Eugene R. Warren argued the cause for appellants. With him on the brief was *Bruce T. Bullion.*

Don Langston, Assistant Attorney General of Arkansas, argued the cause for appellee. With him on the brief was *Joe Purcell,* Attorney General.

Briefs of *amici curiae,* urging reversal, were filed by *Leo Pfeffer, Melvin L. Wulf,* and *Joseph B. Robinson* for the American Civil Liberties Union et al., and by *Philip J. Hirschkrop* for the National Education Association of the United States et al.

MR. JUSTICE FORTAS delivered the opinion of the Court.

I.

This appeal challenges the constitutionality of the "anti-evolution" statute which the State of Arkansas adopted in 1928 to prohibit the teaching in its public schools and universities of the theory that man evolved from other species of life. The statute was a product of the upsurge of "fundamentalist" religious fervor of the twenties. The Arkansas statute was an adaptation of the famous Tennessee "monkey law" which the State adopted in 1925.[1] The constitutionality of the Tennessee law was upheld by the Tennessee Supreme Court in the celebrated *Scopes* case in 1927.[2]

The Arkansas law makes it unlawful for a teacher in any state-supported school or university "to teach the theory or doctrine that mankind ascended or descended from a lower order of animals," or "to adopt or use in any such institution a textbook that teaches" this theory. Violation is a misdemeanor and subjects the violator to dismissal from his position.[3]

[1]Chapter 27, Tenn. Acts 1925; Tenn. Code Ann. §49–1922 (1966 Repl. Vol.).

[2]*Scopes* v. *State,* 154 Tenn. 105, 289 S. W. 363 (1927). The Tennessee court, however, reversed Scopes' conviction on the ground that the jury and not the judge should have assessed the fine of $100. Since Scopes was no longer in the State's employ, it saw "nothing to be gained by prolonging the life of this bizarre case." It directed that a *nolle prosequi* be entered, in the interests of "the peace and dignity of the State." 154 Tenn., at 121, 289 S. W., at 367.

[3]Initiated Act No. 1, Ark, Acts 1929; Ark. Stat. Ann. §§ 80–1627, 80–1628 (1960 Repl. Vol.). The text of the law is as follows:

"§ 80–1627.—Doctrine of ascent or descent of man from lower order of animals prohibited.—It shall be unlawful for any teacher or other instruc-

The present case concerns the teaching of biology in a high school in Little Rock. According to the testimony, until the events here in litigation, the official textbook furnished for the high school biology course did not have a section on the Darwinian Theory. Then, for the academic year 1965–1966, the school administration, on recommendation of the teachers of biology in the school system, adopted and prescribed a textbook which contained a chapter setting forth "the theory about the origin . . . of man from a lower form of animal."

Susan Epperson, a young woman who graduated from Arkansas' school system and then obtained her master's degree in zoology at the University of Illinois, was employed by the Little Rock school system in the fall of 1964 to teach 10th grade biology at Central High School. At the start of the academic year, 1965, she was confronted by the new textbook (which one surmises from the record was not unwelcome to her.) She faced at least a literal dilemma because she was supposed to use the new textbook for classroom instruction and presumably to teach the statutorily condemned chapter; but to do so would be a criminal offense and subject her to dismissal.

She instituted the present action in the Chancery Court of the State, seeking a declaration that the Arkansas statute is void and enjoining the State and the defendant officials of the Little Rock school system from dismissing her for violation of the statute's

---

tor in any University, College, Normal, Public School, or other institution of the State, which is supported in whole or in part from public funds derived by State and local taxation to teach the theory or doctrine that mankind ascended or descended from a lower order of animals and also it shall be unlawful for any teacher, textbook commission, or other authority exercising the power to select textbooks for above mentioned educational institutions to adopt or use in any such institution a textbook that teaches the doctrine or theory that mankind descended or ascended from a lower order of animals.

§ 80–1628.—Teaching doctrine or adopting textbook mentioning doctrine—Penalties—Positions to be vacated.—Any teacher or other instructor or textbook commissioner who is found guilty of violation of this act by teaching the theory or doctrine mentioned in section 1 hereof, or by using, or adopting any such textbooks in any such educational institution shall be guilty of a misdemeanor and upon conviction shall be fined not exceeding five hundred dollars; and upon conviction shall vacate the position thus held in any educational institutions of the character above mentioned or any commission of which he may be a member."

provisions. H. H. Blanchard, a parent of children attending the public schools, intervened in support of the action.

The Chancery Court, in an opinion by Chancellor Murray O. Reed, held that the statute violated the Fourteenth Amendment to the United States Constitution.[4] The court noted that this Amendment encompasses the prohibitions upon state interference with freedom of speech and thought which are contained in the First Amendment. Accordingly, it held that the challenged statute is unconstitutional because, in violation of the First Amendment, it "tends to hinder the quest for knowledge, restrict the freedom to learn, and restrain the freedom to teach."[5] In this perspective, the Act, it held, was an unconstitutional and void restraint upon the freedom of speech guaranteed by the Constitution.

On appeal, the Supreme Court of Arkansas reversed.[6] Its two-sentence opinion is set forth in the margin.[7] It sustained the statute as an exercise of the State's power to specify the curriculum in public schools. It did not address itself to the competing constitutional considerations.

Appeal was duly prosecuted to this Court under 28 U. S. C. § 1257 (2). Only Arkansas and Mississippi have such "anti-evolution" or

[4]The opinion of the Chancery Court is not officially reported.

[5]The Chancery Court analyzed the holding of its sister State of Tennessee in the *Scopes* case sustaining Tennessee's similar statute. It refused to follow Tennessee's 1927 example. It declined to confine the judicial horizon to a view of the law as merely a direction by the State as employer to its employees. This sort of astigmatism, it held, would ignore overriding constitutional values, and "should not be followed," and it proceeded to confront the substance of the law and its effect.

[6]242 Ark. 922, 416 S. W. 2d 322 (1967).

[7]"Per Curiam. Upon the principal issue, that of constitutionality, the court holds that Initiated Measure No. 1 of 1928, Ark. Stat. Ann. § 80–1627 and § 80–1628 (Repl. 1960), is a valid exercise of the state's power to specify the curriculum in its public schools. The court expresses no opinion on the question whether the Act prohibits any explanation of the theory of evolution or merely prohibits teaching that the theory is true; the answer not being necessary to a decision in the case, and the issue not having been raised.

"The decree is reversed and the cause dismissed.

"Ward, J., concurs. Brown, J., dissents.

"Paul Ward, Justice, concurring. I agree with the first sentence in the majority opinion.

"To my mind, the rest of the opinion beclouds the clear announcement made in the first sentence."

"monkey" laws on their books.[8] There is no record of any prosecutions in Arkansas under its statute. It is possible that the statute is presently more of a curiosity than a vital fact of life in these States.[9] Nevertheless, the present case was brought, the appeal as of right is properly here, and it is our duty to decide the issues presented.

II.

At the outset, it is urged upon us that the challenged statute is vague and uncertain and therefore within the condemnation of the Due Process Clause of the Fourteenth Amendment. The contention that the Act is vague and uncertain is supported by language in the brief opinion of Arkansas' Supreme Court. That court, perhaps reflecting the discomfort which the statute's quixotic prohibition necessarily engenders in the modern mind,[10] stated that it "expresses no opinion" as to whether the Act prohibits "explanation" of the theory of evolution or merely forbids "teaching that the theory is true." Regardless of this uncertainty, the court held that the statute is constitutional.

On the other hand, counsel for the State, in oral argument in this Court, candidly stated that, despite the State Supreme Court's equivocation, Arkansas would interpret the statute "to mean that to make a student aware of the theory . . . just to teach that there was such a theory" would be grounds for dismissal and for prosecution under

[8]Miss. Code Ann. §§ 6798, 6799 (1942). Ark. Stat. Ann. §§ 80–1627, 80–1628 (1960 Repl. Vol.). The Tennessee law was repealed in 1967. Oklahoma enacted an anti-evolution law, but it was repealed in 1926. The Florida and Texas Legislatures, in the period between 1921 and 1929, adopted resolutions against teaching the doctrine of evolution. In all, during that period, bills to this effect were introduced in 20 States. American Civil Liberties Union (ACLU), The Gag on Teaching 8 (2d ed., 1937).

[9]Clarence Darrow, who was counsel for the defense in the *Scopes* trial, in his biography published in 1932, somewhat sardonically pointed out that States with anti-evolution laws did not insist upon the fundamentalist theory in all respects. He said: "I understand that the States of Tennessee and Mississippi both continue to teach that the earth is round and that the revolution on its axis brings the day and night, in spite of all opposition." The Story of My Life 247 (1932).

[10]R. Hofstadter & W. Metzger, in The Development of Academic Freedom in the United States 324 (1955), refer to some of Darwin's opponents as "exhibiting a kind of phylogenetic snobbery [which led them] to think that Darwin had libeled the [human] race by discovering simian rather than seraphic ancestors."

the statute; and he said "that the Supreme Court of Arkansas' opinion should be interpreted in that manner." He said: "If Mrs. Epperson would tell her students that 'Here is Darwin's theory, that man ascended or descended from a lower form of being,' then I think she would be under this statute liable for prosecution."

In any event, we do not rest our decision upon the asserted vagueness of the statute. On either interpretation of its language, Arkansas' statute cannot stand. It is of no moment whether the law is deemed to prohibit mention of Darwin's theory, or to forbid any or all of the infinite varieties of communication embraced within the term "teaching." Under either interpretation, the law must be stricken because of its conflict with the constitutional prohibition of state laws respecting an establishment of religion or prohibiting the free exercise thereof. The overriding fact is that Arkansas' law selects from the body of knowledge a particular segment which it proscribes for the sole reason that it is deemed to conflict with a particular religious doctrine; that is, with a particular interpretation of the Book of Genesis by a particular religious group.[11]

III.

The antecedents of today's decision are many and unmistakable. They are rooted in the foundation soil of our Nation. They are fundamental to freedom.

Government in our democracy, state and national, must be neutral in matters of religious theory, doctrine, and practice. It may not be hostile to any religion or to the advocacy of no-religion; and it may not aid, foster, or promote one religion or religious theory against another or even against the militant opposite. The First Amendment mandates governmental neutrality between religion and religion, and between religion and nonreligion.[12]

As early as 1872, this Court said: "The law knows no heresy, and is committed to the support of no dogma, the establishment of

[11]In *Scopes* v. *States*, 154 Tenn. 105, 126, 289 S. W. 363, 369 (1927), Judge Chambliss, concurring, referred to the defense contention that Tennessee's anti-evolution law gives a "preference" to "religious establishments which have as one of their tenets or dogmas the instantaneous creation of man."

[12]*Everson v. Board of Education*, 330 U. S. 1, 18 (1947); *McCollum* v. *Board of Education*, 333 U. S. 203 (1948): *Zorach* v. *Clauson*, 343 U. S. 306, 313–314 (1952); *Fowler* v. *Rhode Island*, 345 U. S. 67 (1953); *Torcaso* v. *Watkins*, 367 U. S. 488, 495 (1961).

no sect." *Watson* v. *Jones*, 13 Wall. 679, 728. This has been the interpretation of the great First Amendment which this Court has applied in the many and subtle problems which the ferment of our national life has presented for decision within the Amendment's broad command.

Judicial interposition in the operation of the public school system of the Nation raises problems requiring care and restraint. Our courts, however, have not failed to apply the First Amendment's mandate in our educational system where essential to safeguard the fundamental values of freedom of speech and inquiry and of belief. By and large, public education in our Nation is committed to the control of state and local authorities. Courts do not and cannot intervene in the resolution of conflicts which arise in the daily operation of school systems and which do not directly and sharply implicate basic constitutional values.[13] On the other hand, "[t]he vigilant protection of constitutional freedoms is nowhere more vital than in the community of American schools," *Shelton* v. *Tucker*, 364 U. S. 479, 487 (1960). As this Court said in *Keyishian* v. *Board of Regents*, the First Amendment "does not tolerate laws that cast a pall of orthodoxy over the classroom." 385 U. S. 589, 603 (1967).

The earliest cases in this Court on the subject of the impact of constitutional guarantees upon the classroom were decided before the Court expressly applied the specific prohibitions of the First Amendment to the States. But as early as 1923, the Court did not hesitate to condemn under the Due Process Clause "arbitrary" restrictions upon the freedom of teachers to teach and of students to learn. In that year, the Court, in an opinion by Justice McReynolds, held unconstitutional an Act of the State of Nebraska making it a crime to teach any subject in any language other than English to pupils who had not passed the eighth grade.[14] The State's purpose in enacting the law was to promote civic cohesiveness by encouraging the learning of English and to combat the "baneful effect" of permitting foreigners to rear and educate their children in the language of the parents' native land. The Court recognized these purposes, and it acknowledged the State's power to prescribe the school curriculum, but it held that these were not adequate to support the restriction upon the liberty of teacher and pupil. The challenged statute, it held,

[13]See the discussion in Developments in The Law—Academic Freedom, 81 Harv. L. Rev. 1045, 1051–1055 (1968).

[14]The case involved a conviction for teaching "the subject of reading in the German language" to a child of 10 years.

unconstitutionally interfered with the right of the individual, guaranteed by the Due Process Clause, to engage in any of the common occupations of life and to acquire useful knowledge. *Meyer* v. *Nebraska*, 262 U. S. 390 (1923). See also *Bartels* v. *Iowa*, 262 U. S. 404 (1923).

For purposes of the present case, we need not re-enter the difficult terrain which the Court, in 1923, traversed without apparent misgivings. We need not take advantage of the broad premise which the Court's decision in *Meyer* furnishes, nor need we explore the implications of that decision in terms of the justiciability of the multitude of controversies that beset our campuses today. Today's problem is capable of resolution in the narrower terms of the First Amendment's prohibition of laws respecting an establishment of religion or prohibiting the free exercise thereof.

There is and can be no doubt that the First Amendment does not permit the State to require that teaching and learning must be tailored to the principles or prohibitions of any religious sect or dogma. In *Everson* v. *Board of Education*, this Court, in upholding a state law to provide free bus service to school children, including those attending parochial schools, said: "Neither [a State nor the Federal Government] can pass laws which aid one religion, aid all religions, or prefer one religion over another." 330 U.S. 1, 15 (1947).

At the following Term of Court, in *McCollum* v. *Board of Education*, 333 U. S. 203 (1948), the Court held that Illinois could not release pupils from class to attend classes of instruction in the school buildings in the religion of their choice. This, it said, would involve the State in using tax-supported property for religious purposes, thereby breaching the "wall of separation" which, according to Jefferson, the First Amendment was intended to erect between church and state. *Id.*, at 211. See also *Engel* v. *Vitale*, 370 U. S. 421 (1962); *Abington School District* v. *Schempp*, 374 U. S. 203 (1963). While study of religions and of the Bible from a literary and historic viewpoint, presented objectively as part of a secular program of education, need not collide with the First Amendment's prohibition, the State may not adopt programs or practices in its public schools or colleges which "aid or oppose" any religion. *Id.*, at 225. This prohibition is absolute. It forbids alike the preference of a religious doctrine or the prohibition of theory which is deemed antagonistic to a particular dogma. As Mr. Justice Clark stated in *Joseph Burstyn, Inc.* v. *Wilson*, "the state has no legitimate interest in protecting any or all religions from views distasteful to them. . . ." 343 U. S. 495, 505 (1952). The test was stated as follows in *Abington School District* v.

Schempp, supra, at 222: "[W]hat are the purpose and the primary effect of the enactment? If either is the advancement or prohibition of religion then the enactment exceeds the scope of legislative power as circumscribed by the Constitution."

These precedents inevitably determine the result in the present case. The State's undoubted right to prescribe the curriculum for its public schools does not carry with it the right to prohibit, on pain of criminal penalty, the teaching of a scientific theory or doctrine where that prohibition is based upon reasons that violate the First Amendment. It is much too late to argue that the State may impose upon the teachers in its schools any conditions that it chooses, however restrictive they may be of constitutional guarantees. *Keyishian* v. *Board of Regents,* 385 U. S. 589, 605–606 (1967).

In the present case, there can be no doubt that Arkansas has sought to prevent its teachers from discussing the theory of evolution because it is contrary to the belief of some that the Book of Genesis must be the exclusive source of doctrine as to the origin of man. No suggestion has been made that Arkansas' law may be justified by considerations of state policy other than the religious views of its citizens.[15] It is clear that fundamental sectarian conviction was and is the law's reason for existence.[16] Its antecedent, Tennessee's

[15]Former Dean Leflar of the University of Arkansas School of Law has stated that "the same ideological considerations underlie the anti-evolution enactment" as underlie the typical blasphemy statute. He says that the purpose of these statutes is an "ideological" one which "involves an effort to prevent (by censorship) or punish the presentation of intellectually significant matter which contradicts accepted social, moral or religious ideas." Leflar, Legal Liability for the Exercise of Free Speech, 10 Ark. L. Rev. 155, 158 (1956). See also R. Hofstadter & W. Metzger, The Development of Academic Freedom in the United States 320–366 (1955) (*passim*); H. Beale, A History of Freedom of Teaching in American Schools 202–207 (1941); Emerson & Haber, The *Scopes* Case in Modern Dress, 27 U. Chi. L. Rev. 522 (1960); Waller, The Constitutionality of the Tennessee Anti-Evolution Act, 35 Yale L. J. 191 (1925) (*passim*); ACLU, The Gag on Teaching 7 (2d ed., 1937); J. Scopes & J. Presley, Center of the Storm 45–53 (1967).

[16]The following advertisement is typical of the public appeal which was used in the campaign to secure adoption of the statute:

"THE BIBLE OR ATHEISM, WHICH?

"All atheists favor evolution. If you agree with atheism vote against Act No. 1. If you agree with the Bible vote for Act No. 1. . . . Shall conscientious church members be forced to pay taxes to support teachers to teach evolution which will undermine the faith of their children? The "monkey law," candidly stated its purpose: to make it unlawful "to teach any theory that denies the story of the Divine Creation of man as taught in the Bible, and to teach instead that man has descended from a lower order of animals."[17] Perhaps the sensational publicity attendant upon the *Scopes* trial induced Arkansas to adopt less explicit language.[18] It eliminated Tennessee's reference to "the story of the Divine Creation of man" as taught in the Bible, but there is no doubt that the motivation for the law was the same: to suppress the teaching of a theory which, it was thought, "denied" the divine creation of man.

Arkansas' law cannot be defended as an act of religious neutrality. Arkansas did not seek to excise from the curricula of its schools and universities all discussion of the origin of man. The law's effort was confined to an attempt to blot out a particular theory because of its supposed conflict with the Biblical account, literally read. Plainly, the law is contrary to the mandate of the First, and in violation of the Fourteenth, Amendment to the Constitution.

The judgment of the Supreme Court of Arkansas is

Reversed.

MR. JUSTICE BLACK, concurring.

I am by no means sure that this case presents a genuinely justiciable case or controversy. Although Arkansas Initiated Act No. 1, the statute alleged to be unconstitutional, was passed by the voters of

---

Gazette said Russian Bolshevists laughed at Tennessee. True, and that sort will laugh at Arkansas. Who cares? Vote FOR ACT NO. 1." The Arkansas Gazette, Little Rock, Nov. 4, 1928, p. 12, cols. 4–5.

Letters from the public expressed the fear that teaching of evolution would be "subversive of Christianity," *id.*, Oct. 24, 1928, p. 7, col. 2; see also *id*, Nov. 4, 1928, p. 19, col. 4; and that it would cause school children "to disrespect the Bible," *id.*, Oct. 27, 1928, p. 15, col. 5. One letter read: "The cosmogony taught by [evolution] runs contrary to that of Moses and Jesus, and as such is nothing, if anything at all, but atheism. . . . Now let the mothers and fathers of our state that are trying to raise their children in the Christian faith arise in their might and vote for this anti-evolution bill that will take it out of our tax supported schools. When they have saved the children, they have saved the state." *Id.*, at cols. 4–5.

[17]Arkansas' law was adopted by popular initiative in 1928, three years after Tennessee's law was enacted and one year after the Tennessee Supreme Court's decision in the *Scopes* case, *supra.*

[18]In its brief, the State says that the Arkansas statute was passed with the holding of the *Scopes* case in mind. Brief for Appellee 1.

Arkansas in 1928, we are informed that there has never been even a single attempt by the State to enforce it. And the pallid, unenthusiastic, even apologetic defense of the Act presented by the State in the Court indicates that the State would make no attempt to enforce the law should it remain on the books for the next century. Now, nearly 40 years after the law has slumbered on the books as though dead, a teacher alleging fear that the State might arouse from its lethargy and try to punish her has asked for a declaratory judgment holding the law unconstitutional. She was subsequently joined by a parent who alleged his interest in seeing that his two then school-age sons "be informed of all scientific theories and hypotheses. . . ." But whether this Arkansas teacher is still a teacher, fearful of punishment under the Act, we do not know. It may be, as has been published in the daily press, that she has long since given up her job as a teacher and moved to a distant city, thereby escaping the dangers she had imagined might befall her under this lifeless Arkansas Act. And there is not one iota of concrete evidence to show that the parent-intervenor's sons have not been or will not be taught about evolution. The textbook adopted for use in biology classes in Little Rock includes an entire chapter dealing with evolution. There is no evidence that this chapter is not being freely taught in the schools that use the textbook and no evidence that the intervenor's sons, who were 15 and 17 years old when this suit was brought three years ago, are still in high school or yet to take biology. Unfortunately, however, the State's languid interest in the case has not prompted it to keep this Court informed concerning facts that might easily justify dismissal of this alleged lawsuit as moot or as lacking the qualities of a genuine case or controversy.

Notwithstanding my own doubts as to whether the case presents a justiciable controversy, the Court brushes aside these doubts and leaps headlong into the middle of the very broad problems involved in federal intrusion into state powers to decide what subjects and schoolbooks it may wish to use in teaching state pupils. While I hesitate to enter into the consideration and decision of such sensitive state-federal relationships, I reluctantly acquiesce. But, agreeing to consider this as a genuine case or controversy, I cannot agree to thrust the Federal Government's long arm the least bit further into state school curriculums than decision of this particular case requires. And the Court, in order to invalidate the Arkansas law as a violation of the First Amendment, has been compelled to give the State's law a broader meaning than the State Supreme Court was willing to give it. The Arkansas Supreme Court's opinion, in its entirety, stated that:

> Upon the principal issue, that of constitutionality, the court holds that Initiated Measure No. 1 of 1928, Ark. Stat. Ann. § 80–1627 and § 80–1628 (Repl. 1960), is a valid exercise of the state's power to specify the curriculum in its public schools. The court expresses no opinion on the question whether the Act prohibits any explanation of the theory of evolution or merely prohibits teaching that the theory is true; the answer not being necessary to a decision in the case, and the issue not having been raised.

It is plain that a state law prohibiting all teaching of human development or biology is constitutionally quite different from a law that compels a teacher to teach as true only one theory of a given doctrine. It would be difficult to make a First Amendment case out of a state law eliminating the subject of higher mathematics, or astronomy, or biology from its curriculum. And, for all the Supreme Court of Arkansas has said, this particular Act may prohibit that and nothing else. This Court, however, treats the Arkansas Act as though it made it a misdemeanor to teach or to use a book that teaches that evolution is true. But it is not for this Court to arrogate to itself the power to determine the scope of Arkansas statutes. Since the highest court of Arkansas has deliberately refused to give its statute that meaning, we should not presume to do so.

It seems to me that in this situation the statute is too vague for us to strike it down on any ground but that: vagueness. Under this statute as construed by the Arkansas Supreme Court, a teacher cannot know whether he is forbidden to mention Darwin's theory at all or only free to discuss it as long as he refrains from contending that it is true. It is an established rule that a statute which leaves an ordinary man so doubtful about its meaning that he cannot know when he has violated it denies him the first essential of due process. See, *e. g., Connally* v. *General Construction Co.,* 269 U.S. 385, 391 (1926). Holding the statute too vague to enforce would not only follow long-standing constitutional precedents but it would avoid having this Court take unto itself the duty of a State's highest court to interpret and mark the boundaries of the State's laws. And, more important, it would not place this Court in the unenviable position of violating the principle of leaving the States absolutely free to choose their own curriculums for their own schools so long as their action does not palpably conflict with a clear constitutional command.

The Court, not content to strike down this Arkansas Act on the unchallengeable ground of its plain vagueness, chooses rather to invalidate it as a violation of the Establishment of Religion Clause of the First Amendment. I would not decide this case on such a sweeping ground for the following reasons, among others.

1. In the first place I find it difficult to agree with the Court's statement that "there can be no doubt that Arkansas has sought to prevent its teachers from discussing the theory of evolution because it is contrary to the belief of some that the Book of Genesis must be the exclusive source of doctrine as to the origin of man." It may be instead that the people's motive was merely that it would be best to remove this controversial subject from its schools; there is no reason I can imagine why a State is without power to withdraw from its curriculum any subject deemed too emotional and controversial for its public schools. And this Court has consistently held that it is not for us to invalidate a statute because of our views that the "motives" behind its passage were improper; it is simply too difficult to determine what those motives were. See, *e.g., United States* v. *O'Brien,* 391 U. S. 367, 382–383 (1968).

2. A second question that arises for me is whether this Court's decision forbidding a State to exclude the subject of evolution from its school infringes the religious freedom of those who consider evolution an anti-religious doctrine. If the theory is considered anti-religious, as the Court indicates, how can the State be bound by the Federal Constitution to permit its teachers to advocate such an "anti-religious" doctrine to school children? The very cases cited by the Court as supporting its conclusion hold that the State must be neutral, not favoring one religious or anti-religious view over another. The Darwinian theory is said to challenge the Bible's story of creation; so too have some of those who believe in the Bible, along with many others, challenged the Darwinian theory. Since there is no indication that the literal Biblical doctrine of the origin of man is included in the curriculum of Arkansas schools, does not the removal of the subject of evolution leave the State in a neutral position toward these supposedly competing religious and anti-religious doctrines? Unless this Court is prepared simply to write off as pure nonsense the views of those who consider evolution an anti-religious doctrine, then this issue presents problems under the Establishment Clause far more troublesome than are discussed in the Court's opinion.

3. I am not ready to hold that a person hired to teach school children takes with him into the classroom a constitutional right to teach sociological, economic, political, or religious subjects that the school's managers do not want discussed. This Court has said that the rights of free speech "while fundamental in our democratic

society, still do not mean that everyone with opinions or beliefs to express may address a group at any public place and at any time." *Cox* v. *Louisiana,* 379 U.S. 536, 554; *Cox* v. *Louisiana,* 379 U.S. 559, 574. I question whether it is absolutely certain, as the Court's opinion indicates, that "academic freedom" permits a teacher to breach his contractual agreement to teach only the subjects designated by the school authorities who hired him.

Certainly the Darwinian theory, precisely like the Genesis story of the creation of man, is not above challenge. In fact the Darwinian theory has not merely been criticized by religionists but by scientists, and perhaps no scientist would be willing to take an oath and swear that everything announced in the Darwinian theory is unquestionably true. The Court, it seems to me, makes a serious mistake in bypassing the plain, unconstitutional vagueness of this statute in order to reach out and decide this troublesome, to me, First Amendment question. However wise this Court may be or may become hereafter, it is doubtful that, sitting in Washington, it can successfully supervise and censor the curriculum of every public school in every hamlet and city in the United States. I doubt that our wisdom is so nearly infallible.

I would either strike down the Arkansas Act as too vague to enforce, or remand to the State Supreme Court for clarification of its holding and opinion.

MR. JUSTICE HARLAN, concurring.

I think it deplorable that this case should have come to us with such an opaque opinion by the State's highest court. With all respect, that court's handling of the case savors of a studied effort to avoid coming to grips with this anachronistic statute and to "pass the buck" to this Court. This sort of temporizing does not make for healthy operations between the state and federal judiciaries. Despite these observations, I am in agreement with this Court's opinion that, the constitutional claims having been properly raised and necessarily decided below, resolution of the matter by us cannot properly be avoided.* See, *e.g., Chicago Life Insurance Co.* v. *Needles,* 113 U.S. 574, 579 (1885).

*Short of reading the Arkansas Supreme Court's opinion to have proceeded on the premise that it need not consider appellants' "establishment" contention, clearly raised in the state courts and here, in view of its holding that the State possesses plenary power to fix the curriculum in its public schools, I can perceive no tenable basis for remanding the case to

I concur in so much of the Court's opinion as holds that the Arkansas statute constitutes an "establishment of religion" forbidden to the States by the Fourteenth Amendment. I do not understand, however, why the Court finds it necessary to explore at length appellants' contentions that the statute is unconstitutionally vague and that it interferes with free speech, only to conclude that these issues need not be decided in this case. In the process of *not* deciding them, the Court obscures its otherwise straightforward holding, and opens its opinion to possible implications from which I am constrained to disassociate myself.

MR. JUSTICE STEWART, concurring in the result.

The States are most assuredly free "to choose their own curriculums for their own schools." A State is entirely free, for example, to decide that the only foreign language to be taught in its public school system shall be Spanish. But would a State be constitutionally free to punish a teacher for letting his students know that other languages are also spoken in the world? I think not.

It is one thing for a State to determine that "the subject of higher mathematics, or astronomy, or biology" shall or shall not be included in its public school curriculum. It is quite another thing for a State to make it a criminal offense for a public school teacher so much as to mention the very existence of an entire system of respected human thought. That kind of criminal law, I think, would clearly impinge upon the guarantees of free communication contained in the First Amendment, and made applicable to the States by the Fourteenth.

The Arkansas Supreme Court has said that the statute before us may or may not be just such a law. The result, as MR. JUSTICE BLACK points out, is that "a teacher cannot know whether he is forbidden to mention Darwin's theory at all." Since I believe that no State could constitutionally forbid a teacher "to mention Darwin's theory at all," and since Arkansas may, or may not, have done just that, I conclude that the statute before us is so vague as to be invalid under the Fourteenth Amendment. See *Cramp* v. *Board of Pub. Instruction*, 368 U.S. 278.

---

the state court for an explication of the purpose and meaning of the statute in question. I am unwilling to ascribe to the Arkansas Supreme Court any such quixotic approach to constitutional adjudication. I take the first sentence of its opinion (*ante*, at 101, n. 7) to encompass an overruling of appellants' "establishment" point, and the second sentence to refer only to their "vagueness" claim.

TINKER *v.* DES MOINES SCHOOL DIST.

Syllabus.

TINKER ET AL. *v.* DES MOINES INDEPENDENT COMMUNITY SCHOOL DISTRICT ET AL.

CERTIORARI TO THE UNITED STATES COURT OF APPEALS FOR THE EIGHTH CIRCUIT.

No. 21. Argued November 12, 1968.—Decided February 24, 1969.

Petitioners, three public school pupils in Des Moines, Iowa, were suspended from school for wearing black armbands to protest the Government's policy in Vietnam. They sought nominal damages and an injunction against a regulation that the respondents had promulgated banning the wearing of armbands. The District Court dismissed the complaint on the ground that the regulation was within the Board's power, despite the absence of any finding of substantial interference with the conduct of school activities. The Court of Appeals, sitting *en banc,* affirmed by an equally divided court. *Held:*

1. In wearing armbands, the petitioners were quiet and passive. They were not disruptive and did not impinge upon the rights of others. In these circumstances, their conduct was within the proection of the Free Speech Clause of the First Amendment and the Due Process Clause of the Fourteenth. Pp. 505–506.
2. First Amendment rights are available to teachers and student, subject to application in light of the special characteristics of the school environment. Pp. 506–507.
3. A prohibition against expression of opinion without any evidence that the rule is necessary to avoid substantial interference with school discipline or the rights of others, is not permissible under the First and Fourteenth Amendments. Pp. 507–514. 383 F. 2d 988, reversed and remanded.

Dan L. Johnston argued the cause for petitioners. With him on the brief were *Melvin L. Wulf* and *David N. Ellenhorn.*

Allan A. Herrick argued the cause for respondents. With him on the brief were *Herschel G. Langdon* and *David W. Belin.*

Charles Morgan, Jr., filed a brief for the United States National Student Association, as *amicus curiae,* urging reversal.

MR. JUSTICE FORTAS delivered the opinion of the Court.

Petitioner John F. Tinker, 15 years old, and petitioner Christopher Eckhardt, 16 years old, attended high schools in Des Moines, Iowa. Petitioner Mary Beth Tinker, John's sister, was a 13-year-old student in junior high school.

In December 1965, a group of adults and students in Des Moines held a meeting at the Eckhardt home. The group determined to publicize their objections to the hostilities in Vietnam and their support for a truce by wearing black armbands during the holiday season and by fasting on December 16 and New Year's Eve. Petitioners and their parents had previously engaged in similar activities, and they decided to participate in the program.

The principals of the Des Moines schools became aware of the plan to wear armbands. On December 14, 1965, they met and adopted a policy that any student wearing an armband to school would be asked to remove it, and if he refused he would be suspended until he returned without the armband. Petitioners were aware of the regulation that the school authorities adopted.

On December 16, Mary Beth and Christopher wore black armbands to their schools. John Tinker wore his armband the next day. They were all sent home and suspended from school until they would come back without their armbands. They did not return to school until after the planned period for wearing armbands had expired—that is, until after New Year's Day.

This complaint was filed in the United States District Court by petitioners, through their fathers, under § 1983 of Title 42 of the United States Code. It prayed for an injunction restraining the respondent school officials and the respondent members of the board of directors of the school district from disciplining the petitioners, and it sought nominal damages. After an evidentiary hearing the District Court dismissed the complaint. It upheld the constitutionality of the school authorities' action on the ground that it was reasonable in order to prevent disturbance of school discipline. 258 F. Supp. 971 (1966). The court referred to but expressly declined to follow the Fifth Circuit's holding in a similar case that the wearing of symbols like the armbands cannot be prohibited unless it "materially and substantially interfere[s] with the requirements of appropriate discipline in the operation of the school." *Burnside* v. *Byars*, 363 F. 2d 744, 749 (1966).[1]

[1]In *Burnside*, the Fifth Circuit ordered that high school authorities be enjoined from enforcing a regulation forbidding students to wear "freedom buttons." It is instructive that in *Blackwell* v. *Issaquena County Board of Education*, 363 F. 2d 749 (1966), the same panel on the same day reached

On appeal, the Court of Appeals for the Eighth Circuit considered the case *en banc*. The court was equally divided, and the District Court's decision was accordingly affirmed, without opinion. 383 F. 2d 988 (1967). We granted certiorari. 390 U.S. 942 (1968).

I.

The District Court recognized that the wearing of an armband for the purpose of expressing certain views is the type of symbolic act that is within the Free Speech Clause of the First Amendment. See *West Virginia* v. *Barnette*, 319 U.S. 624 (1943); *Stromberg* v. *California*, 283 U.S. 359 (1931). Cf. *Thornhill* v. *Alabama*, 310 U.S. 88 (1940); *Edwards* v. *South Carolina*, 372 U.S. 229 (1963); *Brown* v. *Louisiana*, 383 U.S. 131 (1966). As we shall discuss, the wearing of armbands in the circumstances of this case was entirely divorced from actually or potentially disruptive conduct by those participating in it. It was closely akin to "pure speech" which, we have repeatedly held, is entitled to comprehensive protection under the First Amendment. Cf. *Cox* v. *Louisiana*, 379 U.S. 536, 555 (1965); *Adderley* v. *Florida*, 385 U.S. 39 (1966).

First Amendment rights, applied in light of the special characteristics of the school environment, are available to teachers and students. It can hardly be argued that either students or teachers shed their constitutional rights to freedom of speech or expression at the schoolhouse gate. This has been the unmistakable holding of this Court for almost 50 years. In *Meyer* v. *Nebraska*, 262 U.S. 390 (1923), and *Bartels* v. *Iowa*, 262 U.S. 404 (1923), this Court, in opinions by Mr. Justice McReynolds, held that the Due Process Clause of the Fourteenth Amendment prevents States from forbidding the teaching of a foreign language to young students. Statutes to this effect, the Court held, unconstitutionally interfere with the liberty of teacher, student, and parent.[2] See also *Pierce* v.

---

the opposite result on different facts. It declined to enjoin enforcement of such a regulation in another high school where the students wearing freedom buttons harassed students who did not wear them and created much disturbance.

[2]*Hamilton* v. *Regents of Univ. of Cal.*, 293 U. S. 245 (1934), is sometimes cited for the broad proposition that the State may attach conditions to attendance at a state university that require individuals to violate their religious convictions. The case involved dismissal of members of a religious denomination from a land grant college for refusal to participate in military training. Narrowly viewed, the case turns upon the Court's

Society of Sisters, 268 U.S. 510 (1925); *West Virginia* v. *Barnette*, 319 U.S. 624 (1943); *McCollum* v. *Board of Education*, 333 U.S. 203 (1948); *Wieman* v. *Updegraff*, 344 U.S. 183, 195 (1952) (concurring opinion); *Sweezy* v. *New Hampshire*, 354 U.S. 234 (1957); *Shelton* v. *Tucker*, 364 U.S. 479, 487 (1960); *Engel* v. *Vitale*, 370 U.S. 421 (1962); *Keyishian* v. *Board of Regents*, 385 U.S. 589, 603 (1967); *Epperson* v. *Arkansas*, *ante*, p. 97 (1968).

In *West Virginia* v. *Barnette*, *supra*, this Court held that under the First Amendment, the student in public school may not be compelled to salute the flag. Speaking through Mr. Justice Jackson, the Court said:

> *The Fourteenth Amendment, as now applied to the States, protects the citizen against the State itself and all of its creatures—Boards of Education not excepted. These have, of course, important, delicate, and highly discretionary functions, but none that they may not perform within the limits of the Bill of Rights. That they are educating the young for citizenship is reason for scrupulous protection of Constitutional freedoms of the individuals, if we are not to strangle the free mind at its source and teach youth to discount important principles of our government as mere platitudes. 319 U.S., at 637.*

On the other hand, the Court has repeatedly emphasized the need for affirming the comprehensive authority of the States and of school officials, consistent with fundamental constitutional safeguards, to prescribe and control conduct in the schools. See *Epperson* v. *Arkansas*, *supra*, at 104; *Meyer* v. *Nebraska*, *supra*, at 402. Our problem lies in the area where students in the exercise of First Amendment rights collide with the rules of the school authorities.

---

conclusion that merely requiring a student to participate in school training in military "science" could not conflict with his constitutionally protected freedom of conscience. The decision cannot be taken as establishing that the State may impose and enforce any conditions that it chooses upon attendance at public institutions of learning, however violative they may be of fundamental constitutional guarantees. See, *e.g.*, *West Virginia* v. *Barnette*, 319 U. S. 624 (1943); *Dixon* v. *Alabama State Board of Education*, 294 F. 2d 150 (C. A. 5th Cir. 1961); *Knight* v. *State Board of Education*, 200 F. Supp. 174 (D. C. M. D. Tenn. 1961); *Dickey* v. *Alabama State Board of Education*, 273 F. Supp. 613 (D. C. M. D. Ala. 1967). See also Note, Unconstitutional Conditions, 73 Harv. L. Rev. 1595 (1960); Note, Academic Freedom, 81 Harv. L. Rev. 1045 (1968).

II.

The problem posed by the present case does not relate to regulation of the length of skirts or the type of clothing, to hair style, or deportment. Cf. *Ferrell* v. *Dallas Independent School District*, 392 F. 2d 697 (1968); *Pugsley* v. *Sellmeyer*, 158 Ark, 247, 250 S.W. 538 (1923). It does not concern aggressive, disruptive action or even group demonstrations. Our problem involves direct, primary First Amendment rights akin to "pure speech."

The school officials banned and sought to punish petitioners for a silent, passive expression of opinion, unaccompanied by any disorder or disturbance on the part of petitioners. There is here no evidence whatever of petitioners' interference, actual or nascent, with the schools' work or of collision with the rights of other students to be secure and to be let alone. Accordingly, this case does not concern speech or action that intrudes upon the work of the schools or the rights of other students.

Only a few of the 18,000 students in the school system wore the black armbands. Only five students were suspended for wearing them. There is no indication that the work of the schools or any class was disrupted. Outside the classrooms, a few students made hostile remarks to the children wearing armbands, but there were no threats or acts of violence on school premises.

The District Court concluded that the action of the school authorities was reasonable because it was based upon their fear of a disturbance from the wearing of the armbands. But, in our system, undifferentiated fear or apprehension of disturbance is not enough to overcome the right to freedom of expression. Any departure from absolute regimentation may cause trouble. Any variation from the majority's opinion may inspire fear. Any word spoken, in class, in the lunchroom, or on the campus, that deviates from the views of another person may start an argument or cause a disturbance. But our Constitution says we must take this risk, *Terminiello* v. *Chicago*, 337 U.S. 1 (1949); and our history says that it is this sort of hazardous freedom—this kind of openness—that is the basis of our national strength and of the independence and vigor of Americans who grow up and live in this relatively permissive, often disputatious, society.

In order for the State in the person of school officials to justify prohibition of a particular expression of opinion, it must be able to show that its action was caused by something more than a mere desire to avoid the discomfort and unpleasantness that always accompany an unpopular viewpoint. Certainly where there is no finding and no showing that engaging in the forbidden conduct would "materially and substantially interfere with the requirements of appropriate discipline in the operation of the school," the prohibition cannot be sustained. *Burnside* v. *Byars, supra,* at 749.

In the present case, the District Court made no such finding, and our independent examination of the record fails to yield evidence that the school authorities had reason to anticipate that the wearing of the armbands would substantially interfere with the work of the school or impinge upon the rights of other students. Even an official memorandum prepared after the suspension that listed the reasons for the ban on wearing the armbands made no reference to the anticipation of such disruption.[3]

On the contrary, the action of the school authorities appears to have been based upon an urgent wish to avoid the controversy which might result from the expression, even by the silent symbol of armbands, of opposition to this Nation's part in the conflagration in Vietnam.[4] It is revealing, in this respect, that the meeting at

[3]The only suggestions of fear of disorder in the report are these:

"A former student of one of our high schools was killed in Viet Nam. Some of his friends are still in school and it was felt that if any kind of a demonstration existed, it might evolve into something which would be difficult to control."

"Students at one of the high schools were heard to say they would wear arm bands of other colors if the black bands prevailed."

Moreover, the testimony of school authorities at trial indicates that it was not fear of disruption that motivated the regulation prohibiting the armbands; the regulation was directed against "the principle of the demonstration" itself. School authorities simply felt that "the schools are no place for demonstrations," and if the students "didn't like the way our elected officials were handling things, it should be handled with the ballot box and not in the halls of our public schools."

[4]The District Court found that the school authorities in prohibiting black arbands, were influenced by the fact that "[t]he Viet Nam war and the involvement of the United States therein has been the subject of a major controversy for some time. When the arm band regulation involved herein was promulgated, debate over the Viet Nam war had become vehement in many localities. A protest march against the war had been recently held in Washington, D. C. A wave of draft card burning incidents protesting the war had swept the country. At that time two highly publicized draft card burning cases were pending in this court. Both individuals supporting the war and those opposing it were quite vocal in expressing their views." 258 F. Supp., at 972–973.

which the school principals decided to issue the contested regulation was called in response to a student's statement to the journalism teacher in one of the schools that he wanted to write an article on Vietnam and have it published in the school paper. (The student was dissuaded.[5])

It is also relevant that the school authorities did not purport to prohibit the wearing of all symbols of political or controversial significance. The record shows that students in some of the schools wore buttons relating to national political campaigns, and some even wore the Iron Cross, traditionally a symbol of Nazism. The order prohibiting the wearing of armbands did not extend to these. Instead, a particular symbol—black armbands worn to exhibit opposition to this Nation's involvement in Vietnam—was singled out for prohibition. Clearly, the prohibition of expression of one particular opinion, at least without evidence that it is necessary to avoid material and substantial interference with schoolwork or discipline, is not constitutionally permissible.

In our system, state-operated schools may not be enclaves of totalitarianism. School officials do not possess absolute authority over their students. Students in school as well as out of school are "persons" under our Constitution. They are possessed of fundamental rights which the State must respect, just as they themselves must respect their obligations to the State. In our system, students may not be regarded as closed-circuit recipients of only that which the State chooses to communicate. They may not be confined to the expression of those sentiments that are officially approved. In the absence of a specific showing of constitutionally valid reasons to regulate their speech, students are entitled to freedom of expression of their views. As Judge Gewin, speaking for the Fifth Circuit, said, school officials cannot suppress "expressions of feelings with which they do not wish to contend." *Burnside* v. *Byars, supra,* at 749.

In *Meyer* v. *Nebraska, supra,* at 402, Mr. Justice McReynolds expressed this Nation's repudiation of the principle that a State might so conduct its schools as to "foster a homogeneous people." He said:

In order to submerge the individual and develop ideal citizens,

[5]After the principals' meeting, the director of secondary education and the principal of the high school informed the student that the principals were opposed to publication of his article. They reported that "we felt that it was a very friendly conversation, although we did not feel that we had convinced the student that our decision was a just one."

Sparta assembled the males at seven into barracks and intrusted their subsequent education and training to official guardians. Although such measures have been deliberately approved by men of great genius, their ideas touching the relation between individual and State were wholly different from those upon which our institutions rest; and it hardly will be affirmed that any legislature could impose such restrictions upon the people of a State without doing violence to both letter and spirit of the Constitution.

This principle has been repeated by this Court on numerous occasions during the intervening years. In *Keyishian* v. *Board of Regents,* 385 U.S. 589, 603, Mr. Justice Brennan, speaking for the Court, said:

"The vigilant protection of constitutional freedoms is nowhere more vital than in the community of American schools." Shelton *v.* Tucker, *[364 U.S. 479], at 487. The classroom is peculiarly the "marketplace of ideas." The Nation's future depends upon leaders trained through wide exposure to that robust exchange of ideas which discovers truth "out of a multitude of tongues, [rather] than through any kind of authoritative selection."*

The principle of these cases is not confined to the supervised and ordained discussion which takes place in the classroom. The principal use to which the schools are dedicated is to accommodate students during prescribed hours for the purpose of certain types of activities. Among those activities is personal intercommunication among the students.[6] This is not only an inevitable part of the process of attending school; it is also an important part of the educational process. A student's rights, therefore, do not embrace merely the classroom hours. When he is in the cafeteria, or on the playing field, or on the campus during the authorized hours, he may express his opinions, even on controversial subjects like the conflict in

[6]In *Hammond* v. *South Carolina College,* 272 F. Supp. 947 (D. C. S. C. 1967), District Judge Hemphill had before him a case involving a meeting on campus of 300 students to express their views on school practices. He pointed out that a school is not like a hospital or a jail enclosure. Cf. *Cox* v. *Louisiana,* 379 U. S. 536 (1965); *Adderley* v. *Florida,* 385 U. S. 39 (1966). It is a public place, and its dedication to specific uses does not imply that the constitutional rights of persons entitled to be there are to be gauged as if the premises were purely property. Cf. *Edwards* v. *South Carolina,* 372 U. S. 229 (1963); *Brown* v. *Louisiana,* 383 U. S. 131 (1966).

Vietnam, if he does so without "materially and substantially interfer[ing] with the requirements of appropriate discipline in the operation of the school" and without colliding with the rights of others. *Burnside* v. *Byars, supra,* at 749. But conduct by the student, in class or out of it, which for any reason—whether it stems from time, place, or type of behavior—materially disrupts classwork or involves substantial disorder or invasion of the rights of others is, of course, not immunized by the constitutional guarantee of freedom of speech. Cf. *Blackwell* v. *Issaquena County Board of Education,* 363 F. 2d 749 (C. A. 5th Cir. 1966).

Under our Constitution, free speech is not a right that is given only to be so circumscribed that it exists in principle but not in fact. Freedom of expression would not truly exist if the right could be exercised only in an area that a benevolent government has provided as a safe haven for crackpots. The Constitution says that Congress (and the States) may not abridge the right to free speech. This provision means what it says. We properly read it to permit reasonable regulation of speech-connected activities in carefully restricted circumstances. But we do not confine the permissible exercise of First Amendment rights to a telephone booth or the four corners of a pamphlet, or to supervised and ordained discussion in a school classroom.

If a regulation were adopted by school officials forbidding discussion of the Vietnam conflict, or the expression by any student of opposition to it anywhere on school property except as part of a prescribed classroom exercise, it would be obvious that the regulation would violate the constitutional rights of students, at least if it could not be justified by a showing that the students' activities would materially and substantially disrupt the work and discipline of the school. Cf. *Hammond* v. *South Carolina State College,* 272 F. Supp. 947 (D. C. S. C. 1967) (orderly protest meeting on state college campus); *Dickey* v. *Alabama State Board of Education,* 273 F. Supp. 613 (D. C. M. D. Ala. 1967) (expulsion of student editor of college newspaper). In the circumstances of the present case, the prohibition of the silent, passive "witness of the armbands," as one of the children called it, is no less offensive to the Constitution's guarantees.

As we have discussed, the record does not demonstrate any facts which might reasonably have led school authorities to forecast substantial disruption of or material interference with school activities, and no disturbances or disorders on the school premises in fact occurred. These petitioners merely went about their ordained rounds in school. Their deviation consisted only in wearing on their sleeve a band of black cloth, not more than two inches wide. They wore it to exhibit their disapproval of the Vietnam hostilities and their advocacy of a truce, to make their views known, and, by their example, to influence others to adopt them. They neither interrupted school activities nor sought to intrude in the school affairs or the lives of others. They caused discussion outside of the classrooms, but no interference with work and no disorder. In the circumstances, our Constitution does not permit officials of the State to deny their form of expression.

We express no opinion as to the form of relief which should be granted, this being a matter for the lower courts to determine. We reverse and remand for further proceedings consistent with this opinion.

Reversed and remanded.

MR. JUSTICE STEWART, concurring.

Although I agree with much of what is said in the Court's opinion, and with its judgment in this case, I cannot share the Court's uncritical assumption that, school discipline aside, the First Amendment rights of children are co-extensive with those of adults. Indeed, I had thought the Court decided otherwise just last Term in *Ginsberg* v. *New York*, 390 U.S. 629. I continue to hold the view I expressed in that case: "[A] State may permissibly determine that, at least in some precisely delineated areas, a child—like someone in a captive audience—is not possessed of that full capacity for individual choice which is the presupposition of First Amendment guarantees." *Id.*, at 649–650 (concurring in result). Cf. *Prince* v. *Massachusetts*, 321 U.S. 158.

MR. JUSTICE WHITE, concurring.

While I join the Court's opinion, I deem it appropriate to note, first, that the Court continues to recognize a distinction between communicating by words and communicating by acts or conduct which sufficiently impinges on some valid state interest; and, second, that I do not subscribe to everything the Court of Appeals said about free speech in its opinion in *Burnside* v. *Byars*, 363 F. 2d 744, 748 (C. A. 5th Cir. 1966), a case relied upon by the Court in the matter now before us.

MR. JUSTICE BLACK, dissenting.

The Court's holding in this case ushers in what I deem to be an entirely new era in which the power to control pupils by the elected "officials of state supported public schools . . ." in the United States is in ultimate effect transferred to the Supreme Court.[1] The Court brought this particular case here on a petition for certiorari urging that the First and Fourteenth Amendments protect the right of school pupils to express their political views all the way "from kindergarten through high school." Here the constitutional right to "political expression" asserted was a right to wear black armbands during school hours and at classes in order to demonstrate to the other students that the petitioners were mourning because of the death of United States soldiers in Vietnam and to protest that war which they were against. Ordered to refrain from wearing the armbands in school by the elected school officials and the teachers vested with state authority to do so, apparently only seven out of the school system's 18,000 pupils deliberately refused to obey the order. One defying pupil was Paul Tinker, 8 years old, who was in the second grade; another, Hope Tinker, was 11 years old and in the fifth grade; a third of the Tinker family was 13, in the eighth grade; and a fourth member of the same family was John Tinker, 15 years old, an 11th grade high school pupil. Their father, a Methodist minister without a church, is paid a salary by the American Friends Service Committee. Another student who defied the school order and insisted on wearing an armband in school was Christopher Eckhardt, an 11th grade pupil and a petitioner in this case. His mother is an official in the Women's International League for Peace and Freedom.

As I read the Court's opinion it relies upon the following grounds for holding unconstitutional the judgment of the Des Moines school officials and the two courts below. First, the Court concludes that the wearing of armbands is "symbolic speech" which is "akin to 'pure speech' " and therefore protected by the First and Fourteenth Amendments. Secondly, the Court decides that the public schools are an appropriate place to exercise "symbolic speech" as long as normal school functions are not "unreasonably" disrupted. Finally, the Court arrogates to itself, rather than to the State's elected officials charged with running the schools, the decision as to which school disciplinary regulations are "reasonable."

Assuming that the Court is correct in holding that the conduct

[1]The petition for certiorari here presented this single question:

"Whether the First and Fourteenth Amendments permit officials of state supported public schools to prohibit students from wearing symbols of political views within school premises where the symbols are not disruptive of school discipline or decorum."

of wearing armbands for the purpose of conveying political ideas is protected by the First Amendment, cf., *e.g., Giboney* v. *Empire Storage & Ice Co.,* 336 U.S. 490 (1949), the crucial remaining questions are whether students and teachers may use the schools at their whim as a platform for the exercise of free speech—"symbolic" or "pure"—and whether the courts will allocate to themselves the function of deciding how the pupil's school day will be spent. While I have always believed that under the First and Fourteenth Amendments neither the State nor the Federal Government has any authority to regulate or censor the content of speech, I have never believed that any person has a right to give speeches or engage in demonstrations where he pleases and when he pleases. This Court has already rejected such a notion. In *Cox* v. *Louisiana,* 379 U.S. 536, 554 (1965), for example, the Court clearly stated that the rights of free speech and assembly "do not mean that everyone with opinions or beliefs to express may address a group at any public place and at any time."

While the record does not show that any of these armband students shouted, used profane language, or were violent in any manner, detailed testimony by some of them shows their armbands caused comments, warnings by other students, the poking of fun at them, and a warning by an older football player that other, nonprotesting students had better let them alone. There is also evidence that a teacher of mathematics had his lesson period practically "wrecked" chiefly by disputes with Mary Beth Tinker, who wore her armband for her "demonstration." Even a casual reading of the record shows that this armband did divert students' minds from their regular lessons, and that talk, comments, etc., made John Tinker "self-conscious" in attending school with his armband. While the absence of obscene remarks or boisterous and loud disorder perhaps justifies the Court's statement that the few armband students did not actually "disrupt" the classwork, I think the record overwhelmingly shows that the armbands did exactly what the elected school officials and principals foresaw they would, that is, took the students' minds off their classwork and diverted them to thoughts about the highly emotional subject of the Vietnam war. And I repeat that if the time has come when pupils of state-supported schools, kindergartens, grammar schools, or high schools, can defy and flout orders of school officials to keep their minds on their own schoolwork, it is the beginning of a new revolutionary era of permissiveness in this country fostered by the judiciary. The next logical step, it appears to me, would be to hold unconstitutional laws that bar pupils under 21 or

18 from voting, or from being elected members of the boards of education.[2]

The United States District Court refused to hold that the state school order violated the First and Fourteenth Amendments. 258 F. Supp. 971. Holding that the protest was akin to speech, which is protected by the First and Fourteenth Amendments, that court held that the school order was "reasonable" and hence constitutional. There was at one time a line of cases holding "reasonableness" as the court saw it to be the test of a "due process" violation. Two cases upon which the Court today heavily relies for striking down this school order used this test of reasonableness, *Meyer* v. *Nebraska*, 262 U.S. 390 (1923), and *Bartels* v. *Iowa*, 262 U.S. 404 (1923). The opinions in both cases were written by Mr. Justice McReynolds; Mr. Justice Holmes, who opposed this reasonableness test, dissented from the holdings as did Mr. Justice Sutherland. This constitutional test of reasonableness prevailed in this Court for a season. It was this test that brought on President Franklin Roosevelt's well-known Court fight. His proposed legislation did not pass, but the fight left the "reasonableness" constitutional test dead on the battlefield, so much so that this Court in *Ferguson* v. *Skrupa*, 372 U.S. 726, 729, 730, after a thorough review of the old cases, was able to conclude in 1963:

There was a time when the Due Process Clause was used by this Court to strike down laws which were thought unreasonable, that is, unwise or incompatible with some particular economic or social philosophy.

. . . . .

"The doctrine that prevailed in Lochner, Coppage, Adkins, Burns, *and like cases—that due process authorizes courts to hold laws un-*

[2]The following Associated Press article appeared in the Washington Evening Star, January 11, 1969, p. A–2, col. 1:

"BELLINGHAM, Mass. (AP)—Todd R. Hennessy, 16, has filed nominating papers to run for town park commissioner in the March election.

"'I can see nothing illegal in the youth's seeking the elective office,' said Lee Ambler, the town counsel. 'But I can't overlook the possibility that if he is elected any legal contract entered into by the park commissioner would be void because he is a juvenile.'

"Todd is a junior in Mount St. Charles Academy, where he has a top scholastic record."

constitutional when they believe the legislature has acted unwisely—has long since been discarded."

The Ferguson case totally repudiated the old reasonableness-due process test, the doctrine that judges have the power to hold laws unconstitutional upon the belief of judges that they "shock the conscience" or that they are "unreasonable," "arbitrary," "irrational," "contrary to fundamental 'decency,'" or some other such flexible term without precise boundaries. I have many times expressed my opposition to that concept on the ground that it gives judges power to strike down any law they do not like. If the majority of the Court today, by agreeing to the opinion of my Brother Fortas, is resurrecting that old reasonableness-due process test, I think the constitutional change should be plainly, unequivocally, and forthrightly stated for the benefit of the bench and bar. It will be a sad day for the country, I believe, when the present-day Court returns to the McReynolds due process concept. Other cases cited by the Court do not, as implied, follow the McReynolds reasonableness doctrine. *West Virginia* v. *Barnette,* 319 U.S. 624, clearly rejecting the "reasonableness" test, held that the Fourteenth Amendment made the First applicable to the States, and that the two forbade a State to *compel* little schoolchildren to salute the United States flag when they had religious scruples against doing so.[3] Neither *Thornhill* v. *Alabama,* 310 U.S. 88; *Stromberg* v. *California,* 283 U.S. 359; *Edwards* v. *South Carolina,* 372 U.S. 229; nor *Brown* v. *Louisiana,* 383 U.S. 131, related to schoolchildren at all, and none of these cases embraced Mr. Justice McReynolds' reasonableness test; and *Thorn-*

[3]In *Cantwell* v. *Connecticut,* 310 U. S. 296, 303–304 (1940), this Court said:

"The First Amendment declares that Congress shall make no law respecting an establishment of religion or prohibiting the free exercise thereof. The Fourteenth Amendment has rendered the legislatures of the states as incompetent as Congress to enact such laws. The constitutional inhibition of legislation on the subject of religion has a double aspect. On the one hand, it forestalls compulsion by law of the acceptance of any creed or the practice of any form of worship. Freedom of conscience and freedom to adhere to such religious organization or form of worship as the individual may choose cannot be restricted by law. On the other hand, it safeguards the free exercise of the chosen form of religion. Thus the Amendment embraces two concepts,—freedom to believe and freedom to act. The first is absolute but, in the nature of things, the second cannot be. Conduct remains subject to regulation for the protection of society.

hill, Edwards, and *Brown* relied on the vagueness of state statutes under scrutiny to hold them unconstitutional. *Cox* v. *Louisiana,* 379 U.S. 536, 555, and *Adderley* v. *Florida,* 385 U.S. 39, cited by the Court as a "compare," indicating, I suppose, that these two cases are no longer the law, were not rested to the slightest extent on the *Meyer* and *Bartels* "reasonableness-due process-McReynolds" constitutional test.

I deny, therefore, that it has been the "unmistakable holding of this Court for almost 50 years" that "students" and "teachers" take with them into the "schoolhouse gate" constitutional rights to "freedom of speech or expression." Even *Meyer* did not hold that. It makes no reference to "symbolic speech" at all; what it did was to strike down as "unreasonable" and therefore unconstitutional a Nebraska law barring the teaching of the German language before the children reached the eighth grade. One can well agree with Mr. Justice Holmes and Mr. Justice Sutherland, as I do, that such a law was no more unreasonable than it would be to bar teaching of Latin and Greek to pupils who have not reached the eighth grade. In fact, I think the majority's reason for invalidating the Nebraska law was that it did not like it or in legal jargon that it "shocked the Court's conscience," "offended its sense of justice," or was "contrary to fundamental concepts of the English-speaking world," as the Court has sometimes said. See, *e.g., Rochin* v. *California,* 342 U.S. 165, and *Irvine* v. *California,* 347 U.S. 128. The truth is that a teacher of kindergarten, grammar school, or high school pupils no more carries into a school with him a complete right to freedom of speech and expression than an anti-Catholic or anti-Semite carries with him a complete freedom of speech and religion into a Catholic church or Jewish synagogue. Nor does a person carry with him into the United States Senate or House, or into the Supreme Court, or any other court, a complete constitutional right to go into those places contrary to their rules and speak his mind on any subject he pleases. It is a myth to say that any person has a constitutional right to say what he pleases, where he pleases, and when he pleases. Our Court has decided precisely the opposite. See, *e.g., Cox* v. *Louisiana,* 379 U.S. 536, 555; *Adderley* v. *Florida,* 385 U.S. 39.

In my view, teachers in state-controlled public schools are hired to teach there. Although Mr. Justice McReynolds may have intimated to the contrary in *Meyer* v. *Nebraska, supra,* certainly a teacher is not paid to go into school and teach subjects the State does not hire him to teach as a part of its selected curriculum. Nor are public school students sent to the schools at public expense to broadcast political or any other views to educate and inform the public. The original idea of schools, which I do not believe is yet abandoned as worthless or out of date, was that children had not yet reached the point of experience and wisdom which enabled them to teach all of their elders. It may be that the Nation has outworn the old-fashioned slogan that "children are to be seen not heard," but one may, I hope, be permitted to harbor the thought that taxpayers send children to school on the premise that at their age they need to learn, not teach.

The true principles on this whole subject were in my judgment spoken by Mr. Justice McKenna for the Court in *Waugh* v. *Mississippi University* in 237 U.S. 589, 596–597. The State had there passed a law barring students from peaceably assembling in Greek letter fraternities and providing that students who joined them could be expelled from school. This law would appear on the surface to run afoul of the First Amendment's freedom of assembly clause. The law was attacked as violative of due process and of the privileges and immunities clause and as a deprivation of property and of liberty, under the Fourteenth Amendment. It was argued that the fraternity made its members more moral, taught discipline, and inspired its members to study harder and to obey better the rules of discipline and order. This Court rejected all the "fervid" pleas of the fraternities advocates and decided unanimously against these Fourteenth Amendment arguments. The Court in its next to the last paragraph made this statement which has complete relevance for us today:

> *It is said that the fraternity to which complainant belongs is a moral and of itself a disciplinary force. This need not be denied. But whether such membership makes against discipline was for the State of Mississippi to determine. It is to be remembered that the University was established by the State and is under the control of the State, and the enactment of the statute may have been induced by the opinion that* membership in the prohibited societies divided the attention of the students and distracted from that singleness of purpose which the State desired to exist in its public educational institutions. *It is not for us to entertain conjectures in opposition to the views of the States and annul its regulations upon disputable considerations of their wisdom or necessity. (Emphasis supplied.)*

It was on the foregoing argument that this Court sustained the power of Mississippi to curtail the First Amendment's right of peaceable assembly. And the same reasons are equally applicable to curtailing in the States' public schools the right to complete freedom of expression. Iowa's public schools, like Mississippi's university, are operated to give students an opportunity to learn, not to talk politics by actual speech, or by "symbolic" speech. And, as I have pointed out before, the record amply shows that public protest in the school classes against the Vietnam war "distracted from that singleness of purpose which the State [here Iowa] desired to exist in its public educational institutions." Here the Court should accord Iowa educational institutions the same right to determine for themselves to what extent free expression should be allowed in its schools as it accorded Mississippi with reference to freedom of assembly. But even if the record were silent as to protests against the Vietnam war distracting students from their assigned class work, members of this Court, like all other citizens, know, without being told, that the disputes over the wisdom of the Vietnam war have disrupted and divided this country as few other issues ever have. Of course students, like other people, cannot concentrate on lesser issues when black armbands are being ostentatiously displayed in their presence to call attention to the wounded and dead of the war, some of the wounded and the dead being their friends and neighbors. It was, of course, to distract the attention of other students that some students insisted up to the very point of their own suspension from school that they were determined to sit in school with their symbolic armbands.

Change has been said to be truly the law of life but sometimes the old and the tried and true are worth holding. The schools of this Nation have undoubtedly contributed to giving us tranquility and to making us a more law-abiding people. Uncontrolled and uncontrollable liberty is an enemy to domestic peace. We cannot close our eyes to the fact that some of the country's greatest problems are crimes committed by the youth, too many of school age. School discipline, like parental discipline, is an integral and important part of training our children to be good citizens—to be better citizens. Here a very small number of students have crisply and summarily refused to obey a school order designed to give pupils who want to learn the opportunity to do so. One does not need to be a prophet or the son of a prophet to know that after the Court's holding today some students in Iowa schools and indeed in all schools will be ready, able, and willing to defy their teachers on practically all orders. This is the more unfortunate for the schools since groups of students all over the land are already running loose, conducting break-ins, sit-ins, lie-ins, and smash-ins. Many of these student groups, as is all too familiar to all who read the newspapers and watch the television news programs, have already engaged in rioting, property seizures, and destruction. They have picketed schools to force students not to cross their picket lines and have too often violently attacked earnest but frightened students who wanted an education that the pickets did not want them to get. Students engaged in such activities are apparently confident that they know far more about how to operate public school systems than do their parents, teachers, and elected school officials. It is no answer to say that the particular students here have not yet reached such high points in their demands to attend classes in order to exercise their political pressures. Turned loose with lawsuits for damages and injunctions against their teachers as they are here, it is nothing but wishful thinking to imagine that young, immature students will not soon believe it is their right to control the schools rather than the right of the States that collect the taxes to hire the teachers for the benefit of the pupils. This case, therefore, wholly without constitutional reasons in my judgment, subjects all the public schools in the country to the whims and caprices of their loudest-mouthed, but maybe not their brightest, students. I, for one, am not fully persuaded that school pupils are wise enough, even with this Court's expert help from Washington, to run the 23,390 public school systems[4] in our 50 States. I wish, therefore, wholly to disclaim any purpose on my part to hold that the Federal Constitution compels the teachers, parents, and elected school officials to surrender control of the American public school system to public school students. I dissent.

MR. JUSTICE HARLAN, dissenting.

I certainly agree that state public school authorities in the discharge of their responsibilities are not wholly exempt from the requirements of the Fourteenth Amendment respecting the freedoms of expression and association. At the same time I am reluctant to believe that there is any disagreement between the majority and myself on the proposition that school officials should be accorded the widest authority in maintaining discipline and good order in their institutions. To translate that proposition into a workable constitutional rule, I would, in cases like this, cast upon those complaining the burden of showing that a particular school measure was motivated by other than legitimate school concerns—for example, a desire

[4]Statistical Abstract of the United States (1968), Table No. 578, p. 406.

to prohibit the expression of an unpopular point of view, while permitting expression of the dominant opinion.

Finding nothing in this record which impugns the good faith of respondents in promulgating the armband regulation, I would affirm the judgment below.

Suggestions for classroom use

The people who read this book, as well as the professors who use it, vary considerably. They come to it with different backgrounds, with different purposes, and with variations in their previous knowledge of civil rights and constitutional law. Consequently, the suggestions that follow may be useful to some of the readers and not to others. They are probably most applicable to classroom situations where instructors and students have little knowledge of civil rights law, legal procedures, or public reactions to constitutional principles.

1. Interview or invite to class a local attorney acquainted with both trial and appeal procedures. Prepare questions that will elicit information about:
   a. Court costs and legal fees; how much are they and who pays them?
   b. How long do cases take from initial disagreement to final resolution? Why do they take so long?
   c. What is the structure of the court system of your state? What courts have jurisdiction over what kinds of problems?
   d. How are judges selected in your state? How are they removed?
   e. Other items of interest to your class.
2. Interview officials of the local NEA, AFT, and ACLU chapters

to find out what assistance a teacher might expect in enforcing his civil rights.

3. Using volunteers from the class, role play selected cases. In each of these civil rights cases as well as in conflicts that never reach the courts, there are important ideas and powerful feelings represented on both sides of an issue. Through role playing the alternative positions become explicit, and their logic as well as emotional appeal can be more clearly examined.
4. With the help of student volunteers, role play the controversies briefly described in Chapter 1. Create all the supporting roles you deem necessary for full presentation of the conflicting interests.
5. Construct a questionnaire based on cases and controversies presented in this book and administer it to local groups of students, teachers, administrators, and parents. Analyze their responses to see if there are any systematic differences among these groups as they view the civil rights of teachers.
6. Take the questionnaire constructed for no. 5 above and administer it to civic and social groups like the League of Women Voters, the American Legion, campus Young Republicans, campus Young Democrats, the Chamber of Commerce, and others. Hypothesize the probable outcomes and test your hypotheses.
7. Look up the reports based on the Purdue Opinion Polls (POP) (H. H. Remmers and R. D. Franklin, "Sweet Land of Liberty," *Phi Delta Kappan,* October 1962, pp. 22–27), and see whether the answers to your questionnaire support the findings or challenge them.
8. Administer POP no. 30 before and after studying the civil rights of teachers. Are there significant differences in the responses? The poll may be obtained from earlier reports or from the Measurement and Research Center, Purdue University.
9. Search your local papers and those of a contrasting rural or urban area for news items related to school controversies. Keep a scrapbook for the period of your school term and analyze the accounts to see how many controversies involved civil rights and which civil rights seem to be most problematic in your area.
10. Have members of the class look up the constitution of their particular state and check whether it has civil rights provisions similar to those of the national Constitution.
11. It has come to our attention that the expression "civil rights" has leftist connotations, while "constitutional rights" has a rightist flavor. Do you find this to be the case? Do people in your area

react differently to the same questions if they refer to "constitutional rights of teachers" than if they deal with "civil rights of teachers"?

12. Have members of the class make a wall chart or transparencies showing the structure of the local and state court systems together with the kinds of cases each court handles.

13. Find out the calendars of nearby courts and have students sit in on some of the cases.

14. Have students look through recent Supreme Court reports and report their findings on recent civil rights cases.

15. If there are law schools in your area, third-year law students could be an excellent resource in helping the class or individual students in understanding and discussing technical legal questions. It would also be good experience for the law students to explain constitutional and procedural matters to teachers.

16. In this book we do not explain the law of contracts or torts, yet these areas are of interest and relevance to teachers. Third-year law students could be of great assistance in explaining basic principles and illustrating them with examples.

17. Not all states have tenure laws. Have students find out whether or not their states grant tenure either by law or by contract. Interviews with school administrators or officials of teacher organizations will provide this information. What are the provisions of their tenure laws? What procedural safeguards exist for tenured teachers that do not exist for probationary ones?

18. Are there forces at work in your state attempting to alter existing tenure laws? What changes are proposed, and what are the reasons for and against such changes?

19. Are civil rights absolute or relative? If they are relative, relative to what—the personal views of the judge, community mores, situational variables, or "changing times"? Although on most matters the law is quite settled and clear, the following four items should point up the tension prevailing at the edges of the law as well as in its application to particular situations.

a. A Florida District Court of Appeals upheld the dismissal of a band instructor on the grounds of immorality and incompetence. The facts showed that the teacher made some remarks "in the classroom of mixed boys and girls (teenagers), relating to sex and virginity and premarital sex relations." The school board deemed his remarks sufficiently serious to warrant suspension pending a hearing on charges of immorality and incompetence. Allegations were also made about lack of discipline in his classes. The Court, in upholding the action of the board, said that

There are many factors which may have a material bearing upon the competency of the instructor, among which could be his attitude toward the students, his manner of speaking to them and his general lack of proper personality conducive to a mutual understanding. The instructor's attitude and expression on moral conduct, sex questions and such, could also affect his competency. In addition, as to the immorality charge, there was evidence of unbecoming and unnecessary risqué remarks made by the petitioner in a class of mixed teenage boys and girls which we agree with the School Board were of an immoral nature. It may be that topless waitresses and entertainers are in vogue in certain areas of our country and our federal courts may try to enjoin our state courts from stopping the sale of lewd and obscene literature and the showing of obscene films, but we are still of the opinion that instructors in our schools should not be permitted to so risquély discuss sex problems in our teenage mixed classes as to cause embarrassment to the children or to invoke in them other feelings not incident to the courses of study being pursued. (Pyle *v.* Washington County School Board, *238 So. 2d 121 [1970]*).

b. For all human kind, justice is relative, not absolute. In spite of the long tradition that 'justice' is absolute and eternal, the tradition has always been incorrect. *Fiat justitia ruat coelum* (Let right be done, though the heaven should fall) is a phrase impressive mainly because of its being in Latin and not understandable. When the skies begin to fall, Justice removes the blindfold from her eyes and tilts the scales. (Arthur Corbin, *Contracts,* Vol. 1, St. Paul, Minn., West Publishing, 1963, p. 3)

c. My analysis of the judicial process comes then to this and little more: logic and history and custom and utility and the accepted standards of right conduct are the forces which singly or in combination shape the progress of the law.

Which of these forces shall dominate in any case, must depend largely upon the comparative importance or value of the social interests that will be thereby promoted or impaired. . . . The social interests served by symmetry or certainty must be balanced against the social interests served by equity and fairness. . . . (Justice Cordozo, *Nature of the Judicial Process,* New Haven, Conn., Yale University Press, 1921, pp. 71–73)

d. This page is taken from *My Name Is Arnold: A Ghetto Primer*, by Essie G. Branch (The DuSable Museum of Negro History, 3806 S. Michigan Ave., Chicago, Ill., 1971). Would you have the right to use it to teach beginning reading in some situations but not in others?

At school I like lunch hour pretty good because we can play and I can see Floyd. They gives us free hot lunch every day. But they don't give us nothing with soul. Somedays it be chopped suey and jellio and somedays it be brocli and sour kraut. Me and Floyd, we don't like none of that stuff. It taste like shit.

20. To desegregate faculty and staff pursuant to the Fourteenth Amendment, the courts have proposed "objective criteria" for selection, promotion, demotion, or dismissal. For example, a court in Alabama has required that the schools provide the following information:

(1) The system's nonracial objective criteria used in selecting the staff member(s) dismissed or demoted;

(2) The name, address, race, type of certificate held, degree or degrees held, total teaching experience and experience in the in the system and position during the 1969–1970 school year of each person to be dismissed, or demoted as hereinabove defined; and in the case of demotion, the person's new position during the 1970–1971 school year and his salaries for 1969–1970 and 1970–1971;

(3) The basis for the dismissal or demotion of each person, including the procedure employed in applying the system's nonracial objective criteria;

(4) Whether or not the person to be dismissed or demoted was offered any other staff vacancy; and, if so, the outcome; and, if not, the reason. (*Lee* v. *Macon County Board of Education*, Civil Action No. 604-E, slip Op. [U.S.D.C.M.D. Ala. E.D. February 12, 1970])

In your estimate is this type of information useful in avoiding racial discrimination in personnel practices? Is the information sufficient, or would you include other requirements? Do we know enough about teaching to base our decision on "objective criteria"? If we do not, how can we avoid the kind of subjectivity that is camouflage for racial discrimination?

21. What would your reactions be if during a school assembly a teacher stood up and with brief comments and gestures led a group of students out of the room? Assume that the assembly was properly called by the school authorities and that the teacher had honest and serious objections to its content. The teacher claimed to be exercising his First Amendment rights, while the school officials claimed that his behavior was disruptive of orderly and organized schooling. See what the court said in *State* v. *Besson*, 266 A. 2d 175 (N.J. County Court, 1970).

22. Loyalty oaths are used by thousands of school districts, colleges, and other public institutions. The one reproduced is used by many states. What are your reactions to it in light of what you have read? Does your state have a similar oath?

I, ———, do solemnly swear (or affirm) that I will support and defend the Constitution of the United States and the Constitution of the State of ——— against all enemies, foreign and domestic; and I will bear true faith and allegiance to the same; that I take this obligation freely, without any mental reservation or purpose of evasion; and that I will well and faithfully discharge the duties of the office or position in which I am employed, SO HELP ME GOD.

23. The following quotes might be of interest to you:

a. If a state may compel surrender of one constitutional right as a condition of its favor, it may, in like manner, compel a surrender of all. It is inconceivable that guarantees imbedded in the Constitution of the United States may thus be manipulated out of existence. (The Supreme Court, in *Frost Trucking Co.* v. *Railroad Comm.*, 271 U.S., 583, 594, 46 S.Ct. 605 [1926])

b. Freedom from belief in force and violence as a justifiable weapon for the destruction of Government is the very essence of the teacher's qualifications. . . . In the current struggle for men's minds, the state is well within its province in ensuring the integrity of the educational process against those who would pervert it to subversive ends. (Robert R. Hamilton, *Legal Rights and Liabilities of Teachers,* Wyoming, School Law Publications, 1956, p. 84)

c. Because of this policy (of intellectual freedom), public officials cannot be constitutionally vested with powers to select the ideas people can think about, censor the public views they can express, or choose the persons or groups people can associate with. Public officials with such powers are not public servants; they are public masters. (Justice Hugo Black, in *Adler* v. *Board of Education,* 342 U.S. 485, 497 [1952])

d. "Respect for law," my late revered colleague Mr. Justice Frankfurter warned, "cannot be turned off and on as though it were a hot water faucet." Those who flout the law when the law displeases them only undermine the system they need to save them. (Justice William J. Brennan, "Progress and the Bill of Rights," speech delivered at The Third Independent Day Dinner at the Earl Warren Institute of The University of Judaism, Los Angeles, June 30, 1966, p. 15)

e. While a great many people "believe" in the Bill of Rights as a somewhat familiar, friendly fiction, they really do not believe in the principles set forth within it. And this becomes all the more true when, as you will find often happens, the Bill of Rights is attacked—or some provision of it is attacked—in the name of some presumably great virtue. Attacks on the rights of individuals by those in power, those in control of the government, always come in the name of some great virtue. (Justice William J. Brennan, "Progress and The Bill of Rights," pp. 12–13)

f. I would expect that constitutional change will be a concomitant of the changes in our society which the future will bring. Just as we have learned that what our constitutional fundamentals meant to the wisdom of other times cannot be their measure to the vision of our time, similarly, what those fundamentals mean for us, our descendants will learn, cannot be the measure to the vision of their time. In sum, "freedom is an unstable compound. Because one man's liberty can be another man's constraint, because conditions of life in our dynamic society continue to change and because freedom at large is grand but elusive in the particular, the task of formulation is never ending. . . . We must bear in mind that our Bill of Rights was written in another age for another society. This heritage with its noble concepts of liberty and freedom has to be re-defined and re-defended by every generation." Pedrick, 49 Cornell L.Q. 581, 608 (1964). (Justice William J. Brennan, "Progress and The Bill of Rights," pp. 10–11)

g. What our Constitution says, what our legislatures do, and what our courts write are vitally important. But the reality of freedom in our daily lives is shown by the attitudes and policies of people toward each other in the very block or township where we live. There we will find the real measure of a living Bill of Rights. (Justice William J. Brennan, "Progress and The Bill of Rights," p. 11)

h. Right here in enlightened California we have had our dark pages of racism. In the records of our state Supreme Court is the case of *People* v. *Hall,* 4 Cal. 399. This 1854 case involved a California statute which provided, "No Black, or Mulatto person, or Indian shall be allowed to give evidence in favor of, or against a White man." In the *Hall* case the defendant was convicted of murder upon the testimony of Chinese witnesses. The court found that Indians were actually Oriental and therefore Chinese as Orientals were excluded from the right to testify in any case for or against a white man. And then the highest court in our state went on to say in this crude racist language:

"The same rule which would admit them (the Chinese) to

testify, would admit them to all the equal rights of citizenship, and we might soon see them at the polls, in the jury box, upon the bench, and in our legislative halls." How prophetic —with Judges Wong and Aiso on our bench, and Assemblyman Song in Sacramento, all from this area. (Justice Mosk of the California Supreme Court)

i. Many long years ago a great philosopher in Athens, Solon, was asked how justice could be attained in his land. Said Solon, "Justice can be attained in a society only when those who are not injured feel as indignant as those who are." (Justice Mosk of the California Supreme Court)

24. The following excerpts from various newspapers present recent civil rights controversies related to teachers and teaching. What rights are involved, and how would your class resolve them after reading this book?

a. *Poughkeepsie, N.Y.* Vincent Tasciotti, Americanism chairman of the Pleasant Valley American Legion, presented a petition signed by about fifty persons asking that Austin Bentley, a suspended Arlington School District sixth-grade teacher, be fired for "conduct unbecoming to a teacher." Bentley was accused of distributing copies of *Common Sense,* a controversial newspaper, on Main Street in Poughkeepsie. At a hearing before a three-man panel appointed by the state board of education, Tasciotti said the Legion is dedicated to upholding the U.S. Constitution against enemies, both foreign and domestic, and perpetuation of 100 percent Americanism. He objected to *Common Sense* articles supporting Angela Davis and condemning American education. Bentley was represented at the hearing by Stephen E. Bass, a White Plains Civil Liberties Union attorney. Tasciotti said, "The people who put out that rag have a right to print it, but a teacher has a responsibility to the children he's teaching, the educational system, and the parents." After testimony from several persons the hearing was adjourned until a later date. The panel was charged with reporting its findings to the state board of education after completion of the hearing. (*Poughkeepsie Journal,* 21 March 1971)

b. *Northampton, Mass.* Police Chief James Whalen threatened to file a criminal complaint against the school committee unless it removes Claude Browne's *Manchild in the Promised Land* from use in a black history course. Whalen says the book is "pornographic literature" and contains "428 incidents of impure words." He said the book violates state laws dealing with pornographic literature. (*Daily Defender*, 25 May 1971)

c. *Carmel, N.Y.* In response to parental objections, school district administrators are re-evaluating the book *The Pre-School Years,* used in home economics classes. Prepared and distributed by the New York State Department of Health, the book contains a section on masturbation which closely follows a similar essay in a Boy Scout handbook. Some thirty-five parents attended a meeting of the board to protest "sex education," including, in addition to complaints about the booklet, a demand for an explanation of a discussion concerning contraceptive devices during a recent 10th-grade science-class discussion. Assistant Superintendent James O'Connell is checking parents' complaints about the booklet and will report to the board of education with recommendations at the next meeting. (*Putnam Courier*, 17 March 1971)

d. *Cincinnati, Ohio.* Susan C. Richmond, an English teacher since 1956 and an advocate of an "open classroom," told the Cincinnati School Board she will teach "any book I feel is appropriate to the course." She objects strenuously to a new policy which sets up three levels of review for books teachers want to use in classrooms: the school's own English department, a city-wide committee comprised of about twenty-two teachers, and the school board for final approval. Mrs. Richmond disapproves of the policy because, "Some teachers feel that since four-letter words are in it and certain allusions to sexual incidents, they can't handle the book before a class. They seem to think that if they can't handle it, no other teacher can handle it either. I don't feel I have the right to say another teacher might not try." *Cincinnati Enquirer*, 26 March 1971

e. *Susquehanna Valley, N.Y.* About sixty residents of the district protested to the school board the use of the novel, *Hog Butcher,* in sophomore English classes. The book by R. L. Fair relates an incident in the life of a 10-year-old boy in a Chicago ghetto. Complaints centered on the allegedly obscene language of the book. Supported by Board Members Mrs. Dorothy Chantry and Joseph Peone, the book was reportedly not prohibited from curriculum use after a stormy board meeting March 18. (*Binghampton Press*, 4 April 1971)

f. *Burlington, Conn.* Regional District 10 Board of Education reaffirmed the right of school and administrative personnel to select the reading material used at Lewis School. In response to a complaint from a group of approximately sixty Harwinton parents who objected to some books on a reading list because the books, in their opinion, contain obscenities, the board said: "Any parent may request that their child be excused from reading a particular book, since parents differ in interpretations of what is obscene, vulgar or perverted. . . . This board of education reaffirms the three resolutions adopted April 10, 1967." The resolutions referred to were in response to a similar complaint about the book *To Kill a Mockingbird,* by Harper Lee. At this time, the board went on record as approving assigned reading material and noted the selection of books would be continued by administrative personnel, department heads, and teachers. Books included in the recent complaint were: *The Learning Tree,* by Gordon Parks; *Down These Mean Streets,* by Piri Thomas; and *The Cool World,* by Warren Miller. (*Hartford Courant,* 25 April 1971)

g. *Fort Lauderdale, Fla.* A black civics teacher who refused to pledge allegiance to the American flag because "there isn't liberty and justice for all" has been suspended. "I don't consider myself anti-American," says Leroy Bates. "The words in the pledge are just untrue. Since I was in the ninth grade I've seen very little equality. "There isn't liberty and justice for all," Mr. Bates said. "As far as I can see these are not even goals people are subscribing to." Broward County School Superintendent Benjamin C. Willis has ordered Mr. Bates suspended from his post at Henry D. Middle School. Mr. Bates was scheduled to be charged before a school board meeting Thursday with "gross insubordination" for refusing a direct order to participate in the pledge of allegiance at the school. Mr. Bates said he has retained a lawyer and will fight the suspension. The father of two said he stood outside his classroom when the pledge was recited and during his three years as a teacher he had never recited it. Last year he taught social studies at then all-black Dillard High School in Fort Lauderdale. "I guessed it surprised my white students this year," Mr. Bates said. "In black schools there was not much notice because we all had somewhat the same feeling." (*The Christian Science Monitor,* 4 April 1970)

h. *Sacramento, California.* A Sacramento State College coed has been criticized by a school official for "unprofessional" conduct—living temporarily in the back of a station wagon to cut costs. After nationwide publicity about her unusual—and since abandoned—dwelling, Cherie Gordon, a physical education major, said she received a memorandum from Dorothy R. Mohr, chairman of the women's physical education department, which read: "If you persist in your present attitudes and modes of behavior, the probability is high that the faculty of the department . . . would find you unacceptable as a teacher credential candidate." The memorandum said the faculty and many physical education students believed the 21-year-old coed's conduct to be "unprofessional." "They say your newspaper and television publicity has been in poor taste, and has been detrimental to the reputation of the college and the department," the letter said. Almost in tears, Cherie said, "It has turned out to be a malicious and frightening experience." Even before the memorandum, Cherie, as planned, gave up bedding down in her sleeping bag in the back of the vehicle she had named "Old Green Moose." She now lives in a dormitory. Mrs. Mohr's note said local school officials had called the college, saying Cherie "would never be hired in their schools." However, Cherie says she has received more than two dozen letters from around the country praising her determination and resourcefulness. (*Los Angeles Times*, 1969)

i. *Cranston, R.I.* A school committeeman who sharply criticized a prostitute's talk to a high-school class says he wants to know why criminals also have been allowed to address the students. Meanwhile, support grew Thursday for two teachers and their department chairman who were given letters of reprimand in connection with a March 10 speech by the prostitute to 40 seniors in a class at Cranston West High School. The class is designed to deal with real contemporary social problems. Committeeman Aram G. Garabedian Thursday called for a "full disclosure" of why pupils in Project EPIC have been permitted to listen to a murderer, a rapist, and a man who nearly beat someone to death. He said he and other committee members did not learn of these guest speakers until they read student comments in newspaper reports. The prime issue, he said, is who should decide what takes place in the classroom. While conceding that the administration, faculty, and students should be included in decision-making, the school board "has been delegated the final say by the General Assembly," he said. Mr. Garabedian also criticized the Rhode Island Education Association for backing the teachers and opposing a public hearing on Project EPIC next week. Three other board members, including one who previously supported the forum at which the public would be asked to comment, said Thursday in a letter to the board chairman that "we believe the scheduled public hearing on Tuesday will serve no useful purpose except to further polarize the community." The Rhode Island Social Studies Association supported the teachers in a statement Thursday, saying that "all available evidence indicates that the examination of the victimless crime in the EPIC program, including [the prostitute speaker], was carefully planned as an integral part of the instructional program." Albert K. Aubin, director of youth activities for the Cranston Council 1738, Knights of Columbus, also backed the teachers Thursday and said he was speaking for himself. In a prepared statement, he said, "the tinhorn headline-grabbers are the ones of whom to be suspicious, not the academic community with its genuine pedagogic objectives." It also was announced Thursday that Attorney General Richard J. Israel will address the class next Friday on "victimless crimes," the same subject the prostitute was invited to discuss. (*The Christian Science Monitor*, 18 March 1972)

j. *Tucson, Arizona.* Superior Court Judge John Collins ordered the reinstatement of a high school teacher, Ms. Ann Stewart, who had been fired for, among other things, "teaching about withcraft in such a way that it affects students psychologically." Supposedly, she stated in class that she was a witch. But, Mrs. Stewart denied saying such a thing. She said she told her students she has the "physical characteristics of a witch." The decision for reinstatement was based on the school board's failure to provide proper notification and to institute a hearing date. (*New York Times*, 5, December 1971)

73 74 75 76 9 8 7 6 5 4 3 2 1